REFERENCE

OXFORD STUDIES IN MODERN
LEGAL HISTORY

General Editor: A. W. BRIAN SIMPSON
Professor of Law, University of Michigan

OXFORD STUDIES IN MODERN LEGAL HISTORY

The series aims to publish monographs of high quality and originality on history covering the period 1750 onwards.

Broken Engagements

*The Action for Breach of Promise of Marriage
and the Feminine Ideal, 1800–1940*

SASKIA LETTMAIER

OXFORD
UNIVERSITY PRESS

OXFORD
UNIVERSITY PRESS

Great Clarendon Street, Oxford OX2 6DP

Oxford University Press is a department of the University of Oxford.
It furthers the University's objective of excellence in research, scholarship,
and education by publishing worldwide in

Oxford New York

Auckland Cape Town Dar es Salaam Hong Kong Karachi
Kuala Lumpur Madrid Melbourne Mexico City Nairobi
New Delhi Shanghai Taipei Toronto

With offices in

Argentina Austria Brazil Chile Czech Republic France Greece
Guatemala Hungary Italy Japan Poland Portugal Singapore
South Korea Switzerland Thailand Turkey Ukraine Vietnam

Oxford is a registered trade mark of Oxford University Press
in the UK and in certain other countries

Published in the United States
by Oxford University Press Inc., New York

British Library Cataloguing in Publication Data

Data available

Library of Congress Cataloging in Publication Data

Data available

Typeset by Newgen Imaging Systems (P) Ltd., Chennai, India
Printed in Great Britain
on acid-free paper by the
MPG Books Group, Bodmin and King's Lynn

ISBN 978–0–19–956997–7

1 3 5 7 9 10 8 6 4 2

Meinen Eltern, Sebastian und allen meinen Lieben

General Editor's Preface

I first became aware of the action for breach of promise of marriage in 1948 when as a schoolboy I sang the part of the defendant in Gilbert and Sullivan's *Trial by Jury*. By that date, real suits for breach of promise hardly ever took place, and when I studied law in Oxford in the 1950s actions for breach of promise had come to seem comical. They were formally abolished in the United Kingdom, except in Scotland, in 1970, and in 1984 in Scotland too. But there was an earlier time, extending from the seventeenth century until the nineteenth and a little later when this action, located somewhat uneasily in either contract law, or perhaps tort law, or even I suppose in family law, flourished, and gave rise to much litigation. Accounts of such cases naturally enough excited very considerable public interest at the time. Dr. Lettmaier, concentrating primarily on the nineteenth century, makes use of such accounts, locating them in their social and legal context, to investigate the changing perceptions of the ideal woman, which were reflected in the treatment of litigants in breach of promise actions, and which would, eventually, cause its demise. And in addition to basing her analysis on the actual practice of litigation Dr. Lettmaier also makes fascinating use of the treatment of breach of promise actions in contemporary imaginative literature. So this book is not simply a legal history of an extinct form of action, but a work of social and cultural history, and is most welcome as a highly original contribution to *Oxford Studies in Modern Legal History*.

A.W. Brian Simpson

Epigraph

All laughed, all scorned the idea of sueing [sic] for money the man who should have disdained their love. The two Lucillas vied with each other in expressions of contempt for such cupidity. '*Nous verrons*,' said Renard, 'if such a thing should ever come to pass.'

Harriet Maria Smythies,
The Breach of Promise (1845)

Acknowledgements

This book grew out of a DPhil thesis researched and written from 2003 to 2007. It is a pleasure now to be able to acknowledge the many people who and institutions which have made a special contribution towards its existence. First of all, I would like to thank my doctoral supervisors, Christa Jansohn and Reinhard Zimmermann, for their kindness and wisdom. This work would not have taken the shape it did without their continued encouragement and generous support down to its final publication. Many other scholars, in Germany, England, and the United States, have been gracious enough to privilege me with their time and expertise, and for this I am grateful to Sir John Baker, Stephen Cretney, Charles Donahue Jr, Janet Halley, Jonathan Herring, Hans-Dieter Spengler, and Klaus Vieweg. It is a pity that the late David Westfall, in whose family law class on heartbalm actions at Harvard in the spring of 2003 the idea for this study was first conceived, never became aware of his influence on this work. I am also grateful to my three anonymous readers at Oxford University Press and to the distinguished editor of this series, Brian Simpson, who read and commented insightfully on the entire manuscript and suggested various improvements. Any errors that remain are, of course, entirely my own responsibility.

A great number of other people have contributed to the success of this project. I am indebted to many librarians and archivists on both sides of the Atlantic: in Germany, I am grateful for the assistance of the staff of Staatsbibliothek Bamberg, particularly Otmar Singer; in England, I must acknowledge the staffs of the British Library at both Bloomsbury and Colindale, the University of London Institute for Advanced Legal Studies, especially Katherine Reid, the Bodleian Library, Oxford, the William Salt Library, Stafford, and the Lichfield, Staffordshire, and Warwickshire County Record Offices; at Harvard, the staff of the Law School Library was unfailingly helpful, as was the staff at the Beinecke Rare Books and Manuscripts Library at Yale. Lee Wicks and Will Stevens made invaluable contributions to Chapter 4 by helping me retrace the winding path of Mary E Newbolt, née Smith, to her death in Liverpool. Papers relating to this project were given at the Third Prague Conference on Linguistics and Literary Studies at Charles University in the spring of 2007 and at Janet Halley's family law workshop at Harvard in the spring of 2009. I am grateful to the organizers of and participants in these events for affording me the opportunity to present my ideas. Generous financial assistance in the form of a dissertation fellowship was provided by Cusanuswerk, Bischöfliche Studienstiftung. My dear friends Suzanne Taylor, Mags Reilly, and Edward Flood saved me from experiencing the scholar's proverbial isolation during my research in London and Oxford. I would also like to thank John Louth, Alex Flach, Chris Champion, Natasha Knight, Emma Hawes, Caroline Quinnell, and everyone else at Oxford University Press who assisted with the production of this book.

My deepest gratitude is to my family, especially to my parents, Karl-Otto and Eva-Maria Lettmaier, and to my brother, Sebastian. It is no easy task to bear with the strains and stresses of life with a family member engaged in a long-term and time-consuming project. Not only have my family accomplished that—with admirable flexibility and patience—I have also been the beneficiary of their prodigious research, technological, and textual talents. As always, my father's computer wizardry has proved invaluable. He performed all of the calculations that appear in this study. Over the long course of this book's gestation, my mother has probably spent sufficient hours hunched over small print to last a lifetime. For her painstaking work, unquenchable optimism, constant good fellowship, intelligence, and wisdom, I am inexpressibly grateful. My family's boundless love and support gave me the necessary strength and confidence to believe in this book's progress even during those difficult stages when things seemed to be falling apart rather than coming together. More times than I can remember they have belied the popular notion that supportive kin networks are a thing of the past.

Saskia Lettmaier

Cambridge,
9 November 2009

Contents

List of Abbreviations

AC	Appeal Cases
Bing NC	Bingham's New Cases, English Common Pleas
Car & P	Carrington & Payne's Nisi Prius Reports
CB	Common Bench Reports
CJ	Chief Justice
Dougl	Douglas' Reports
E & B	Ellis & Blackburn's Queen's Bench Reports
EB & E	Ellis, Blackburn & Ellis' Queen's Bench Reports
ER	English Reports
esp	especially
Ex	Exchequer Reports
Geo	George
HMSO	Her Majesty's Stationery Office
ie	id est
J	Justice
KB	King's Bench
Lev Reports	Levinz' Reports
LJCP	Law Journal Reports, Common Pleas New Series
LR CP	Law Reports, Common Pleas
M & S	Maule & Selwyn's Reports
Mass	Massachusetts
NYS	New York Supplement
Peake's Addl C	Peake's Additional Cases
QB	Queen's Bench
QBD	Queen's Bench Division
QC	Queen's Counsel
rpt edn	reprint edition
rev edn	revised edition
UCQB	Upper Canada Queen's Bench Reports
Vict	Victoria

Table of Cases

Table of Statutes and Restatements

Introduction

This work is an empirical and literary study of a tiny speck of English legal history: the common law action for breach of promise of marriage, available in England from the mid-seventeenth to the late twentieth century, which could be used to recover pecuniary damages against a faithless lover for the breach of an engagement. Although boasting a history of over 300 years, the common law action for breach of promise of marriage saw its rise to cultural prominence and its subsequent fall from favour in the 'long nineteenth century', a time of dramatic political, social, cultural, and legal upheaval extending from the early 1800s to the period just after the two World Wars.[1] It was during this period that the breach-of-promise action acquired its defining characteristics; that breach-of-promise suits increased in number, becoming part of the daily diet at county assizes and the Westminster courts; that they were given increasingly extensive treatment in regional and even national newspapers; and ultimately inspired what Shakespeare's Hamlet has so aptly called the 'abstracts and brief chronicles of the time':[2] works of literature. Just as the 'long nineteenth century' witnessed the rise of the breach-of-promise action, so it witnessed its decline. At the close of this historical period, during the 1920s and the 1930s, the breach-of-promise action became culturally obsolete. As the twentieth century progressed, fewer and fewer actions for breach of promise were brought, and only a handful of this trickle of cases garnered any media attention. The cause of action, become a virtual (legal as well as cultural) dead letter long

---

[1] The 'long nineteenth century' is a familiar concept in historical periodization, but its chronological boundaries are far from certain. The expression is most frequently used to refer to the period between 1789 and 1918. See, for instance, Lynn Abrams, *The Making of Modern Woman: Europe 1789–1918*, Longman History of European Women 5 (London: Longman-Pearson Education, 2002). Other definitions, however, move both the beginning and the endpoint of the period, variously dating it from 1750 to 1914, 1750 to 1925, or even 1750 to 1950. See Edmund Burke, 'Modernity's Histories: Rethinking the Long Nineteenth Century, 1750–1950' in *University of California World History Workshop, Essays and Positions from the World History Workshop*, Paper 1, 25 May 2000 <http://repositories.cdlib.org/ucwhw/ep/1>. In view of this chronological uncertainty and in view of the fact that dominant (male-centred) periodization is difficult to apply to women's history (S Jay Kleinberg (ed), *Retrieving Women's History: Changing Perceptions of the Role of Women in Politics and Society*, Berg/Unesco Comparative Studies (Oxford: Berg; Paris: Unesco, 1988) x), I define the 'long nineteenth century' as the period between the secure establishment of the ideology of true womanhood around 1800 and the consolidation of female emancipation in the wake of the two World Wars.

[2] William Shakespeare, *Hamlet*, Harold Jenkins (ed), The Arden Edition of the Works of William Shakespeare (London: Methuen, 1982) 2.2.520.

before the middle of the twentieth century, lingered on as a marginal suit for
marginal people. It was formally abolished in England in 1970.[3]

This book explores this seminal period in the life of the breach-of-promise
action. In its survey of three consecutive historical periods—the early nineteenth century (1800–1850), the high Victorian (1850–1900), and the
post-Victorian (1900–1940) periods—it traces the evolution of the breach-
of-promise suit from when it first became important until after it fell into
desuetude and subsequently ceased to exist as a cause of action recognized in
English law.

I. Situating the Project: Law, Cultural Ideology, and Nineteenth-Century Women's History

This project has links with two fields of scholarship whose relevance to my
work I should like to acknowledge in this introduction. The first body of
work in relation to which my endeavour can usefully be situated is that
which examines the interaction between the law and social forces extrane-
ous to the law or, put more crudely, the permeability of the law to cultural
ideology. At least since the school of historical jurisprudence, associated
with men like Sir Henry Maine and Sir Paul Vinogradoff, the structures of
the law have been conceived of as the highly contingent product of time
and place, a part of wider social structures rather than apart from them.
Conscious (and more often still subconscious) cultural sensibilities are now
seen as playing a vital role in shaping the structure of a legal system and the
content of legal rules. In the words of Oliver Wendell Holmes, customarily
called America's greatest jurist, it is a fallacy to suppose 'that the only force
at work in the development of the law is logic'.[4] Research into the law's relation to ideology has been taken up by a number of legal schools, such as the
Marxist tradition, the school of legal realism of the 1920s, and the critical
legal studies movement of the 1970s and 1980s. One of the most ambitious
projects in the field of law and ideology to date is Alan Harding's *A Social
History of English Law*, first published in 1966.[5] In his study, which sweeps
across the vast temporal expanse from Anglo-Saxon times to the present,
Harding's aim is to relate 'the development of English law as a whole, and
forwards, to the development of English society'.[6] Proceeding from the

---

[3] The cause of action was abolished by the Law Reform (Miscellaneous Provisions) Act 1970, c 33.
[4] Oliver Wendell Holmes, Jr, 'The Path of the Law' (1897) 10(8) *Harvard Law Review* 465.
[5] Alan Harding, *A Social History of English Law* (rpt edn) (Gloucester, MA: Peter Smith, 1973).
[6] Ibid, 9.

Holmesian premise that the law does not beget itself by a process of logical deduction, but is an expression of variable social needs and cultural pressures, Harding 'reads' the laws governing English society at any given period as a window on the social and cultural standards of the times. More recently, and working within a somewhat narrower compass, Peter Gabel and Jay M Feinman, echoing Marxist views about the ways in which the interests of the powerful shape law, have placed the evolution of the law of contracts in relation to the development of capitalist ideology.[7] The aim of the present study is far more limited. Rather than attempting to explain the entire process of legal evolution, or even the development of the law of contracts in terms of a dominant ideology or succession of ideologies, its concern is with only one particular action framed *ex contractu*, the action for breach of promise of marriage, and its transformation in relation to one specific facet of the social and cultural framework of the England of the 'long nineteenth century.'

The facet of this social and cultural framework that I reference for my analysis of the breach-of-promise action is the nineteenth-century ideology of femininity: the ideal of the true and virtuous woman, which developed from around the middle of the eighteenth century and which was to provide the cultural definition of womanhood throughout the 1800s and the Victorian age. This choice of ideology situates my project within the second corpus of work that I should like to consider here: research into the history of gender or, more particularly, into nineteenth-century women's history. Women's history is an area of study that has seen a rapid transition from famine to feast since its emergence as a historical school in the 1960s.[8] *Gender and History, Journal of the History of Sexuality, Journal of Women's History, Signs,* and *Women's History Review,* to name but five, are all journals devoted exclusively to studies in the history of gender. Books on historical themes about gender are multiplying, and there is an ever-increasing array of Internet sources on many aspects of women's history. The present-day quantity of material on 'the conditions in which women lived' would surely delight the English essayist and novelist Virginia Woolf, who, in 1929, had vainly looked 'about the shelves for books [about women] that were not there'.[9] The nineteenth century has proved especially popular with historians of women. This is hardly to be wondered at: history is, after

---

[7] Peter Gabel and Jay M Feinman, 'Contract Law as Ideology' in *The Politics of Law: A Progressive Critique*, David Kairys (ed), 3rd edn (New York: Basic Books, 1998) 497–510.

[8] An excellent overview over the theoretical directions taken by gender history and the diversity of research in the field is provided in Anna Green and Kathleen Troup, 'Gender and History' in *The Houses of History: A Critical Reader in Twentieth-Century History and Theory*, Anna Green and Kathleen Troup (eds) (Manchester: Manchester University Press, 1999) 253–62.

[9] Virginia Woolf, *A Room of One's Own* (London: Hogarth Press, 1974) 62, 68.

all, the study of change over time, as is evidenced by the fact that gender, a variable social construct, and not sex, the biological difference between men and women—which is only rarely subject to change—is the key concept used in gender history.[10] The nineteenth century, then, is popular with historians of women, because it was a century of great change for women, both in social and in legal terms. Socially, the nineteenth century was, of course, the great age of the middle class, the century when the formulation of a specifically middle-class culture welded together the middling ranks of society, whilst simultaneously separating them off from the aristocracy and gentry above and the working classes below them. Catherine Hall, for one, has argued that the development of the middle class was gendered, that class formation went hand in hand with 'a sharpened division between men and women, between the public and the private'.[11] Women, who had taken more of an active part in social life prior to the nineteenth century,[12] now found themselves assigned a separate sphere, the home, and a special function, the guardianship of the domestic virtues.[13] This 'separate spheres' account has recently been questioned by a number of scholars, who have pointed to the late eighteenth and early nineteenth centuries as a time of increasing opportunities for women, basing their argument on a rise in female literacy and on women's growing participation in the economy.[14] While this reappraisal has much to recommend it—not least because it serves as a helpful reminder that social developments are often considerably more complex and 'messy' than historical accounts of

---

[10] For the sex/gender distinction, see Ann Oakley, *Sex, Gender and Society* (rev edn), Towards a New Society (Aldershot: Gower Publishing, 1985) 16. In women's history, there is now 'a preoccupation with gender as a category of analysis'. Joan Wallach Scott, 'The Problem of Invisibility,' Kleinberg 16.

[11] Catherine Hall, *White, Male and Middle Class: Explorations in Feminism and History* (Cambridge: Polity Press, 1992) 96.

[12] The nineteenth-century world of separate spheres is usually contrasted to the eighteenth century, which is portrayed as a golden age for women (Hall 95, 99). The deterioration in women's social position post-1800 is accounted for by the nineteenth-century advent of industrialization with its male-oriented machines and factories. Patricia Branca, *Women in Europe since 1750* (London: Croom Helm, 1978) 11. The vision of the eighteenth century as a golden age for women has been questioned by a number of scholars. See, for instance, Amanda Vickery, 'Golden Age to Separate Spheres? A Review of the Categories and Chronology of English Women's History' (1993) 36(2) *Historical Journal* 400, 402. See also G J Barker-Benfield, *The Culture of Sensibility: Sex and Society in Eighteenth-Century Britain* (Chicago: University of Chicago Press, 1992) 155.

[13] The classic work on the development and the strength of the ideology of separate spheres and the break it marked with a less restricted past is the massive Leonore Davidoff and Catherine Hall, *Family Fortunes: Men and Women of the English Middle Class, 1780–1850*, Women in Culture and Society (Chicago: University of Chicago Press, 1987). For another work that analyses the doctrine of separate spheres, see Deborah Gorham, *The Victorian Girl and the Feminine Ideal* (Bloomington: Indiana University Press, 1982).

[14] See, for instance, Vickery 412. See also Hannah Barker and Elaine Chalus (eds), *Gender in Eighteenth-Century England: Roles, Representations, and Responsibilities* (London: Longman, 1997) 8–24, where the original separate spheres literature and the more recent revisionist accounts are helpfully reviewed. See also Barker-Benfield 154–350.

them would have us believe—the broad outlines of the original analysis of separate spheres, as Nicola Lacey, for one, has argued, remain persuasive. Thus, it is generally acknowledged that women constituted a lower proportion of those in paid employment in the second half of the nineteenth century than they had in the late eighteenth century—a surprising statistic in the context of general capitalist growth and development—and that their practical access to theoretically burgeoning opportunities was heavily circumscribed, not only by social and financial obstacles to education and independence, but also by the emergence of constraining norms of feminine comportment, which provided the baseline for defining propriety and conditioned women's access to their (shrinking) social terrain.[15] While nineteenth-century women engaged in an impressive range of activities and played many roles in society—'daughter, sister, spinster, mother, wife, widow, neighbour, employer, worker, professional, philanthropist, recipient of charity, churchgoer, consumer, reader, imperialist, political activist, public servant, and monarch, among others'[16]—they did not enjoy infinite possibilities. The economic and cultural limitations they experienced were severe.[17] It therefore remains true to say that the gathering shadows of domesticity made the first half of the nineteenth century an age of great change, in the direction of social restriction, for women, while the declining decades of that same century brought great change in the opposite direction, as more and more women, under the influence of the first feminist movement, declined the dubious honour of being an 'angel in the house'.[18]

Nineteenth-century women's legal history parallels the double shift displayed by the social development. The nineteenth century witnessed, first, the imposition of legal disabilities on women—it is worth remembering that the formal bar on women's political participation was introduced by the Reform Act of 1832, prior to which women ratepayers had been eligible to vote in local elections[19]—and then the piecemeal and hard-won removal of these disabilities as the century wore on. Most of the work in the field of nineteenth-century women's legal history focuses on either the political or the marital bondage of women in that century: either their non-existence for the purposes of public law or the civil death suffered by women on entering the married state. Once

---

[15] Nicola Lacey, *Women, Crime, and Character: From Moll Flanders to Tess of the D'Urbervilles* (Oxford: Oxford University Press, 2008) 95–6.

[16] Susie Steinbach, *Women in England 1760–1914: A Social History* (London: Weidenfeld & Nicolson, 2004) 2.

[17] Ibid.

[18] This catchphrase comes from a poem of the same name by Coventry Patmore. See Coventry Patmore, The Angel in the House *together with* The Victories of Love, Alice Meynell (introd) (London: Routledge, 1905). Although this Victorian poem is little known today, its title has become a byword for domestic womanly perfection.

[19] Robert Shoemaker, *Gender in English Society 1660–1850: The Emergence of Separate Spheres?* (London: Longman, 1998) ch 6.

again, this research emphasis may reflect the historian's concern with change, since it was the public law status of women and the private law status of married women that saw the most dramatic revision during the nineteenth century. The public law position of women, single and married, at the dawn of the nineteenth century is easily explained: 'in public law there was no place for them, except on the throne'.[20] And in private law, when a woman married, her legal identity became suspended in that of her husband, and she 'fell prey to a whole series of disabilities which placed her in the same legal category as wards, lunatics, idiots, and outlaws'.[21] This radical alteration in status was the effect of the doctrine of coverture, according to which by marriage, 'the husband and wife [. . . became] one person in law',[22] that one person and bearer of all rights being the husband. Both the public law status of women and the private law status of married women were extensively revised during the course of the nineteenth century and beyond, culminating in the extension of the franchise to women in 1918, the removal of sex disqualifications in relation to professional and public life by the Sex Disqualification (Removal) Act of 1919, and a succession of family law reforms, one of the most significant of which was the introduction of gender-neutral grounds for divorce in 1923.[23]

While the public law position of women and the private law position of married women are therefore well researched,[24] comparatively little work has been done on the private law position of *single* women in the nineteenth century. In fact, it was (and still is) a widely held belief that in private law single women enjoyed the same rights and liabilities as men. A belief in the private law equality of single women was entertained and propagated, for instance, by leading members of the first women's rights movement. Thus, Barbara Leigh Smith Bodichon, a key figure

[20] Janelle Greenberg, 'The Legal Status of the English Woman in Early Eighteenth-Century Common Law and Equity' in *Studies in Eighteenth-Century Culture*, Harold E Pagliaro (ed), vol 4 (Madison: University of Wisconsin Press, 1975) 172.

[21] Ibid.

[22] William Blackstone, *Commentaries on the Laws of England* (Philadelphia, 1879) 1: 442.

[23] The reforms further included the Divorce Act of 1857 (introducing civil divorce), the Married Women's Property Acts of 1870 and 1882 (allowing a married woman to retain her own wages, possessions, and capital, rather than renounce them to her husband), the Matrimonial Causes Act of 1878 (giving magistrates' courts the power to grant a separation order, with maintenance and custody of children under 10, to a wife who had been beaten by her husband, extended in 1886 to one who had been deserted), and the Infant Custody Act of 1886 (giving mothers the right to appeal for custody of their children). On these reforms, see Mary Lyndon Shanley's book *Feminism, Marriage, and the Law in Victorian England, 1850–1895* (London: I. B. Tauris, 1989).

[24] Lee Holcombe, *Wives and Property: Reform of the Married Women's Property Law in Nineteenth-Century England* (Toronto: University of Toronto Press, 1983) and Shanley's *Feminism, Marriage, and the Law*, for instance, chart the emergence and evolution of the women's rights movement and its impact on, especially, the legal status of married women. A similar emphasis is displayed in David Rubinstein, *Before the Suffragettes: Women's Emancipation in the 1890s* (Brighton: Harvester Press, 1986), which looks at women in employment and politics.

in the campaign for women's suffrage and higher education, in her 1854 pamphlet, deploring women's legal disadvantages, never doubted that single women 'are affected by all the laws and incur the same responsibilities in all their contracts and doings as men'.[25] The same unquestioning belief in the private law equality of single women can still be met with today. Janelle Greenberg, for instance, stated in 1978 that the '*feme sole* enjoyed…the same rights and responsibilities as did men.…She made contracts; she sued and was sued.'[26] This orthodoxy has only recently been challenged. Writing in 1996 in the context of redress in tort for sexual injuries, Lea VanderVelde first questioned the correctness of the claim that single women enjoyed the same private law protection as men. While acknowledging that in many respects single women were independent legal entities, VanderVelde observed that 'in one centrally important way, they were not. Until the midnineteenth [sic] century, single women had no effective pattern of direct rights of action in tort for sexual injuries.'[27]

As a contractual and hence a private law cause of action brought almost by definition by a single woman, the action for breach of promise affords a valuable opportunity for further investigating the relevance of gender in private law. Like the seduction action, already claimed as an instance of the private law inequality of single women by VanderVelde, breach of promise to marry is one of four causes of action, which in American textbooks are frequently grouped under the rubric 'heartbalm'. The term appears to be an American coinage. There is no evidence of its widespread use in England. In addition to breach of promise and seduction, the remaining two 'heartbalm' actions are criminal conversation and alienation of affections. Unlike seduction and breach of promise, the so-called non-marital heartbalm actions, criminal conversation and alienation of affections, are both marital torts. Criminal conversation is the civil cause of action corresponding to the crime of adultery. Abolished in England in 1857, it could be brought by a husband against any man who had committed adultery with his wife. By contrast, alienation of affections, likewise a cause of action open only to the husband, did not have to involve adultery. The gravamen of the injury here was not the interference with a husband's right of exclusive sexual access to his wife's body, but the destruction of the affection or consortium subsisting between husband and wife. Alienation of affections became a distinct tort by the latter half of the nineteenth century and was a purely American kind of lawsuit, which never existed under that label in England. However,

---

[25] Barbara Leigh Smith Bodichon, *A Brief Summary, in Plain Language, of the Most Important Laws Concerning Women* (London, 1854) 4.
[26] Greenberg 172.
[27] Lea VanderVelde, 'The Legal Ways of Seduction' (1996) 48 *Stanford Law Review* 822.

an English husband might recover in tort where a third party induced his wife to leave him or remain away from him against his will.[28]

The common denominator of the heartbalm actions is that they provide legal 'balm' for broken, or at least bruised, hearts. In addition to belonging to the same legal family, seduction and breach of promise to marry share a similar dynamic. Both causes of action revolve around male/female relationships, illegitimate (seduction) in the one case and legitimate (intended marriage) in the other. Of course, there are also substantial differences: seduction is an action in tort, while the breach-of-promise action, formally at least, always remained within the economy of contract. Also, although the relations between a man and a woman, legitimate or illegitimate as the case may be, are at the heart of both, it was only in breach of promise that the man and the woman were the parties to the action. In common law seduction actions, the woman did not have standing to sue. As the action was conceived of as one for the loss of services (*actio per quod servitium amisit*), the right to sue was granted to those entitled to the woman's services, usually her master or her father. Still, the actions are similar in that questions of sex and of socially-prescribed sex-specific norms of behaviour are central to both.

The goal of this study is to explore the impact of these socially constructed sex-specific norms, gender for short, on the litigation of broken engagements in nineteenth-century England. The aim is to provide a consideration of the assimilation and reproduction of a particular cultural construct in a specific legal context and to expose the underlying pattern of sexual typification that informed the law.[29] The claim advanced is that a particular construction of

---

[28] See John W Salmond, *The Law of Torts: A Treatise on the English Law of Liability for Civil Injuries* (London: Stevens & Haynes, 1907) 379. The English cases stress procuring or enticing the plaintiff's spouse to leave the home. There is no English decision squarely holding alienation of affections per se sufficient to sustain an action. See Nathan P Feinsinger, 'Legislative Attack on "Heart Balm"' (1935) 33(7) *Michigan Law Review* 992 n 75. For a history of criminal conversation in England, see Lawrence Stone, *Road to Divorce: England 1530–1987* (Oxford: Oxford University Press, 1990) 231–300. For a discussion of the American law on the subject, see Feinsinger 989–92 and Laura Hanft Korobkin's excellent legal-literary study *Criminal Conversations: Sentimentality and Nineteenth-Century Legal Stories of Adultery*, The Social Foundations of Aesthetic Forms (New York: Columbia University Press, 1998). For a history of alienation of affections, see Thomas K Leeper, 'Alienation of Affections: Flourishing Anachronism' (1977) 13 *Wake Forest Law Review* 586–90.

[29] Arguments linking legal developments and prevalent cultural constructs of femininity—particularly in the context of courtship, marriage, and divorce—have been advanced by a number of scholars in recent years. Michael Grossberg, for instance, has argued that nineteenth-century American 'breach-of-promise suits allowed the courts to promote republican notions of marriage and gender responsibilities'. See Michael Grossberg, *Governing the Hearth: Law and the Family in Nineteenth-Century America*, Studies in Legal History (Chapel Hill: University of North Carolina Press, 1985) 35. Like me, Grossberg ties the twentieth-century demise of these suits to changing cultural ideals for women that included independence and sexuality (55). In a similar vein, Laura Hanft Korobkin's study of criminal conversation asks how twentieth-century 'changes in America's images of women, sexuality, and marriage ... changed women's relation to the law' (5) and concludes that

gender, the nineteenth-century ideal of the true woman, controlled the simultaneous transformation of the action for breach of promise.[30] The ideal of the delicate, virtuous, and submissive woman can be seen as the *fons et origo* of and the unifying construct behind the idiosyncratic complex of rules that governed the breach-of-promise action in the period in question. An analysis of the common law action for breach of promise of marriage reveals that, just as within the range of intentional tort actions, as VanderVelde has shown, sex was *sui generis*, so also within the range of contractual actions sex was *sui generis*. The breach-of-promise action, while formally gender-neutral throughout its history, was lived out as in fact highly gender-conscious during the nineteenth century. In the context of the private law action for breach of promise of marriage, where, exceptionally for the age, single women asserted their legal identity in large numbers, that identity was understood to be, first and foremost, a feminine one.

II. Tools of Analysis: Empiricism and Literature

This study does not stop short at providing evidence for the claim that the nineteenth-century breach-of-promise action was the legal 'codification'[31] of the ideal of true womanhood. Rather, I should like to continue my exploration of the symbiotic relationship between the nineteenth-century feminine ideal and the legal action with an analysis of the effects and wider implications of that alliance.

legal and social developments, most notably acts granting legal rights to married women and attempts by wives to sue the lovers of their adulterous husbands, undermined the sentimental foundations of the suit and deprived it of its attractions and legitimacy. For another work relating cultural ideals to legal and literary history, see Norma Basch's book *Framing American Divorce: From the Revolutionary Generation to the Victorians* (Berkeley: University of California Press, 1999), which traces the legal, social, and cultural experience of divorce in America to provide an innovative exploration of the limits of nineteenth-century ideals of domesticity and conjugal love and their legacy for us today.

[30] A similar argument, with respect to the tort of seduction, is made by M B W Sinclair. Sinclair's central claim is that 'the prevalent conception of women and their social role—the myth of the ideal woman—has controlled the evolution of the tort of seduction'. Sinclair explains the seduction action's initial property-based rationale, as an action by the master for loss of the seduced woman's services, in terms of the then prevalent conception of women as property, 'economically valuable for the services they could provide', and its remoulding as an action 'based on the loss of virtue, not services' by the development of the nineteenth-century feminine ideal. See M B W Sinclair, 'Seduction and the Myth of the Ideal Woman' (1987) 5(33) *Law and Inequality* 33.

[31] For this term, see Ann M Garfinkle, Carol Lefcourt, and Diane B Schulder, 'Women's Servitude under Law' in *Law against the People: Essays to Demystify Law, Order and the Courts*, Robert Lefcourt (ed) (New York: Random House, 1971), who argue that in essence, 'the laws are a formal codification of attitudes toward women that permeate our culture' (120).

For a rigorous effects-oriented analysis of a legal development, it is necessary to turn to academic disciplines other than law. If one is interested in projecting the *likely* impact of a legal rule, then, in the context of contract, the most extensively used discipline to date is microeconomics. An economic projection, despite its many advantages, must, however, by its very nature remain hypothetical. It can never yield more than 'theoretical models of the likely impact of a rule of law under certain, often quite limiting, assumptions'.[32] Against that, the great beauty of the historical perspective is, of course, that, at least as regards effects, one is dealing with actualities, rather than potentialities and hypotheses. The results are there already, waiting, not to be predicted, but to be unearthed. The tool to use in historical analysis, therefore, is empirical investigation.

Accordingly, I analysed over 250 actual breach-of-promise cases, decided by a variety of English courts over the 300-year period extending from the action's common law beginnings in the mid-seventeenth century to its statutory abolition in 1970. The vast majority of these cases date from what I have described as the seminal period in the life of the breach-of-promise action, the period of the action's rise and fall between 1800 and 1940. The cases provide ample evidence of the postulated symbiosis, but since they cover more than a century, they are also revealing for what they tell us about its short- and longer-term effects. Nearly all of my cases are drawn from period newspapers, rather than law reports. There are two reasons for this. For a start, only a small percentage of breach-of-promise cases ever made it into the law reports. Confining one's attention to reported decisions would therefore import the danger of proceeding from too narrow a base. Secondly, judgments that did get reported and thus became judgments of record are appellate decisions. This means that the danger of insufficient material is compounded by a risk of bias, as a case that gets appealed is always likely to be exceptional in some way.[33]

The work of the lower courts, as recorded in period newspapers, offers a rich, but potentially unwieldy, source of information. The bulk of the material, when allied to the constraints of time and money with which all scholars contend, makes it necessary to resort to sampling. My aim in collecting a sample of cases on breach of promise was to ensure that it was

---

[32] H G Beale, W D Bishop, and M P Furmston, *Contract: Cases and Materials*, 5th edn (London: Oxford University Press, 2008) 11.

[33] For advice on the difficult question of whether to draw on newspaper accounts or reported decisions, I am indebted to Stephen Cretney of All Souls College, Oxford. Professor Cretney shared my objections to relying on reported cases and agreed that newspaper accounts were far more likely to be revealing (Stephen Cretney, email to the author, 18 January 2004). He also gave valuable advice on identifying newspapers likely to contain cases on breach of promise.

statistically unbiased, sufficiently broad to pick up trends over time, and sufficiently detailed to get at the human stories behind the legal facts. I sampled from three national and three regional newspapers in England: the *Times, Morning Chronicle, News of the World, Lancaster Gazette, Taunton Courier,* and *Norwich Mercury.* Taken together, these papers, all of which operated throughout at least most of the nineteenth century, cover the country geographically, extending from Taunton and surrounding neighbourhoods in the South over the East Coast to Lancashire in the North West; they cover the country culturally, collectively targeting the population in the metropolis and the provinces, the working classes and the well-to-do; and they cover the country politically, ranging from conservative (*Lancaster Gazette*), over neutral or moderate (*Taunton Courier, Times, Morning Chronicle*), to liberal (*Norwich Mercury, News of the World*). From these papers, I consulted the March and April issues of every fifth year for the period between 1800 and 1940,[34] so as to get coverage of the local assizes[35] as well as reports on cases outside the locality.

An application of these sampling criteria yielded a total of 242 cases. Each case was analysed and coded into seven main (and 64 sub-) categories relating to the parties involved, the making out and defence of the case, the amount of damages, the presence of aggravating or mitigating circumstances, and the strategies and arguments used at the trial. The individuals featured in the sample cases comprise a very diverse lot. They come from different age and socio-economic groups,[36] and the circumstances and length of their engagements vary. The participants in these actions have but one thing in common: they all experienced a significant upset in the transition from the single to the married state, which brought them into court. The records they left provide the statistical basis for this study.

When looking at a large number of cases with familiar plot constellations, mainly for the purpose of statistical analysis, it is easy to forget that each case embodies the skeletal remains of a unique human situation. In so sensitive an

---

[34] Some of the newspapers I consulted did not operate throughout the 1800–1940 period. In this case, I was restricted to sampling from those parts of the period during which the newspaper was published.

[35] The Easter assizes took place sometime in March or April of each year, depending on the courts' schedule.

[36] For statistical purposes, I assigned every participant in my sample a class status, based on (in the case of a man) income, profession, and the terms used by counsel in describing him and (in the case of a woman) the status group of her parents or family, her (non-)participation in the world of work, and the terms used by counsel in describing her. The lowest status group is class 1, which is made up of working-class people with a very tenuous hold on respectability. The highest class (6) is reserved to the aristocracy. Class groups 3–5 are given over to the middle classes, with class 3 describing the lower middle class. Class 2 is made up of the upper working class.

area as love, courtship, break-up, and heartbreak, only detailed accounts can bring out the nuances. I have therefore included three representative case studies, one for each of the three periods that form the major blocks of research effort, to add qualitative dimensions to quantitative data and to illustrate in depth the points I am trying to make. In so doing, I am utilizing the stock historical methodology of demonstrating by example, popularized by the work of Lawrence Stone[37] and put to very effective use by Norma Basch in her study of divorce in nineteenth-century America. The cases selected for study are both representative and exceptional. They are representative in that they are perfect illustrations of what I consider to have been the distinguishing trends of the historical periods from which they date: *Orford v Cole*, selected from the early nineteenth century (1800–1850), demonstrates that period's central concern with the plaintiff's true womanhood as key to her success at trial. *Smith v The Earl Ferrers*, which takes the field for the high Victorian period (1850–1900), furnishes what I regard as the best illustration of this second period's characteristic equation of the breach-of-promise plaintiff with morally bankrupt womanhood. And *Shaw v Shaw*, included for the post-Victorian period (1900–1940), brings out the disintegration and shapelessness of a cause of action past its cultural sell-by date. The three cases studied are exceptional in that each can claim to embody a superlative of some sort.[38] *Orford v Cole* resulted in what appears to have been the highest English jury award for breach of promise in the nineteenth century. *Smith v The Earl Ferrers* was perhaps the most famous breach-of-promise suit of all time.[39] And *Shaw v Shaw* typified the only breach-of-promise constellation that would, in a way, survive the action's abolition.[40]

---

[37] Lawrence Stone is probably the leading historian on sexuality, marriage, divorce, and family structure in England. His work on those subjects includes two collections of case studies: *Broken Lives: Separation and Divorce in England, 1660–1857* (Oxford: Oxford University Press, 1993) and *Uncertain Unions: Marriage in England, 1660–1753* (New York: Oxford University Press, 1992).

[38] Since all of these cases are standouts, they are also unusually well documented. The superior quality of the documentation is yet another circumstance tending to recommend these cases for detailed study.

[39] The case continues to attract phenomenal amounts of scholarly attention today. Almost any modern analysis of breach of promise at least touches on *Smith v The Earl Ferrers*. Discussions of the case are included in Ginger S Frost, *Promises Broken: Courtship, Class, and Gender in Victorian England*, Victorian Literature and Culture Series (Charlottesville: University Press of Virginia, 1995) 118–23 and Karin L Kellogg, ' "Blighted Prospects and Wounded Feelings": Breach of Promise in Victorian Law and Literature', master's thesis, University of Alberta, 1995, 41–8. The case is also routinely included in anthologies of famous Victorian trials. See, for instance, Michael Harrison, *Painful Details: Twelve Victorian Scandals* (London: Max Parish, 1962) 24–37.

[40] The wrong complained of in *Shaw v Shaw* (1954) 2 QB 429 was not that the defendant had broken his promise to marry the plaintiff, but that the plaintiff had entered a marriage which, unknown to her, was void, because her 'husband' was already married. When he died and the truth was discovered, she sued his estate for damages. She recovered on the grounds that the

As the goal of this study is to explore the interaction between the law, in the form of the action for breach of promise, and culture, in the form of the nineteenth-century feminine ideal, the source materials employed are also drawn from both sides of the law/culture divide. Accordingly, alongside actual cases—the principal output of the courts as the chief arbiters on law—the second set of materials consulted is the output of writers as the chief arbiters on culture. References to the legal culture and the larger culture reflect the professional versus lay components at work in breach of promise.[41] Although the focus is on the breach-of-promise action as it was lived out in nineteenth and early twentieth-century England, I have decided to include American literary and cinematic representations of breach of promise in my analysis. Treating America, in this instance, as essentially an adjunct of the mother country is defensible, since the two countries were culturally very homogeneous during the Victorian age. Daniel Walker Howe has demonstrated that Victorian culture was a transatlantic phenomenon, shared by English-speaking countries throughout the Western world:

The Victorian cultural community constituted an international reference group in the nineteenth-century world. . . . The communications system of Victorianism was based on the English language and the media of print and (in due course) the telegraph and telephone. Knowledge of English put one in potential contact with a particular cultural heritage, including law, religion, and science . . .[42]

Howe's belief in a nineteenth-century transatlantic network of ideas is echoed by Steven Mintz, who notes that the 'burgeoning Anglo-American connection' was founded on 'a flood of moral tracts, periodicals, schoolbooks, and advice manuals published on both sides of the Atlantic [. . . which] defined models of character, manners, sensibility, and respectability and helped to create a mass middle-class reading public, responsive to a common set of moral standards and cultural symbols'.[43]

---

deceased was in breach of his promise to marry her and in breach of his implied warranty that he was in a position to marry her.

  When the Law Commission recommended the statutory removal of breach-of-promise actions in 1969, it suggested that a legal remedy (albeit one outside of breach of promise) should be available in constellations like the one in *Shaw v Shaw*. Law Commission, *Breach of Promise of Marriage*, Law Com No 26 (London: HMSO, 1969) 16–18. The Commission's proposals were subsequently enacted into law.

  [41] A similar approach is adopted by Norma Basch in her study of divorce in nineteenth-century America. Drawing on legal texts, newspaper coverage, trial pamphlets, and sentimental fiction, Basch probes the interplay between the legal culture and the larger culture, successively viewing divorce 'as a legal form, a social option, and a cultural symbol' (9).

  [42] Daniel Walker Howe, 'Victorian Culture in America' in *Victorian America*, Daniel Walker Howe (ed) (n p: University of Pennsylvania Press, 1976) 16–17.

  [43] Steven Mintz, *A Prison of Expectations: The Family in Victorian Culture* (New York: New York University Press, 1983) 26–7.

To unearth literature and film dealing with the legal aspects of breach of promise, I conducted systematic searches in the public catalogues of eight leading libraries in England and the United States as well as researching Internet databases. I looked for accounts of breach of promise dating from between 1800 and 1940, rather than 'modern' historical novels and films that seek to bring the age of breach of promise alive retrospectively for the contemporary reader/spectator.[44] The research confirmed what isolated instances of enduringly famous fictional breach-of-promise suits—notably Dickens's *Bardell v Pickwick* (*The Pickwick Papers*[45]) and Gilbert and Sullivan's *Trial by Jury*[46]— had promised: breach-of-promise trials constituted a fertile source of inspiration for nineteenth- and early twentieth-century literature and film. Fictional accounts of breach of promise started to appear in the 1830s, with the turnout increasing somewhat over the second half of the nineteenth century. From the early twentieth century, the breach-of-promise action was picked up by the nascent film industry. That there was a thriving sub-genre of literature and film specifically addressing the legal (and not merely the ever popular social or moral) aspects of a promise of marriage and its breach may surprise us. If works of literature are indeed, as Shakespeare has claimed, the 'brief chronicles of the time',[47] then the fact that the breach-of-promise action was included in the annals is a reflection of its centrality to nineteenth-century Anglo-American culture. Chronicles are highly selective, and only those facts which the writer considers important, are included in the record.

There would be various ways of categorizing this second set of breach-of-promise materials. It is a very diverse group, being made up of short stories, songs, plays, operettas, novels, and films. Some of the productions are canonical, others ephemeral. The methodology that suggests itself for my purposes is to categorize by legal element, with the focus on the plaintiff. One arrives at the following four categories:[48]

>   (A)   Works in which a female character is shown as an in-court breach-of-promise plaintiff ('in-court involvement').

[44] Modern accounts do not provide any insight into how the breach-of-promise action was perceived and represented in the period under investigation and are therefore useless for the purposes of my study.

[45] Charles Dickens, *The Pickwick Papers*, James Kinsley (ed), 1837 (Oxford: Oxford University Press, 1998).

[46] William Schwenck Gilbert and Arthur Sullivan, *Trial by Jury*, *The Savoy Operas: Being the Complete Text of the Gilbert and Sullivan Operas As Originally Produced in the Years 1875–1896*, 1875 (London: Macmillan, 1926) 1–19.

[47] See n 2.

[48] Materials that do not depict a breach-of-promise plaintiff in the sense of one of my four categories or where the treatment of breach of promise seems minor or repetitive are not included in my analysis.

(B) Works in which a female character becomes or at one point has been a breach-of-promise plaintiff, but is not shown as such in court ('out-of-court involvement'). This may happen, for instance, where the breach-of-promise trial takes place off-stage or where the trial predates the time at which the story is set.

(C) Works in which a female character considers bringing, but does not actually bring a breach-of-promise suit ('contemplated involvement'). This may be the case where a female character uses the threat of an action as a means of exerting power over another character.

(D) Works in which a female character is believed by one or more other characters to be considering bringing a breach-of-promise suit, but does not in fact have any such intention ('imputed involvement').

As this study reveals, accounts of breach of promise are not spread evenly over all four categories for each of the three periods under investigation. Instead, in each period, the accounts tend to cluster around one or two of the categories, with the dominant category (or categories) changing from one historical period to the next. This shift in the dominant category is important for what it tells us about the degree of plot-level integration of the breach-of-promise element into the fiction of each period. Works in category A ('in-court involvement'), for instance, where the writer integrates the breach-of-promise element to the extent of allowing the trial to take place before the audience, display a greater degree of plot-level integration than works in category B ('out-of-court involvement'). The degree of plot-level integration, in its turn, however, is a potent indicator of the relevance and meaning of the breach-of-promise action to early nineteenth-century, high, and post-Victorian culture respectively.

In drawing on both empiricism and literature as tools for analysing the effects of the fusion of law and cultural ideology that is embodied in the nineteenth-century action for breach of promise, I am deliberately overstepping the territorial boundaries established by any one discipline. The value of reading in the conceptual in-between space between different methodological approaches lies in highlighting the need to consult a wide variety of historical sources from all areas of cultural activity for a well-rounded picture of the past.

***

This study, then, is an exploration of the use and meaning of the common law action for breach of promise of marriage to early, high, and post-nineteenth-century culture respectively. It advances a particular interpretive model, a particular myth of womanhood, by which we can understand more fully the story of the action's rise and fall. The study adopts for its vantage-point both the evidence of actual cases and the narratives contained in fictional renditions of the breach-of-promise theme.

It begins, in Chapter 1, with the quest to find a unifying construct that would account for the idiosyncratic mixture of rules (a luxuriant blend of both contract and tort) that came to govern the breach-of-promise action from the early 1800s onwards. This unifying construct it locates beyond law, in the socio-cultural context and the emerging feminine ideal of the virtuous, delicate, and submissive woman. The complex of rules applied to the breach-of-promise context during the 'long nineteenth century', the first chapter argues, can be understood as the codification of the nineteenth-century myth of true womanhood.

The second chapter considers the wider implications of this infusion of mythologized femininity for the law, in particular for the position of plaintiffs. It suggests that the feminizing process imported a contradiction to the centre of the action and lodged an inconsistency at the very heart of the plaintiff. By virtue of her position as litigant in a public forum, a woman bringing a breach-of-promise suit put herself in direct opposition to the central tenets of the very femininity the Victorians valorized and in accordance with which the cause of action was shaped. The breach-of-promise plaintiff was structurally very ill fitted for the part she had to play. The nineteenth-century cause of action, as both the legal codification of true womanhood and a platform for not so very true women, may thus be seen as beset from its inception by a fatal structural inconsistency.

Chapters 3–5 provide a consideration of how the action's contradictory potential was realized, sought to be minimized and defused (by the plaintiff's side), or dramatized (by the defendant's) and how it was deployed by writers (and later by film-makers). The three chapters survey three consecutive time periods, the early nineteenth century (1800–1850), the high (1850–1900), and the post-Victorian (1900–1940) periods respectively. Each chapter in the trilogy draws on the empirical evidence and the fictional records as well as incorporating a representative case study. Chapter 3 opens with a case study (*Orford v Cole*) that presents in detail the way the breach-of-promise action was structured around nineteenth-century notions of ideal womanhood. The chapter provides a consideration of the strategies practised by plaintiffs and their legal representatives to obscure the structural inconsistency. It finds evidence for the success of these strategies in both the phenomenal awards secured by early-period breach-of-promise plaintiffs and in the nature of the fictional accounts that date from the early period. In the early period, there is no evidence of any fictional exploitation of the structural inconsistency. Rather, writers display a marked tendency to *create* an inconsistency by inverting the ideal and casting that inversion in the plaintiff role. The effects of this studied miscasting, of putting a widow or virago figure where a true woman should be, are both ludicrous and faintly nauseating. In this disharmony in both the depiction and the reaction it evokes, there is an element of the grotesque, which may be regarded as the dominant aesthetic of early-period breach-of-promise fiction. Chapter 4 considers the high Victorian abandonment of the previously employed strategies of containment and the attendant exposure of the structural inconsistency. The chapter demonstrates that, as the structural inconsistency was rendered more visible, so the breach-of-promise action and, more particularly, the breach-of-promise plaintiff became targets for cultural exclusion and attack. In the high Victorian period, plaintiff success was dampened, and breach-of-promise fiction started to thrive on an exploitation of the structural inconsistency. The fictional plaintiffs of this period are the ideal perverted, their outward true womanhood belying the corruption inside. In the high Victorian period, breach-of-promise comedy takes on the features of satire as it dramatizes the discrepancy between professions of virtue and the practices that contradict them. The fifth and final chapter explores the post-Victorian period, beginning after 1900. The chapter reveals that, as the feminine ideal veered away from the nineteenth-century definition of true womanhood towards the twentieth-century vision of woman as self-sufficient, energetic, and competent, the breach-of-promise action was turned into a legal anachronism, a musty bit of common law machinery only rarely called into action after the 1920s and 1930s. Although the cause of action was not formally abolished in England until 1970, the age of breach of promise was effectively over with the paradigm shift in the feminine ideal. This temporal connection in the decline of both ideal and action once again supports my premise (as did their near-simultaneous birth) that the nineteenth-century feminine ideal and the nineteenth-century breach-of-promise action were uneasily and fatally, but nonetheless inextricably, entwined. In the literary and cinematic versions of this final, post-Victorian period, breach of promise assumes symbolic meaning, signifying a conception of the nature and status of women, which was, quite simply, passé.

1

Codifying Womanhood: The Nineteenth-Century Action for Breach of Promise of Marriage as the Legal Expression of the Ideal of True Womanhood

The action for breach of promise of marriage offers an excellent example of the process of legal evolution. Originating in mid-seventeenth-century England as an action on an *assumpsit*[1] providing compensation for the pecuniary consequences of a broken contract to marry, it reinvented itself in the late eighteenth and early nineteenth centuries: switching its gravamen from the economics of a broken contract to the emotionalism of a woman's wounded feelings and injured affections, the nineteenth-century action lost its moorings both to specific material losses and to conventional contract-based limitations. It emerged as a legal hybrid, which has defied attempts at systematic legal categorization.

This chapter provides a survey and analysis of the evolution of the action for breach of promise of marriage from its mid-seventeenth-century contractual beginnings to its nineteenth-century hybridization. Section I introduces the nineteenth-century action for breach of promise of marriage as a problem in legal classification, a cause of action that has proved resistant to attempts to assign it, lock, stock, and barrel, to conventional legal categories. Section II claims that the action has not always been a legal misfit. Reverting to the

---

[1] The term *assumpsit* came to be commonly employed in the course of the fourteenth century for actions on the case that were based on an allegation that the defendant had undertaken to do something for the plaintiff and had harmed the plaintiff in person or property by doing it badly or wrongly. From the early sixteenth century, *assumpsit* was made available in cases where the defendant had simply failed to comply with what he had agreed to do, ie in cases of a pure nonfeasance. As a result, *assumpsit* became a general action for damages for the breach of a simple contract. Reinhard Zimmermann, *The Law of Obligations: Roman Foundations of the Civilian Tradition* (Oxford: Oxford University Press, 1996) 777–9. For a comprehensive discussion, see A W B Simpson, *A History of the Common Law of Contract: The Rise and Fall of the Action of Assumpsit* (rpt edn) (Oxford: Clarendon Press, 1987) 199–280.

common law action's mid-seventeenth-century origins, it argues that the action, as originally conceived, was firmly rooted in the economy of contract. The claim advanced is that the action's non-contractual features, rather than existing from its inception, were in fact an addition dating from the late eighteenth and early nineteenth centuries. Section III provides a summary of the salient features of the nineteenth-century action for breach of promise of marriage. Drawing on sample cases and statements in contemporary legal treatises, it provides a step-by-step breakdown of a composite nineteenth-century case. Finally, section IV puts forward a unifying construct to account for all the features of the nine-teenth-century action. This construct is found, beyond law, in the socio-cultural context and the reigning feminine ideal. This last section demonstrates that the transformation of the breach-of-promise action at the turn of the nineteenth century can be explained in terms of the simultaneous emergence of the femin-ine ideal of the virtuous, delicate, and submissive woman.

I. The Nineteenth-Century Breach-of-Promise Action as a Problem in Legal Classification

A PROMISE of marriage is in the nature of a contract, of which, if there be any breach or non-performance, the law provides a remedy.[2]

The purpose of the action [for breach of promise of marriage] is to recover compen-sation for a personal wrong, which may probably be irreparable, to obtain damages, perhaps, for loss of health, or loss of happiness, . . . or loss of hitherto unimpeachable honor (that full measure of a woman's ruin), and, sometimes, in addition to all these, loss of property in the disappointment of a settlement for life.[3]

A HETEROGENEOUS mass is disclosed under the auspices of the Action of Breach of Promise of Marriage. Wounded feelings! Loss of position! . . . these are the ingredi-ents of this social mixture.[4]

The above are extracts from three nineteenth-century legal treatises. The first extract is taken from *A Familiar Compendium of the Law of Husband and Wife*, a practitioner's handbook written by an anonymous solicitor in 1831. The second extract comes from J J S Wharton's *Exposition of the Laws Relating to*

---

[2] *A Familiar Compendium of the Law of Husband and Wife; in Two Parts; to Which Is Added a Third Part; Comprising the Laws Relating to Breach of Promise of Marriage, Seduction and Abduction of Women* (London, 1831) 175.

[3] J J S Wharton, *An Exposition of the Laws Relating to the Women of England* (London, 1853) 213.

[4] Charles J MacColla, *Breach of Promise: Its History and Social Considerations; to Which Are Added a Few Pages on the Law of Breach of Promise and a Glance at Many Amusing Cases since the Reign of Queen Elizabeth,* 1879 (Littleton: Fred B Rothman, 1993) vii.

the Women of England, published in 1853. The third extract is the opening to what its author, Charles MacColla, claimed was 'the first book on Breach of Promise':[5] the 1879 *Breach of Promise: Its History and Social Considerations*. Each extract contains its author's attempt to capture in one sentence the quintessence of the nineteenth-century action for breach of promise of marriage.

The *Familiar Compendium* defines a promise of marriage as 'in the nature of a *contract*'. It follows from this definition that the legal remedy for 'any breach or non-performance' of the promise—the action for breach of promise—is also, in essence, contractual. The *Familiar Compendium* thus sees the action for breach of promise of marriage as squarely within the economy of contract and the realm of contractual remedies. The purpose of the action is to provide compensation for the non-performance of a contractual undertaking. Wharton, by contrast, states that the breach-of-promise action is concerned to provide compensation for the commission of a personal wrong. His emphasis is on injury, whether to health, happiness, or honour. Redress for private wrongs and civil injuries, however, is the natural province of the law of *tort*.[6] It is apparent, therefore, that for Wharton, the action for breach of promise is, in essence, a tort action.

In their radically differing accounts of the essential nature of the breach-of-promise action, the two extracts spotlight the problem in legal classification which the action presented for nineteenth-century lawyers. In highlighting the classificatory problem, however, they should also make us suspicious of the clean-cut categorizations—either contract or tort, but not a blend between the two—that they themselves provide. Charles MacColla probably did greater justice to the complexity of the issue, when he in his, admittedly, somewhat racy introduction called the action a 'social mixture,' composed of a 'HETEROGENEOUS mass' of elements. George Lawyer, another nineteenth-century legal commentator and one hailing from the other side of the Atlantic, provided a similar categorization of the action, when he, despondently, described it as being 'distinct from all others of its class'.[7] The virtue of

---

[5]   Ibid, ix.

[6]   The English word tort is a borrowing from the French word *tort*, which in fact means 'wrong'. Analytically, the law of torts is, like the law of contract, part of the law of obligations. However, in tort, the obligation to refrain from doing harm and if harm is done to compensate for it is not imposed by the agreement or contract of the parties, but by force of the general law.

[7]   George Lawyer, 'Are Actions for Breach of the Marriage Contract Immoral?' (1894) 38 *Central Law Journal* 272. Lawyer's reference is to breach of promise as enacted in American courtrooms, but it might with equal fairness be applied to the English situation. While I do not mean to deny that the history of breach of promise was distinct on each side of the Atlantic and varied even between American jurisdictions (surviving or being abolished at different times), there was considerable overlap in the broad outlines of the English and the American breach-of-promise stories. In particular, the peculiar features that turned the breach-of-promise action into a classificatory problem in nineteenth-century England have also been described as characteristic of the breach-of-promise suit in post-Revolutionary America. Thus, Grossberg notes a de facto narrowing of the right of action to female plaintiffs (37);

MacColla's and Lawyer's classification of the action as essentially *sui generis* is that it faces up to and does not gloss over the fact that the nineteenth-century breach-of-promise action seems to have been governed by an altogether idiosyncratic mixture of rules, a lavish combination of contractual elements with elements that were non-contractual in nature or that at least pushed contractual boundaries.[8] Although in theory open to both sexes, the nineteenth-century action for breach of promise of marriage was in practice an action only a female plaintiff could bring (or at least win). The evidentiary standards were set low and were therefore more favourable to the plaintiff's side than in almost any other area of law. And the cognizable heads of damage extended beyond those usual in contract: huge sums were routinely awarded as a pecuniary *solatium* for the injury done to the plaintiff's feelings (from which it was expected that she would never recover) and her decline (as inevitable as it was irreversible, it would seem) in health and spirits.

II. The Common Law Origins of the Action: The Action for Breach of a Marriage Contract

The common law action for breach of promise of marriage has not always displayed the peculiar features that make it such a misfit in conventional legal

lax evidentiary rules (40); a tightening of defences to violations of the strict bourgeois code of feminine sexual morality (41); and a devaluation of the commercial aspects of the breach and stress on emotional losses (36). In fact, the action's standout features were perhaps, if anything, even more pronounced in the United States than in Britain. Thus, one late nineteenth-century English critic of the suit consoled himself with the thought 'that [breach-of-promise suits] never in this country reached that phenomenal state which they apparently attained in the United States'. See J Dundas White, 'Breach of Promise of Marriage' (1894) 38 *Law Quarterly Review* 137.

   [8] It is not only nineteenth-century jurists who have grappled with the problem of classifying the action. Jurists and historians still cannot agree on whether the action is best seen as contractual, tortious, or *sui generis*, with all three positions continuing to claim adherents. An extreme, contractual view of the action is adopted, for instance, by the Law Commission, which writes that the 'action for breach of promise... reflects the refusal of the common law to draw any distinction between commercial and other types of agreement. Hence mutual promises to marry fulfil all the conditions of a legally binding contract and can be enforced in much the same way as, for example, a contract of employment.' Law Commission 2. For a similar stance see Susie L Steinbach, 'Promises, Promises: Not Marrying in England 1780–1920', diss, Yale University, 1996 (Ann Arbor: UMI, 1996) 9632509, esp at 187 and, referring to the Canadian situation, Rosemary J Coombe, '"The Most Disgusting, Disgraceful and Inequitous Proceeding in Our Law": The Action for Breach of Promise of Marriage in Nineteenth-Century Ontario' (1988) 38 *University of Toronto Law Journal* 91. By contrast, the hybrid nature of the action is stressed in Walter Wadlington and Monrad G Paulsen, *Cases and Other Materials on Domestic Relations*, 3rd edn, University Casebook Series (Mineola, NY: Foundation Press, 1978) 96 and Grossberg 33, both referencing the—as I argued above (n 7) closely analogous—situation in America. Finally, the action is described as 'in substance... a tort action' in Robert C Brown, 'Breach of Promise Suits' (1929) 77 *University of Pennsylvania Law Review* 480, another American lawyer.

categories. Its peculiarities, rather than existing from the beginning, are in fact an admixture dating from the late eighteenth and early nineteenth centuries.[9] The birth of the common law action, however, pre-dates the nineteenth century by more than 150 years. Its origins lie in the mid-seventeenth century, in the epoch from the Interregnum to the restoration of the Stuart kings.[10]

Prior to the Interregnum, no remedy for a broken promise of marriage existed at common law. The promise to marry was conceived of as a purely spiritual matter and as such was outside the province of the secular common law courts.[11] The absence of a remedy at common law did not, to be sure, mean that a jilted lover was unprotected. Rather, the jilted party's proper remedy lay in the ecclesiastical court: a suit *causa matrimonialis*.[12] In ecclesiastical law, promises to marry were of two kinds, and as regards the legal consequences, it mattered greatly what kind of promise had been made. Promises made in the present tense (*per verba de praesenti*) were regarded as a valid and indissoluble marriage, and it was the practice of the ecclesiastical courts to require the parties to solemnize their union *in facie ecclesiae*, enforced by the threat of excommunication. By contrast, promises to marry made in the future tense (*per verba de futuro*), the equivalent of what we would now term an engagement, would not be enforced other than by a (toothless) admonition. Only if they had been

---

[9] In this claim I seem, at first sight, to be contradicted by Grossberg, who appears to argue that the hybrid nature of the nineteenth-century action was the result of a mixed parentage, rather than, as claimed by me, a later infiltration. Thus, he writes at page 33: 'From its modern beginnings in the seventeenth century, the breach-of-promise suit has persisted as a curious legal action, a peculiar combination of contract and tort.' However, this statement seems inconsistent with Grossberg's own admission, three pages further on, that the early nineteenth-century American case of *Wightman v Coates* (1818) 15 Mass 1 'engineered a reconstruction of the suit' and brought about 'a fundamental alteration in the suit's logic and role' (36). He also speaks of a 'revamped breach suit', whose function it was to police courtship (38).

[10] In 1649, the English civil wars between royalists and parliamentarians came to their climactic conclusion with the public beheading of Charles I. From 1649 until 1660, the period known as the Interregnum, England was a republic, with Oliver Cromwell at its helm. With Cromwell's death, the republic collapsed, free elections were held, and the Stuart monarchy was restored under Charles II. Kenneth O Morgan (ed), *The Oxford Illustrated History of Britain* (Oxford: Oxford University Press, 1997) 325–9.

[11] There are isolated sixteenth-century instances of jilted lovers suing at common law in circumstances that imply a broken engagement. In 1506, for instance, a disappointed lover successfully brought an action on the case against his former fiancée for money which he had laid out to counsel in maintenance of her lawsuits and for the return of rings and jewels. He carefully avoided any mention of a promise to marry, however, which would have raised jurisdictional problems, and relied instead on words of comfort implying the prospect of marriage. See J H Baker (ed), *The Oxford History of the Laws of England*, vol 6 (Oxford: Oxford University Press, 2003) 855–6.

[12] Although, in modern discussions of the subject, the proper ecclesiastical remedy is sometimes referred to as a suit *causa matrimonii praelocuti*, Charles Donahue, Jr believes that this phrase is in fact unlikely to have been used in the ecclesiastical courts, where the standard term for breach-of-promise actions was simply *causa matrimonialis* (Charles Donahue, Jr, email to the author, 2 March 2009).

followed by sexual intercourse would promises to marry in the future tense be treated as a binding and indissoluble marriage.[13]

During the Interregnum, the ecclesiastical courts were closed and the ecclesiastical remedies thereby suspended.[14] Ingenious plaintiffs (and their even more ingenious counsel) therefore began to bring their grievance up in the common law courts, phrasing their claim in terms of a simple contract.[15] Clearly, the common law judges—unlike their ecclesiastical brethren—had no power to compel the marriage. But if the contractual analogy held, they could award money damages to the disappointed party. The question of whether an action for the breach of a contract to marry lay at common law was finally answered in the affirmative in 1672.[16] In *Holcroft v Dickenson*,[17] Mary Holcroft claimed that as a result of the defendant's failure to perform the contract to marry her, she had suffered expectation damages amounting to £100.[18] The Court of King's Bench held that the loss of the marriage was a temporal loss, of which the secular courts had cognizance and for which a damages remedy would lie at common law. That the common law courts were the appropriate venue for hearing the claim was, however, but the first precedent established by *Holcroft v Dickenson*. In upholding the plaintiff's claim, the court stressed the existence of mutual promises—'a promise that if the plaintiff would marry the defendant within a fortnight' given in exchange for a promise that 'the defendant would marry the plaintiff'[19]—establishing a simple executory contract,[20] 'suf-

[13] See Charles Donahue, Jr, *Law, Marriage, and Society in the Later Middle Ages: Arguments About Marriage in Five Courts* (New York: Cambridge University Press, 2007) 16–17. The most complete statement of the ecclesiastical law on the subject, running to 240 pages, is contained in Henry Swinburne, *A Treatise of Spousals, or Matrimonial Contracts: Wherein All the Questions Relating to That Subject Are Ingeniously Debated and Resolved* (London, 1686).

[14] Marriage was treated as temporal under Cromwell, with parliamentary legislation permitting justices of the peace to marry people instead of priests and the secular courts moving in to handle litigation concerning matrimonial causes formerly dealt with in the church courts. Susan Staves, 'British Seduced Maidens' (1980) 14(2) *Eighteenth-Century Studies* 126.

[15] Although the ecclesiastical courts were reopened after the Interregnum and the ecclesiastical remedies reinstated, with the passage of Lord Hardwicke's Marriage Act, 26 Geo II, c 33, in 1753, the common law action became a jilted lover's sole avenue of redress. The 1753 Act deprived the ecclesiastical courts of the power to compel marriages, so that thereafter all a deserted fiancé(e) could hope for was to win damages in the civil courts (Staves 127).

[16] The common law action seems to have been recognized prior to 1672. Thus, the earliest common law case that may be read as acknowledging a right of action is *Stretch v Parker*, Car Rot 21, decided in 1639. However, it was not until 1672 that the matter was fully discussed and conclusively settled in the leading case of *Holcroft v Dickenson*, 3 Keble 148; 84 ER 645.

[17] 3 Keble 148; 84 ER 645.

[18] In its somewhat more archaic phraseology, the actual claim was that the defendant had 'hindered her preferment' to her damage of £100.

[19] 3 Keble 148; 84 ER 645.

[20] An executory contract is one that has not yet been performed on either side. It has to be distinguished from a part-executed contract, where one side has already entered upon performance, and an executed contract, which has been fully performed on both sides. A contract to marry is the paradigm

ficient alone to support the action'.[21] This contractual rationale for awarding monetary redress for the breach of an engagement accorded well with the
seventeenth-century English conception of marriage and engagements to
marry as essentially property transactions, closely akin to commercial contracts,
whose breach also sounded in damages. Against the background of an understanding of marriage as principally a commercial speculation, the private right
of a rejected lover to seek damages appeared as natural as to allow an action for
the breach of a contract to purchase a horse or a bale of cotton.[22]

   In keeping with its contractual legitimation, the infant common law suit
for breach of promise of marriage presented itself in the garb of a conventional contract action. For a start, like any other contractual action, it was
equally open to both sexes, in practice no less than in theory. In the 1698
case of *Harrison v Cage and Wife*[23] for instance, a male plaintiff, Mr Harrison,
sued a lady who had pledged her vows to him and then gone and married
another. The court expressly refused to draw a distinction between mutual
promises to marry and 'any other mutual agreement'. The plaintiff's sex was
deemed equally irrelevant in both contexts to the issue of who could maintain
an action. Harrison accordingly recovered £400 damages against his fickle mistress, a figure arrived at on the simple calculation that the woman was 'worth
3000l. when the plaintiff courted her'. Further, it was necessary to establish
the existence of *mutual* promises to make out a prima facie case.[24] In fact, in

case of a contract that cannot subsist at all except as a wholly executory arrangement, as it is not possible to have a part-executed promise to marry: no one could ever claim to be 'a little bit married'. See
Patrick S Atiyah, *The Rise and Fall of Freedom of Contract* (Oxford: Clarendon Press, 1979) 204.

   [21] 3 Keble 149; 84 ER 646. That 'mutual promises [...should be] sufficient alone to support
the action', as the presiding judge stated in *Holcroft v Dickenson*, is wholly unexceptionable to the
modern lawyer, acquainted with present-day contract doctrine, which treats the executory contract
as paradigmatic. There has been some controversy amongst legal historians over the history of the
recognition of the actionability of purely executory contracts, though obviously this was accepted
in relation to mutual promises to marry. For discussion see Atiyah, *Rise and Fall* 194–8; Simpson,
History 452–70; Morton J Horwitz, 'The Historical Foundations of Modern Contract Law' (1974)
87 *Harvard Law Review* 917–56; A W B Simpson, 'The Horwitz Thesis and the History of Contracts'
(1979) 46(3) *University of Chicago Law Review* 533–601; J H Baker, *An Introduction to Legal History*,
4th edn (London: Butterworths, 2002) 341; and David Ibbetson, *A Historical Introduction to the Law
of Obligations* (Oxford: Oxford University Press, 2001) 143.

   [22] For this argument see Homer H Clark, Jr, *The Law of Domestic Relations in the United States*, 2nd
edn, vol 1, Hornbook Series (St Paul: West Publishing, 1987), who posits that it was the seventeenth-
century (aristocratic) conception of marriage as a truly contractual affair, meant to create alliances
between families and to consolidate power, that first caused the common law courts to intervene in
the subject matter (2). Of course, aristocratic marriage has to be distinguished from marriage lower
down in society.

   [23] Carthew 467; 90 ER 870.

   [24] In English law, a promise, to be binding, has to be supported by some 'consideration', something of value in the eyes of the law, given in return for the promise. As we have seen, *Holcroft v
Dickenson* had decided that the consideration for the one party's promise to marry was the other party's

its early days, the action was not known as an action for breach of a *promise* of marriage at all, but rather as an action for breach of a *contract* of marriage, stressing the mutuality involved—the fact that A's promise to marry B is given in exchange for B's promise to marry A. The Annual Register[25] for the year 1766, for instance, refers to a case tried at Maidstone Assizes as being for 'the non-performance of a marriage-contract'.[26] That a contractual ethos pervaded the *Urform* of the common law action for breach of promise of marriage is also apparent from the original rules on damages. The contractual rule of recovery is that the plaintiff is entitled to the value of his lost expectations, known as expectation damages.[27] The purpose of the award is to place the plaintiff, so far as money can do so, in the position in which he would have been if the contract had been performed. In two of the early breach-of-promise cases already referred to—*Holcroft v Dickenson* and *Harrison v Cage and Wife*—the plaintiffs clearly claimed or were awarded damages equal to their lost expectations. Mary Holcroft claimed the value of her hindered preferment, while Harrison's damages were calculated on the basis of the 'value' of his bargain—the lady's worth in pecuniary terms. Occasionally, a plaintiff may not be able to prove what he expected to gain from the contract. In such a case, the court cannot award expectation damages. However, it will usually allow recovery of the actual out-of-pocket expenses incurred by the plaintiff in the expectation that the contract would be performed, on the reasonable assumption that a sensible plaintiff will not spend more money in the performance of a contract than he expects to recoup from it. Early breach-of-promise cases, where the plaintiff could not prove the economic value of the marriage, accordingly tied the size

---

counter-promise to marry, the 'mutual promises [. . . being] sufficient alone to support the action' (3 Keble 149; 84 ER 646).

[25] The *Annual Register* is a chronicle of British and world events from 1758 to the present, reporting events from the perspective of a contemporary witness.

[26] *Annual Register for the Year 1766*: 75. For the currency of that term, see also 'Some Early Breach of Promise Cases' (1891) 3 *Green Bag* 3.

[27] This, again, is the modern formulation of the contractual measure of damages. To what extent pre-eighteenth-century law protected the parties' expectations is a matter of dispute. Atiyah's argument that there was at best haphazard enforcement of wholly executory contracts until the late eighteenth century is based on the fact that, as he claims, 'damages for the loss of a mere expectation, unpaid for and unrelied upon, were not [then] generally awarded [. . . and . . .] in the absence of such damages it is not really possible to talk of a proper law of executory contracts' (*Rise and Fall* 200). He admits, however, that actions for breach of a contract of marriage, which 'cannot subsist at all except as wholly executory arrangements', constituted an exception (204). Conventional legal history disagrees with Atiyah: damages were assessed 'upon the principle of compensation for the failure to obtain the thing promised'. See James Barr Ames, *Lectures on Legal History and Miscellaneous Legal Essays* (Cambridge, MA: Harvard University Press; London: Humphrey Milford, 1913) 145. See also William Searle Holdsworth, *A History of English Law* (London: Methuen, 1923) 452, Simpson, *History* 582–7, and Ibbetson 131–2.

of the plaintiff's award to his out-of-pocket loss. In a 1780 case,[28] for instance, the plaintiff, Mr Schreiber, could not prove what precise pecuniary advantage he expected to gain from marrying Mrs Frazer, the widow of a general, since under the terms of their agreement that lady was to continue mistress of her own fortune after marriage. Accordingly, his witnesses proved that, expecting to be soon united in matrimony, Schreiber had bought a house and horses and then resold them at a loss of approximately £600 on account of the anticipated marriage not taking place. The jury returned a verdict of £600 damages, with costs, thus reimbursing Schreiber for his out-of-pocket expenses.

It is apparent that the action for breach of the marriage contract, as originally conceived in the seventeenth century, was a pure contract action. It was not until the late eighteenth and early nineteenth centuries that the action began to depart from 'the broad principles of an older and more universal law'.[29] The nineteenth-century suit for breach of promise of marriage formally stayed within the economy of contractual recovery, but its make-up and cultural message changed. As originally conceived, the action for breach of the marriage contract provided compensation for the pecuniary consequences of a broken contract to marry. With the early nineteenth century, however, the action for breach switched the gravamen of the injury and the level of damages. The nineteenth-century action for breach of promise lost its moorings both to specific material losses and to conventional contract-based limitations and reinvented itself as a hybrid action, composed of a mass of heterogeneous elements, frustrating attempts at systematic legal categorization.

III. 'A HETEROGENEOUS mass':[30] The Nineteenth-Century Action for Breach of Promise of Marriage

By the beginning of the nineteenth century, more was involved in the legal reality of the suit than the breach of a contract. Outwardly, little had changed, and the action formally remained rooted in the old contractual writ. This is apparent from the plaintiff's declaration,[31] which typically continued to aver that a contract had been made and broken:

For that...in consideration that the plaintiff, being unmarried, at the request of the defendant, had...promised the defendant to marry the defendant within a reasonable

---

[28] *Schreiber v Frazer, Annual Register for the Year 1780*: 218–19.
[29] White 142.
[30] MacColla vii.
[31] In common law and probate practice before the Judicature Acts of 1873–1875 the declaration was the first pleading delivered by the plaintiff, stating his claim (Baker, *Introduction* 91).

time after request, he the defendant...promised the plaintiff to marry the plaintiff within a reasonable time after he should be thereunto requested;...and the plaintiff avers, that she, confiding in the said promise of the defendant, hath always...remained and still is unmarried, and was during all the time...ready and willing to marry the defendant...; and although the plaintiff...requested the defendant to marry her..., yet the defendant, disregarding his said promise,...hath wholly neglected and refused so to do, To the plaintiff's damage of £--, and therefore she brings her suit....[32]

Substantively, however, the action had abandoned its contractual roots.

1. Going to court: 'a gentleman should never come into court in such a case'[33]

The most notable change was the practical restriction of the action to female plaintiffs. Of my sample of 242 cases decided in the period between 1800 and 1940, 233 actions (96.3 per cent) involved female plaintiffs. A mere nine cases (3.7 per cent) were brought by a man.[34] This would seem to mark a drastic change from the situation in the seventeenth and eighteenth centuries, where, although a dearth of reported cases makes it difficult to make statistical claims, the sex ratio appears to have been far more evenly balanced. Of the five early breach-of-promise cases I looked at for this study, three, or 60 per cent, featured a male plaintiff.[35] All three plaintiffs recovered substantial damages. If we assume that it was not only men, but also women who broke engagements in the nineteenth century (and the existence of female 'jilts' in nineteenth-century fiction certainly seems to point that way[36]) and that there

[32] Joseph Chitty, *Precedents in Pleading: With Copious Notes on Pleading, Practice and Evidence* (London, 1847) 158–9.

[33] *Townsend v Bennett*, *The Times* 20 April 1875: 11.

[34] These figures accord quite well with those found by Steinbach and Frost in their independent studies of nineteenth-century breach-of-promise cases. Steinbach's database of 322 cases, decided between 1780 and 1920, had women suing men 92 per cent of the time ('Promises' 210). Frost, who only looked at cases from the second half of the nineteenth century, found that 97 per cent of the plaintiffs were women. See Ginger S Frost, 'Promises Broken: Breach of Promise of Marriage in England and Wales 1753–1970', diss, Rice University, 1991, 98.

[35] The three early cases that featured a male plaintiff were: *Harrison v Cage and Wife*, Carthew 467; 90 ER 870; *Schreiber v Frazer*, *Annual Register for the Year 1780*: 218–19; *Foster v Mellish*, *Annual Register for the Year 1802*: 371. A base of five cases is obviously very small, and not too much should be made of the 60 per cent figure. However, an 1891 article on early breach-of-promise cases also discloses a male plaintiff ratio of 50 per cent (two out of a total of four cases). See 'Some Early Breach of Promise Cases' 3. Similarly, Frost claims that until the Hardwicke Act of 1753, 'breach of promise plaintiffs in the civil courts had been predominantly male'. See Ginger S Frost, ' "I Shall Not Sit Down and Crie": Women, Class and Breach of Promise of Marriage Plaintiffs in England, 1850–1900' (1994) 6(2) *Gender and History* 225.

[36] Although Jane Austen's *Sense and Sensibility*, 1811 (London: Penguin, 1994) is perhaps best remembered for Willoughby's heartless desertion of Marianne, we should not forget that Lucy Steele

is nothing intrinsic to male biology that determines men against taking a former sweetheart to court (after all, they had no scruples in doing so in the seventeenth and eighteenth centuries), then the absence of male breach-of-promise plaintiffs in the nineteenth century must be due to a 'filter' within the nineteenth-century breach-of-promise action itself. There is ample evidence that breach-of-promise actions by men were actively discouraged in the nineteenth century. In *Kershaw v Cass*, one of only nine cases in my sample to boast of that rare thing, a male plaintiff, Sergeant Wilkins, as counsel for the widow Cass, did not even bother to plead a defence to Mr Kershaw's claim. Instead, his oratorical skill was expended in a diatribe on men 'booby enough to bring such an action':

> Was there a man among them who did not despise the man who came into court with such a case as this? ... He trusted the jury would teach him a lesson, and how rightly to estimate his conduct by giving him as damages the smallest coin of the realm.[37]

The jury immediately complied, awarding Mr Kershaw contemptuous damages of one farthing. The same misfortune[38] befell all bar one of the remaining eight male plaintiffs: a young draper's assistant of the name of Jack Denny Bower stands alone in having recovered substantial damages for a woman's breach of promise, and his action is the exception that proves the rule, since it was heard in 1910.[39] The sample discloses no nineteenth-century male plaintiff who pulled off a similar feat. Technically, a male plaintiff who recovered even contemptuous damages had 'won' his case, and the fact that the verdict was for the plaintiff expressed the jury's opinion that, legally, he was in the right.[40] However, in awarding contemptuous damages, the jury also gave vent to their feeling that the action, although legally good, was morally wrong and

---

breaks her engagement to Edward Ferrars by marrying Edward's younger brother Robert. Further examples of fictional female jilts of the nineteenth century are provided by Ellen Ap Rice, heroine of Charles Reade's *The Jilt* (London, 1884); Alice Vavasor in Anthony Trollope's *Can You Forgive Her?*, 1864–65 (London: Oxford University Press, 1972); Cynthia Kirkpatrick in Elizabeth Gaskell's *Wives and Daughters*, Frank Glover Smith (ed), 1866, (London: Penguin, 1986) and Maria Bertram in Jane Austen's *Mansfield Park*, Kathryn Sutherland (ed), 1814, (London: Penguin, 2003).

[37] *The Times* 21 March 1849: 7.

[38] Three of the plaintiffs were awarded contemptuous damages. In one case a verdict was taken by consent, with the parties agreeing that the plaintiff should receive no pecuniary compensation. In the remaining three cases, the jury returned a verdict for the female defendant.

[39] *Bower v Ebsworth, The Times* 23 April 1910: 5; 25 April 1910: 3; 28 April 1910: 3. Bower recovered £100 against a widow more than twice his age, who, as Mr Justice Grantham remarked in his summing-up, 'did appear to have led him on' (*The Times* 25 April 1910: 3).

[40] That is to say the jury agreed that a contract to marry had been entered into by the parties and broken by the defendant, so that a verdict for the plaintiff was a foregone conclusion.

should never have been brought. A male plaintiff who was sent away with contemptuous damages did not just fail to derive any benefit from his breach-of-promise action. The judge might also deprive him of his costs[41] or suggest that a motion to this effect by counsel for the defendant would find favour with the court. In *Kershaw v Cass*, for instance, Mr Justice Coleridge reserved judgment on whether 'he would certify to deprive the plaintiff of his costs',[42] and in *Nicholson v Turnbull and Wife* it was reported that 'His Lordship said that…he should, if requested, certify to deprive the plaintiff of costs.'[43] Legal fees could be considerable. For example, in an 1860 case between two people in a humble position in life, where the damages awarded were only £75, the costs of the plaintiff (who was, in that case, a woman) were taxed at over £30.[44] Costs of £30 may therefore be expected to be the minimum a plaintiff would incur in bringing a breach-of-promise action in the mid-nineteenth century. They might be significantly higher where eminent barristers were retained, as they frequently were for breach-of-promise actions (Mr Kershaw, for instance, retained a QC). Occasionally, lawyers might tender their services 'on spec', as Dodson and Fogg famously did in Charles Dickens's *The Pickwick Papers*. Although the established rule of the English bar is supposed to have been that one could not operate what would today be called a contingent fee system, there is evidence that real-life breach-of-promise cases were taken up on a 'no cure, no pay' basis.[45] However, since that effectively put the risk of the action being unsuccessful on the lawyer, it is unlikely that the case of a male plaintiff, whose statistical likelihood of recovering only contemptuous damages was, as we have just seen, overwhelming, would be taken up 'on spec'.

A refusal to award the plaintiff his costs could leave him seriously out of pocket. In *Townsend v Bennett*, another male-plaintiff case, Mr Justice Brett had refused to certify for costs. Mr Digby Seymour, QC, as counsel for Mr Townsend, then moved the court to grant a certificate, arguing that the refusal to certify was 'virtually an absolute condemnation of the action':

The decision seemed to amount to this—that a gentleman should never come into court in such a case.[46]

---

[41] Normally, in the absence of special circumstances, a winning litigant is awarded his costs (ie his legal fees) against the unsuccessful party.

[42] *The Times* 21 March 1849: 7.

[43] *Morning Chronicle* 4 March 1850: 7.

[44] *Parry v Judge*, *The Times* 2 March 1860: 11.

[45] See, for instance, *Webber v Symes and Wife*, *The Times* 22 April 1850: 7 (action by attorney for payment of services rendered to Symes's wife in a breach-of-promise action previous to her coverture). Because cases do turn up in the law reports in which relatively poor people appear to have been able to sue under such an arrangement, it has long been suspected amongst legal historians that—whatever the formal rule—contingent fee agreements did in fact go on.

[46] *The Times* 20 April 1875: 11.

Unmoved by counsel's eloquence, the court steadfastly refused to certify, practically establishing a precedent that, indeed, 'a gentleman should never come into court in such a case'. It can be seen therefore that, although the breach-of-promise action was, throughout its history, theoretically gender-neutral, it was lived out as *in practice* gender-specific in the nineteenth century. The nineteenth-century breach-of-promise action was a ladies' action, an action only female plaintiffs 'should' bring, for only they could win[47] it. The American lawyer Lawrence Friedman has argued that ' "[p]ure" contract doctrine is blind to details of subject matter and person.... In the law of contract, it does not matter if either party is a woman [or] a man ... as soon as it does matter ... we are no longer talking pure contract.'[48] In its practical restriction of the right of action to female plaintiffs, the nineteenth-century breach-of-promise suit then was, in Friedman's terms, no longer 'pure contract'.

2. The in-court processing of a nineteenth-century breach-of-promise suit

In every action for breach of a contract, the first in-court stage of the case is dominated by the plaintiff. The plaintiff normally has to prove that a contract has been entered into between the parties and broken by the defendant. Once the contract and the breach have been established, the burden passes to the defendant to make out a defence to the plaintiff's claim.[49] It is only in the third and final stage of the process that the judge or, as tended to be the case in the nineteenth century, the jury[50] become substantially involved. In the nineteenth century, the jury decided for or against the plaintiff on the issue of contract and breach and for or against the defendant on the issue of defence.

---

[47] I use the word 'win' here in the sense of recovering substantial damages, since, as we have seen, most male plaintiffs also technically won their suits.

[48] Lawrence M Friedman, *Contract Law in America: A Social and Economic Case Study* (Madison: University of Wisconsin Press, 1965) 20.

[49] The normal practice in an action for breach of promise was to plead '*non assumpsit*', which was called the general issue. This enabled the defendant at the trial to deny the promise, or the breach of promise, and to raise any other matters of either fact or law which provided a defence to the action, or were relevant to the assessment of damages. In 1834, under new pleading rules, known as the Hilary Rules, the scope of the general issue was restricted, allowing the defendant who pleaded *non assumpsit* only to deny the promise at the trial; other defences had to be individually raised by what were known as special pleas. This new system proved unsatisfactory and was abandoned in the 1850s; thereafter, actions for breach of promise were handled in much the same way as they had been before 1834. There is no modern comprehensive account of how the Hilary Rules affected contract litigation, but see Baker, *Introduction* 88–92.

[50] In civil cases, the jury normally had to determine the issue of liability as well as the amount of damages. The use of civil juries has steadily declined in the twentieth century, and they survive only exceptionally, usually in libel cases (Baker, *Introduction* 92).

If they found for the plaintiff on the first two issues and against the defendant on the third issue, the jurors had to go on to consider the question of damages. The award of damages was the denouement of any suit for a breach of contract and peculiarly the province of the jury.[51]

In what follows, I will consider the three stages outlined above with reference to the in-court processing of a nineteenth-century breach-of-promise suit. In so doing, I shall not be drawing on any one case. The reason for this is simple. There is no one breach-of-promise case that displays all the quirks and oddities of the cause of action as a whole or at least none that displays all of them to perfection: *Orford v Cole*, *Billing v Smith*, and *Daniel v Bowles*, to name but three, might be interesting on the issue of establishing the contract; *Gough v Farr* on the question of breach; and a different list of cases again on the issues of defences and damages. To fully reveal the 'HETEROGENEOUS mass'[52] of rules that governed the nineteenth-century action for breach of promise, it is necessary to rely on a heterogeneous or composite case, made up of parts gleaned from a multitude of different real-life cases.

(a) *Making out a case*

As was stated above, in order to make out a case, the plaintiff in a contract action has to show, firstly, that a contract subsisted between the parties and, secondly, that the defendant has broken it. The plaintiff's first task, therefore, is to establish the existence of the contract.

The most authoritative definition of a simple contract[53] is probably the one contained in Joseph Chitty's definitive *Practical Treatise on the Law of Contracts*, a work now in its 30th edition that continues to be the leading exposition of English contract law today. According to the 1841 edition of the book, a simple contract is constituted by 'the mutual assent of two … persons, competent to contract, founded on a sufficient and legal motive, inducement, or consideration, to perform some legal act'. The heart of this definition and, by implication, of a contract is the 'mutual assent' of the parties. The assent is composed of two parts: a 'definite promise' on the one hand and a definite acceptance 'by the person claiming the benefit' on the other.[54] In addition to requiring a definite acceptance, a promise, to be binding in English law, has to be supported by some consideration, something of value in the eyes of the law that is given in exchange for the promise. As we have seen,

---

[51] Joseph Chitty, *A Practical Treatise on the Law of Contracts*, 4th edn (London, 1850) 768.
[52] See n 30.
[53] Simple contracts have to be distinguished from contracts under seal, also known as specialties. Unlike a simple contract, a contract under seal does not require consideration to be enforceable. However, special formalities are prescribed for the formation of such a contract. Thus, there cannot be a contract under seal 'without writing, sealing, and delivery' (Chitty, *Practical Treatise*, 4th edn 3).
[54] Chitty, *Practical Treatise*, 3rd edn (London, 1841) 9.

Holcroft v Dickenson had decided that mutual promises to marry were consideration for one another, 'sufficient alone to support the action'.[55] Therefore, applying
conventional contract law, a binding contract to marry should involve a promise to
marry on the one side and a counter-promise to marry on the other. This counter-
promise would constitute both the acceptance of the promise *and* the legal consideration for it.

A nineteenth-century breach-of-promise plaintiff would therefore have to
establish, first of all, that the defendant had made her a promise of marriage.
According to early nineteenth-century rules on civil procedure, neither the
plaintiff nor the defendant could give evidence.[56] The plaintiff could not therefore satisfy the evidentiary burden by her own credible testimony that a promise of marriage had been made to her. Instead, she had to rely on other modes
of substantiating the promise.

(i) The spoken promise of marriage
The first issue that arose was whether it was necessary to have written evidence of
the promise. As a general rule, a simple contract did not have to be reduced into
writing, and the law did not distinguish between spoken and written promises:
both had 'the same efficacy, properties, and effect'.[57] However, by a statute dating from the reign of Charles II, commonly known as the Statute of Frauds,[58]
special provisions had been enacted with regard to the evidence required to
prove certain kinds of simple contracts. Under the terms of that statute, no
action was to be brought on any contract or promise falling under any one of
five classes of transactions, unless the transaction had been embodied in some
writing.[59] The third of these classes of transactions was described as agreements
made upon consideration of marriage. Now, if the promise of marriage was
caught by that provision then, clearly, it was not actionable unless written evidence of it was forthcoming.

For some years after the passage of the seventeenth-century statute, when
the action was still in its strictly contractual phase, 'it was often decided that no

---

[55] See n 21.

[56] Until early in the nineteenth century, no one with a pecuniary interest in the result of an action
was competent to give evidence. In 1843, the Evidence Amendment Act, 6 & 7 Vict, c 85, was passed,
allowing most interested parties in most types of action to bear witness at trial. Breach-of-promise
actions were, however, excluded from the scope of the Act. Despite a number of amendments to
the 1843 Act during the 1850s, that exclusion continued until 9 August 1869, when the Evidence
(Further) Amendment Act of that year (32 & 33 Vict, c 68) made the parties to a breach-of-promise
action competent to give evidence. The impact of the 1869 Act on the litigation of breach-of-promise
suits—and on their depiction in works of literature—will form the subject matter of Chapter 4.

[57] Chitty, *Practical Treatise*, 4th edn 4.

[58] (1677) 29 Charles II, c 3.

[59] Edward Jenks, *A Short History of English Law: From the Earliest Times to the End of the Year 1927*,
4th edn (London: Methuen, 1928) 306.

action for breach of promise of marriage could be sustained unless the promise were in writing, it being considered that such promises came within...this famous statute'.[60] Thus, in *Philpott v Wallet*, a case, like the statute, dating from the reign of Charles II, it was expressly held that 'this promise is directly within the words and not out of the intent of the statute, because the promise is that in consideration the one would marry the other, the other would marry him, and therefore it is a promise in consideration of marriage'.[61] However, this decision was overruled in the eighteenth century, when the court in *Cork v Baker*[62] took the view that the statute only applied to settlements made in consideration of marriage and not to contracts to marry. This made it unnecessary to have the promise in writing. The sufficiency of a spoken promise of marriage was consistently recognized and upheld by the courts in the nineteenth century, although the occasional defendant seems to have laboured under the misconception that an absence of writing meant that there was no case to answer. One nineteenth-century dandy with a fondness for horses, dogs, and the good life (as well as, apparently, making ill-thought-out promises of marriage, for this was his second (!) appearance as defendant in a breach-of-promise suit) thought that, having been burnt once, he had learnt his lesson in making sure that 'he had never written'.[63] With £500 damages awarded against him, he had to learn the hard way that a spoken promise would do and that the only way to be 'safe' from a breach-of-promise suit was not to promise, in any way, shape, or form, in the first place.

A dislike of formality in the proof of the promise of marriage is also evident in the 1818 case of *Orford v Cole*,[64] which we will have occasion to examine in more detail later. In that case, the jury had returned a verdict of £7,000 damages for Miss Orford, 'which bestowed so considerable an addition of fortune on the fair suitor, [and] was hailed with universal satisfaction' by a crowded court, 'containing 3000 persons'.[65] On the subsequent morning, Mr Scarlett, as counsel for Mr Cole, requested a new trial on the ground that his client's

---

[60] MacColla 20. See also Alexander Cairns, *Eversley's Law of the Domestic Relations: Husband and Wife, Parent and Child, Guardian and Ward, Infants, Master and Servant*, 4th edn (London: Sweet & Maxwell, 1926) 81.

[61] 3 Lev Reports 65; 83 ER 579, rpt in MacColla 20–1.

[62] 1 Strange 34; 93 ER 367. See also *Horam v Humfreys* (1771) Lofft 80; 98 ER 543.

[63] *Ellice v Fenwick*, *News of the World* 29 March 1846: 6. In this action, Fenwick was made to pay £500 in damages to Mrs Ellice, a 'very clever, ladylike' widow of about 35. Two years earlier, he had been sued for breach of promise by Miss Lacy, another 'lady possessing considerable personal attractions' (*Lacy v Fenwick*, *The Times* 5 April 1844: 7). *Lacy v Fenwick* was eventually compromised for £1,000.

[64] *Report of the Proceedings in the Cause of Mary Alice Orford, versus Thomas Butler Cole, Esq for Breach of Promise of Marriage; Tried at Lancaster, on Monday, the 30th Day of March, 1818, before the Honorable Sir John Bailey, Knight, and a Special Jury* (Liverpool, 1818).

[65] Ibid, 68.

love letters (which contained the promise of marriage) had been improperly admitted as evidence, because they had not been stamped as required by the Stamp Act,[66] which stated that any evidence to a contract worth £20 or more had to be stamped before being admitted as evidence in court. Surely, he argued, this contract, the breach of which the jury had recompensed with £7,000 in damages, was thought to be worth more than £20. In arguing for the applicability of the Stamp Act, Mr Scarlett was implying that the contract between Miss Orford and Mr Cole was exactly like other contracts and should be governed by the same rules. Mr Justice Bailey, however, rejected the analogy. The contract in question was of a different description from contracts 'measurable in the outset by monies or monies' worth',[67] and the Stamp Act was, therefore, inapplicable. Bailey's distinction is clearly one based on the subject matter of the contract in question. Marriage, according to him, cannot be assigned a monetary value. Pure contract, however, as we saw above, is blind to details of subject matter.[68] Therefore, in relying on the subject matter of the contract in *Orford v Cole* as grounds for distinguishing it from other contracts, Mr Justice Bailey was no longer talking pure contract.

(ii) The implied promise of marriage

> Mr. Joyce: Did you ever hear the defendant say anything about marriage?
>
> Witness: No, I have never heard it; but I have seen it (roars of laughter).—
>
> Mr. Joyce: Give us some idea of that expressive pantomime.—
>
> Witness: I have seen them very deeply in conversation, but I never heard what they said (laughter).
>
> Cross-examination of witness for the plaintiff in *Billing v Smith* (1861)[69]

The preceding sub-section has made clear that the plaintiff did not have to adduce written proof that the defendant had made her a promise of marriage. The next issue that arose was whether it was necessary to prove that the defendant had promised marriage *in totidem verbis*. In other words: did the defendant actually have to have said 'Will you marry me?' or was something short of this sufficient?

All the nineteenth-century legal treatises agree that 'it is not...necessary to prove an express promise...'.[70] Instead, the promise could be inferred from the

---

[66] 55 Geo III, c 184.

[67] *Report of the Proceedings in the Cause of Mary Alice Orford* 69.

[68] See n 48.

[69] *News of the World* 21 April 1861: 5.

[70] Wharton 215. Similar statements can be found in *Familiar Compendium* 176 and in Chitty, *Practical Treatise*, 4th edn 467.

defendant's conduct.[71] Keeping company with the plaintiff, walking or riding out with her, visiting her outside normal visiting hours, or even paying her marked attention was all conduct from which a court might infer a promise of marriage. In the 1861 case of *Billing v Smith*, quoted above, for instance, none of the witnesses for the plaintiff could testify to an express promise of marriage. All their evidence amounted to was that the defendant had been frequently seen in the plaintiff's shop, that his deportment towards her had been 'gallant', and that they had once been 'very deeply in conversation'. Despite the fact that there was a perfectly innocent explanation for the defendant's visits—he was the plaintiff's landlord and therefore obliged to call for his rent from time to time—and although one witness admitted under cross-examination that the defendant's conduct was only 'such as a gentleman would pay to every other female', the jury arrived at the conclusion that Mr Smith had made Mrs Billing an offer of marriage and awarded her £50. The liberality with which nineteenth-century juries were wont to infer promises of marriage is an aspect of breach-of-promise suits satirized by Charles Dickens in *The Pickwick Papers*, first published in 1837. Indeed, if the chronological order were reversed, one might be tempted to think that Dickens had *Billing v Smith* in mind when plotting the famous case of *Bardell v Pickwick*. In *Pickwick*, evidence of a promise is slim, amounting to no more than that Mr Pickwick resided at Mrs Bardell's for two years and that 'during the whole of that time, [she] waited on him, attended to his comforts, cooked his meals'—a circumstance more than accounted for by the fact that she is his landlady; that he occasionally gave money to her little boy; that he had once been discovered holding Mrs Bardell in his arms; and that he had sent her a letter mentioning a warming pan, which counsel for Mrs Bardell was convinced was 'a mere cover for hidden fire—a mere substitute for some endearing word or promise . . .'.[72] Another startling real-life illustration of how low the courts were prepared to go and of what would suffice to make them infer a promise of marriage is provided by *Morris v Maddox*.[73] Ann Morris met John Maddox when she came to Harley to help out at the Unicorn Inn, a small public house run by her brother-in-law. Maddox had been a regular at the inn before Ann's arrival, being partial to its brandy and water. Her relatives claimed to have observed, however, that his visits became more frequent after Ann got there and that he seemed taken with her. He called her 'my dear' and on one occasion gave her a silver watch. 'It did not appear, however, that he made any

---

[71] Thus, Chitty states that 'the contract may be evidenced by the unequivocal conduct of the parties, and by a general, yet definite understanding between them, their friends and relations, that a marriage is to take place' (*Practical Treatise*, 4th edn 467). See also Wharton 216 (the promise of the man is very often but a matter of presumption from his conduct) and MacColla 20.

[72] Dickens, *The Pickwick Papers* 425–6; ch 34.

[73] *Morning Chronicle* 25 March 1856: 8; *News of the World* 30 March 1856: 7.

distinct proposals, or that he walked out with the plaintiff, or introduced her to his friends.' Still, the jury found that Maddox had made Ann Morris a promise of marriage (something he strenuously denied), it being 'stated as a fact of some importance . . . that, after a certain period, he no longer paid for what he drank at the Unicorn, but was entertained by the landlord gratis'.[74] The jury clearly felt that Maddox should not have accepted free drinks, unless he meant to marry Ann, and it accordingly inferred that he had, impliedly, promised to marry her.[75] In other words, the court inferred a promise where, under the circumstances, the defendant *should* have promised, that is to say, it inferred a promise from a moral obligation. In contract law, however, it is not normally permissible to imply a promise from a *moral* (as opposed to a legal) liability.[76] It follows that in its liberal rules on implying promises, the nineteenth-century action for breach of promise of marriage departed, yet again, from conventional contract law.

(iii) The counter-promise

As we have seen, the formation of a contract typically requires that the definite promise of the one party be 'accepted by the person claiming the benefit'[77] and that it be supported by some consideration. A bare promise, unaccepted and unsupported by consideration, is *nudum pactum* and unenforceable.[78] In the case of a contract to marry, we would therefore expect the woman to have to show that she, in her turn, promised to marry the man, her counter-promise constituting both the requisite acceptance and the legal consideration necessary to conclude the contract.

In this instance, too, however, anyone looking for a strict compliance with conventional contractual principles is bound to be disappointed: in an action by a lady for a breach of promise of marriage, we are told, 'it is not necessary, for the purpose of making out the [. . . contract] that the plaintiff by words

---

[74] *Morning Chronicle* 25 March 1856: 8.

[75] It bears stressing that Ann had also been 'too lavish of her favours' and that her intimacy with Maddox had resulted in a child. This may have made the court very eager to find that Maddox had promised to marry her. Thus, Feinsinger has noted that, at least in the American context, there was 'virtually a presumption of a promise to marry . . . where there appears to have been intercourse between the parties' (981). This is borne out by the American case of *Wightman v Coates* (1818) 15 Mass 1, where the court stated that in resolving any doubt on the question of the promise against the defendant, it was merely vindicating his honour as a gentleman. Frost has also noted that a verdict for the plaintiff was likely to result, even on questionable evidence, where the plaintiff had been seduced (Frost, 'I Shall Not Sit Down and Crie' 237).

[76] Chitty, *Practical Treatise*, 4th edn 24.

[77] Ibid, 9.

[78] This is the rule applying to simple contracts. Contracts under seal, by contrast, are special in that they do not require consideration to be binding. Instead, they require the formalities of writing, sealing, and delivery (Chitty, *Practical Treatise*, 4th edn 3, 5).

consented to accept the defendant...'.[79] If the woman countenanced the man's promise 'and behaved as if she agreed to the matter, *although there be no actual promise,* yet it will be sufficient evidence of a promise on her part'.[80] Once again, the leading case, virtually dispensing with the need for a counter-promise, dates from the early nineteenth century.[81] In the 1826 case of *Daniel v Bowles*,[82] Captain Bowles proposed for Miss Daniel, not to that young lady herself, but to her mother. The mother promised to mention the subject to Miss Daniel's father. Captain Bowles afterwards introduced the subject again, when both Mrs and Miss Daniel were present. Mrs Daniel stated that there was no objection to the marriage on the part of herself and Mr Daniel, and Captain Bowles thereupon took *the mother's* hand and said 'from this time consider me as your son'. Although Miss Daniel herself had remained entirely passive throughout and made no observation whatsoever, she was held entitled to maintain an action, Mr Chief Justice Best being of the opinion that she could be taken to have made a promise, simply by virtue of 'being present, and not making any objection'. In other words, anything short of an outright rejection of the defendant would be taken as an implied promise to marry him. By contrast, the general contractual rule is that silence and mere inactivity cannot amount to an acceptance, much less a counter-promise:

The general rule is that silence does not amount to an acceptance and the rule is a good one.... The law would be unduly burdensome if it imposed on people an obligation to take positive steps to reject unwanted offers. Thus it is that the law puts the onus on the person to whom the offer has been made to demonstrate that he has, by some positive conduct on his part, accepted the offer. Silence does not generally constitute such 'positive conduct'. It is, by its nature, equivocal; it could be consistent with a rejection of the offer, indifference to the offer, or acceptance of it.[83]

The practical effect of *Daniel v Bowles* was that the 'contract' to marry was, to all intents and purposes, concluded by the defendant's promise of marriage alone, provided his promise was not actively rejected by the plaintiff. Thus, in a radical break with conventional contract doctrine, a bare promise was, in

---

[79] *Familiar Compendium* 176.

[80] Wharton 215 (emphasis added).

[81] The requirements had already been set very low in the eighteenth-century case of *Hutton v Mansell*, 3 Salk 64; 91 ER 693. Although *Hutton v Mansell* was not explicitly referred to in *Daniel v Bowles* (1826) 2 Car & P 553; 172 ER 251, it was likely looked to as a precedent.

[82] (1826) 2 Car & P 553; 172 ER 251.

[83] Ewan McKendrick, *Contract Law*, Palgrave Macmillan Law Masters (Basingstoke: Palgrave Macmillan, 2007) 106. McKendrick goes on to claim that the law does not recognize an exception to the general rule that silence and mere inactivity cannot amount to an acceptance and cites *Felthouse v Bindley* (1862) 142 ER 1037 in support.

substance, made enforceable, and the action for breach of a *promise* of marriage was born.[84]

(iv) The broken promise of marriage

In addition to establishing the existence of the contract, the plaintiff had to show that the defendant had broken it. In breach-of-promise cases, plaintiffs would frequently delay bringing suit until their former fiancés had married someone else.[85] Marriage with another woman would clearly put it out of the defendant's power to perform his contract with the plaintiff and would therefore, legally, constitute a breach of it.[86] It would also, psychologically, close the relationship for the woman concerned and make her more ready to contemplate legal action. Establishing a breach was similarly unproblematic where the defendant was, unbeknownst to the plaintiff, a married man at the time of making the promise.[87] In such a case, the contract would be broken as soon as it was made.

[84] It is by no means true that, as has been claimed by Brown, '[a]ll suits for breach of contract are technically for the breach of a promise...' (474). English lawyers generally stress that a contract includes a bargain element. See Patrick S Atiyah, *An Introduction to the Law of Contract*, 5th edn, Clarendon Law Series (Oxford: Clarendon Press, 1995) 42. MacColla also felt that it was a misnomer to call a contractual action an action for breach of a promise (17), although he seems to treat the problem as purely linguistic. Brown, of course, was an American, and in fairness to him it must be said that a definition of contract in terms of promises is quite common in American law. Thus, the American Restatement of Contracts reads: 'A contract is a promise or a set of promises for the breach of which the law gives a remedy...' See Restatement (Second) of Contracts § 1 (1979). Also, American contract law recognizes a more extensive estoppel remedy than English law, meaning that bare promises are more often enforceable there.

[85] Frost found that in 30 per cent of cases (259 out of her sample of 875) 'in which much information is known the defendants had married someone else by the time of the suit'. Frost, 'I Shall Not Sit Down and Crie' 234.

[86] The defendant who had married another woman would be deemed to have broken his contract with the plaintiff so as to enable her to bring an action even if the time for performance had not yet arrived. For instance, the defendant may have promised to marry the plaintiff when his father died and then married another woman in his father's lifetime. In such a case, the courts consistently allowed the woman to bring her action at once, applying the conventional contractual doctrine of anticipatory breach, established in *Hochster v De la Tour* (1853) 2 E & B 678, which involved an employment contract. See MacColla 22.

[87] If there was a legal problem in the case of a promise by a married man, it was not whether the defendant had broken his promise, but whether there was a binding promise capable of being broken in the first place. As the man was already married, performance of his promise to marry the plaintiff was either *contra bonos mores* (and therefore void) or legally impossible (and therefore void). Both arguments were made and rejected in the 1849 case of *Wild v Harris*, 7 CB 999. The validity of what Randall Craig has felicitously termed 'bigamous promises' to marry (*Promising Language: Betrothal in Victorian Law and Fiction* (Albany: State University of New York Press, 2000) 92) was affirmed in the 1850 case of *Millward v Littlewood*, 5 Ex 775, and consistently upheld into the twentieth century: *Shaw v Shaw* (1954) 2 QB 429. In my sample, 13 cases, or 5.6 per cent, involved promises to marry by married men.

By contrast, no action would lie on a promise by a married man *whom the plaintiff knew to be married*. Such a contract was deemed contrary to public policy, because it interfered with the contractor's ability to commit to his marriage and was thought to encourage adultery, desertion, or even murder.

Of course, the relationship between the parties could terminate without the defendant marrying someone else, and the woman might wish to bring her breach-of-promise action then, rather than going on hoping for a reconciliation. Normally, to establish a breach where performance of the contract is still possible, the defendant must have clearly refused to perform on being requested to do so by the plaintiff. In *Gough v Farr*,[88] counsel for the defendant maintained that this general rule should apply in breach-of-promise cases. A contract to marry, he submitted, was 'in point of law exactly like any other contract; and [... therefore, where the defendant was as much in a condition to marry the plaintiff as he ever was] there must... be a distinct opportunity given to the defendant to fulfil his engagements, by a tender on the part of the plaintiff...'. In the case before him, Miss Gough, the daughter of a clergyman, had not tendered herself to marry the defendant, and there was no knowing that *if* she had tendered herself to him, he would not have fulfilled his engagement by marrying her. Therefore, counsel argued, there was no evidence that the defendant had broken his contract, and the action was not good. The Court of the Exchequer agreed that 'in cases where the defendant had not married another, there ought to be proof of a tender and refusal'. To that extent, the court applied conventional contract law. However, it added a significant rider:

But if the plaintiff's father go to the defendant, and ask him if he means to fulfil his engagements to his daughter, and he reply, 'Certainly not'; proof of this will be sufficient.

It appeared that in *Gough v Farr*, the plaintiff's father, the Reverend Gough, had gone to ask the young man's intentions and received the above-quoted reply. This point-blank refusal *to the father* was deemed sufficient proof that Mr Farr had broken his contract *with the plaintiff* to entitle her to maintain her action. In other words, in breach-of-promise cases, tender of performance did not have to proceed from the plaintiff herself. It could be made by other persons acting on her behalf or in her best interests, such as family (as in *Gough v Farr*) or friends. Nor did the defendant's refusal have to be directly to the plaintiff. There, too, friends and relations could act as channels of communication. The precedent established in *Gough v Farr* was applied and even taken a little further in *Caldicott v Beagin*.[89] In that case, Miss Caldicott, 'a lady

---

And since the plaintiff knew of the marriage, there was here no countervailing interest in protecting her. See *Spiers v Hunt* [1908] 1 KB 720; *Wilson v Carnley* [1908] 1 KB 729. The House of Lords did, however, carve out an exception for promises of marriage made by one spouse, after a *decree nisi* for the dissolution of the marriage had been pronounced, to marry a third party after the decree had been made absolute. See *Fender v St. John-Mildmay* [1938] AC 1.

88   (1827) 2 Car & P 631.
89   *News of the World* 1 March 1846: 7.

of great personal attractions and accomplishments, only 19 years of age', sued Mr Beagin, a stockbroker making between £800 and £1,000 a year. Mr Beagin denied that he had broken the contract. It appeared that, following a lover's quarrel, Mr Caldicott 'came to demand if the defendant meant to fulfil his obligation to marry his daughter. The defendant said he did not.' Thus far, the case was clearly within the precedent established by *Gough v Farr*, and Mr Beagin would be taken to have broken his contract. However, Beagin had one more card up his sleeve. At the trial, he suddenly declared himself ready to fulfil his engagement with the plaintiff—but without success. The Court of Exchequer held that Beagin had broken his contract once and for all by his refusal to Mr Caldicott, and 'after the turn things had taken, and the length to which things had . . . gone', he could not now turn round and offer to marry the plaintiff. *Gough v Farr* and *Caldicott v Beagin* established that a refusal to marry on being asked to do so by the plaintiff's family or friends would constitute a breach of the contract and that such a breach would be taken as final. A man might also be taken to have broken his contract even where he did not, strictly speaking, refuse. MacColla recounts a case between parties, who, 'at the ripe age of fifty years [. . .] took to courting'.[90] The man had asked the woman to 'put the askings up', but she had declined, 'thinking it was a man's place to do that'.[91] Thereupon, the defendant had looked for company elsewhere. At the trial, he sought to deny that he had broken the contract. The plaintiff, he argued, should have been agreeable and met him halfway: 'I was not going to do it all myself.'[92] The court disagreed with the defendant's notions of a proper courtship. It found that an unwillingness to 'do it all himself' effectively amounted to a breach by the defendant of his contract.

In their rules on when a defendant would be taken to have broken his promise of marriage—in effect whenever he evinced an unwillingness towards the plaintiff, her family, or her friends to do all the running in the relationship— the triplet of cases just considered continued the nineteenth-century breach-of-promise tradition of making exceptions from strict contract law.

(b) Defending the suit

Once the plaintiff had made out her case, the defendant could only hope for a verdict in his favour if he could establish a defence that would bar the plaintiff's action. In my consideration of the defences that a defendant might try to set up in a breach-of-promise suit, I shall limit myself to a discussion of four. These four defences differ, either in their nature or in their treatment by the courts, from those that might be set up in an ordinary contract action.

---

[90] MacColla 66.   [91] Ibid, 67.   [92] Ibid, 70.

The first defence that I should like to consider is one that was different in nature from those that might be put forward in conventional contract actions. The defence was special to the breach-of-promise context and in excess of the 'usual defences to actions upon simple contracts'[93]: the defence of unchastity. In the early nineteenth century, it was a defence for the defendant to prove that, subsequent to making the promise of marriage, he had discovered the plaintiff to be a loose and immodest woman and that he broke his promise on account of her depraved conduct and immorality.[94] Over the course of the century, the defence was restricted to actual bodily unchastity.[95] However, loose or simply 'unfeminine' conduct, although no longer an absolute defence to the action, continued to operate to lower awards, often to contemptuous levels, and I will consider its role as a mitigating factor later, when addressing the question of damages.

The notion of physical unchastity appears to have been applied very literally by the courts. It seems that any sexual intimacy with another man, voluntary or, indeed, *involuntary*, would bar the action. In *Barnett v Abrahams*,[96] the plaintiff appeared to have been raped by a guard on the Metropolitan Railway[97] and had given birth to a child. Despite the fact that she does not seem to have been morally to blame for her misfortune, the jury returned a verdict for the defendant. The rule was simple:

If a man who has made a promise of marriage discovers that the person he has promised to marry is with child by another man, he is justified in breaking such promise...[98]

A verdict for the defendant would, *a fortiori*, be taken, where it appeared that a want of physical chastity was combined with downright immorality. In an action by a theatre actress against a Greek cotton broker, for instance, the plaintiff, under cross-examination, admitted to having been 'somewhat lax in her morality'.[99] The jury found for the defendant.

---

[93] Chitty, *Practical Treatise*, 4th edn 623.

[94] *Familiar Compendium* 178. See also Wharton 217.

[95] Thus, Chitty's 1871 edition states that it would seem that only '*want of chastity* on the part of the woman can be relied upon . . . as a ground for refusing to perform [. . . the] contract' (*Practical Treatise*, 9th edn (London, 1871) 795).

[96] *The Times* 29 April 1870: 10.

[97] Rape, or at least allegations of rape, in a railway carriage were very frequent in the late nineteenth century, when railway travel first became available. There were even proposals to have separate carriages for men and women. Susan S M Edwards, *Female Sexuality and the Law: A Study of Constructs of Female Sexuality as They Inform Statute and Legal Procedure*, Law in Society Series (Oxford: Martin Robertson, 1981) 127.

[98] *Familiar Compendium* 178 (quoting Mr. Chief Justice Abbott in the 1824 case of *Irving v Greenwood* 1 Car & P 350).

[99] *Colebrooke v Ralli*, *News of the World* 2 April 1876: 5.

It would appear, therefore, that a Magdalen[100] could not hope for a very sympathetic hearing in a breach-of-promise courtroom. However, there were four qualifications to this general rule. Firstly, the defendant had to *prove*, not merely assert, that the plaintiff was an abandoned woman.[101] In fact, the defence of unchastity was a double-edged sword. It was a defence a defendant put forward at his peril. If proved, the plaintiff's unchastity would ensure a verdict in his favour. But if not proved, the defendant would be deemed to have cast aspersions on the plaintiff's hitherto unblemished character, which would aggravate the damages he had to pay. Thus, in *Kitteridge v Crow*, the Lord Chief Baron instructed the jury to consider 'the line of defence persisted in at the trial in imputing to the plaintiff that she had been intimate with other men, of the truth of which imputation there was not a shadow of evidence, and whether [. . . this conduct of the defendant's] would not enhance the sum they might think it right to award'.[102] Secondly, the plaintiff's unchastity had to have caused the breach. In other words, the defendant had to show that he broke his promise on account of the want of chastity and not for some other reason. Thirdly, the jury had to be satisfied that the defendant did not know of the plaintiff's want of chastity when he promised to marry her. A promise made to a Madonna was binding; a promise made to a Magdalen the defendant believed to be a Madonna was not binding; but a promise to a Magdalen the defendant knew to be a Magdalen was binding, and he had to keep it or pay damages for its breach. An example of the application of this third proviso is afforded by the early nineteenth-century *cause célèbre* of *Foote v Hayne*,[103] a case that, at the time it was heard, excited 'unexampled interest . . . in the public mind'.[104] The plaintiff, Maria Foote, was an actress, 'of great beauty, of considerable talents, and of extensive accomplishments [. . . and in her profession] possessed of great and almost unrivalled powers'.[105] In her first youth, she had contracted an intimacy with Colonel Berkeley, the eldest son of Lord Berkeley, which had 'entailed the ruin of that unhappy lady'.[106] In 1823, Miss Foote again found herself the object of amorous attentions. Mr Hayne promised to marry her. After this, his first, promise of marriage to Miss Foote, Hayne was informed

---

[100] Eric Trudgill uses the terms Madonna and Magdalen to describe the twin Victorian stereotypes of the ideal pure woman and the fallen woman. Eric Trudgill, *Madonnas and Magdalens: The Origins and Development of Victorian Sexual Attitudes* (New York: Holmes and Meier, 1976).

[101] *Irving v Greenwood* (1824) 1 Car & P 350 (per Abbott, C J).

[102] *The Times* 21 March 1860: 12.

[103] The case is discussed in *Familiar Compendium* 179–94. It also constitutes a focal point of Steinbach's consideration of the breach-of-promise action ('Promises' 34–104).

[104] *Familiar Compendium* 179.

[105] Ibid, 180.

[106] Ibid, 181.

of the nature of the connection that had subsisted between his intended and Colonel Berkeley, and for a time the engagement between Foote and Hayne seemed at an end. Too great, however, was the impression the beauty and bewitching ways of the young actress had made on the heart of the susceptible Hayne, and he again requested Miss Foote to make him the happiest of men, this time with full knowledge of her antecedents. When Hayne finally changed his mind about the marriageability of a woman who had been another man's mistress and the mother of two of his children, the Lord Chief Justice instructed the jury 'that if the connection had ended at the time Mr. Hayne was informed... of Miss Foote's situation, he should have thought himself bound to tell [... them that] he was justified in then breaking off all acquaintance. The connection had, however, been renewed...'.[107] Mr Hayne had to pay £3,000 for breaking his promise of marriage to a woman with a past, because he knew her virtue to be tarnished when he proposed to her. Another illustration of the same principle is provided by *Turner v Wilson*.[108] In that case, the defence raised the point that the plaintiff, 10 years before, had been seduced and had a child nine years old. The defendant had been well aware of this fact while the courtship was going on. Not only did the plaintiff's past *known* unchastity not constitute a defence, but the 'introduction of this topic was severely commented on by the learned counsel for the plaintiff, and also by the learned Judge'. Finally, and perhaps most significantly, it was no defence to show that the plaintiff had been unchaste with the defendant himself. This is important because many plaintiffs had in fact fallen under the defendant's promise of marriage.[109] Fifty-eight cases in my sample, for instance, involved seduction under promise of marriage, followed, in most cases, by the birth of a child. The fact that the woman had fallen to the man she was suing, and under promise of marriage, too, did not stop some defendants from at least trying to argue that she, having lost her virtue, had no right to compensation for the breach of promise. In *Roebuck v Dunderdale*, for example, counsel for the defendant argued that in falling to the defendant in a moment of temptation, Miss Roebuck had lost 'her claim to the defendant's confidence in her future honour... flung away, in

---

[107] Ibid, 193–4.

[108] *The Times* 10 March 1865: 12.

[109] The case where the plaintiff had fallen during the engagement has to be distinguished from the situation where the defendant promised to marry the plaintiff specifically *in consideration that she would have illicit intercourse with him*. Such a contract had been held to be void in *Morton v Fenn* (1783) 3 Dougl 211, although the precedent does not seem to have been applied in any case thereafter. This may be due to the proviso that if the defendant had renewed his promise after the illicit intercourse, this subsequent promise would be binding.

that moment, all her claim to the defendant's respect [. . . and lost] any claim on him to make her his wife':

> [T]he defendant, in refusing to marry her, did so because he felt, that the woman who had fallen as she had, merely because she could not resist temptation, might again become unfaithful; and that he could not have any confidence in her that she would not.[110]

In other cases, counsel for the defence argued that the plaintiff's fall should at least lower her damages. In *Gorst v Hodgson*,[111] it was claimed that to give heavy damages in the case of such 'derelictions from virtue' would be 'in opposition to good sense, to law, to good feeling, and religion', and in *Bell v Sutcliffe*,[112] the jury was requested to consider, in assessing damages, what 'sort of a girl' the plaintiff was. Her seduction 'was a proof at least that she did not attach that great value to character, which was ascribed to her; and in a case where a woman demands damages for her wounded honour, this conduct must naturally reduce the damages a jury would give'. This line of defence consistently failed. Far from barring the action or operating to lower awards, seduction under promise of marriage constituted an aggravating circumstance, which would increase damages.[113] The defence of unchastity then, unique to the breach-of-promise action and a departure from conventional contract law, was not a simple or straightforward defence. Its theoretical basis as a bar to the action was never clearly expressed. The closest the courts came to explaining the defence in terms of general contract law theory was in *Beachey v Brown*,[114] where Cockburn CJ and Crompton J seemed to base it on the non-disclosure of a material fact, going to the very root of the contract of marriage[115] and entitling the other party thereto to rescind it. To that extent, the contract to marry was classed as one *uberrimae fidei*.[116] To raise the unchastity defence could help the defendant's case; but it could also hurt it. Its success or otherwise depended on complicated questions of proof, causation, the defendant's knowledge, and the circumstances of the plaintiff's fall.

A second defence a defendant might put forward in a breach-of-promise action was the plaintiff's poor health, which, it might be claimed, rendered

---

[110] *Morning Chronicle* 9 April 1825: 1. The argument that a woman who had shown herself to be seducible was therefore not marriageable had been familiar since the eighteenth century (Staves 109). In 1767, Hugh Kelly wrote a problem novel about whether a girl seduced under promise of marriage could be depended on to make a chaste wife. Hugh Kelly, *Memoirs of a Magdalen, or, the History, of Louisa Mildmay*, The Flowering of the Novel, 1767 (New York: Garland Publishing, 1974).

[111] *Lancaster Gazette* 27 March 1841: 3.

[112] *The Times* 23 March 1824: 3.

[113] *Berry v Da Costa* (1866) LR 1 CP 331. This is borne out by the statistical evidence. For a discussion of seduction under promise of marriage as an aggravating circumstance, see pp 50–1 below.

[114] (1860) EB & E 796.

[115] Ibid, 800.

[116] The duty to disclose was, however, limited to unchastity. Otherwise, as Crompton J remarked, 'I do not know where we would stop … He [the defendant] might complain that what he took to be a beautiful head of hair turned out to be a wig' (Ibid).

her unfit to perform the duties of a wife. The ill-health defence is interesting because the courts' attitude towards it changed dramatically over the course of the history of the breach-of-promise action. In the eighteenth century, the plaintiff's physical infirmity, arising or becoming known to the defendant after the contract was entered into, afforded a good defence. In the late eighteenth-century case of *Atchinson v Baker*, Lord Kenyon had formulated what was in effect a broad frustration rule (although it anticipated the full development of that doctrine at common law): 'if the condition of the parties were changed after the time of making the contract, it was a good cause for either party to break off the connexion'.[117] During the course of the nineteenth century, how-ever, the availability of the ill-health defence became increasingly doubtful. Thus, the 1871 edition of Chitty's *Practical Treatise* questioned the authority of the eighteenth-century dicta and added that 'the better opinion would seem to be that no [bodily] infirmity...can be relied upon...as a ground for refusing to perform [...the] contract.'[118] One late-nineteenth-century defendant who tried the ill-health defence and failed was Dr Snell.[119] Snell was a medical man and supposedly a specialist in consumption. He claimed that it was one of his inviolable principles not to marry into a consumptive taint and that his engage-ment to Eva Froud had been subject to the express condition that there was no consumption in her family. He 'rescinded' the contract, when he claimed to have discovered that Eva's mother had fallen a victim to the disease. The court's response to Dr Snell's line of defence was twofold. Firstly, it doubted that the engagement had been subject to an express condition: a proposal was 'painful enough without adding to it the formalities of an application to an insurance office'. Secondly, in the absence of an express condition, the rule *caveat emp-tor* applied. In other words, it was for the defendant to ascertain the plaintiff's state of health prior to proposing marriage. If he proposed and afterwards dis-covered her to be affected by some physical infirmity, he was bound to keep his promise or suffer the financial consequences of breaking it.[120] In the nine-teenth century, therefore, the legal position was that a plaintiff's *moral* frailty might, while her *physical* frailty would not, operate to excuse a defendant from his promise to marry her.

The third defence I should like to consider is a defence variously known as release, discharge, or exoneration. Unlike the defence of unchastity, which, as we have seen, was unique to the breach-of-promise action, the defence of

---

[117] (1797) Peake's Addl C 103 (124), quoted in Chitty, *Practical Treatise*, 3rd edn 540.

[118] Chitty, *Practical Treatise*, 9th edn 795.

[119] *Froud v Snell, The Times* 2 April 1895: 13.

[120] The jury awarded Eva Froud £1,000 in damages, more than 140 per cent of Dr Snell's annual income. This represents a very high award, especially for the late nineteenth century. It appears, there-fore, that Dr Snell's defence did not just fail: suggesting that Eva Froud was subject to a consumptive taint (which was not conclusively proved) might, on the contrary, have increased the damages.

release was generally available in actions upon a simple contract. However, the defence of release was *applied* differently by nineteenth-century courts in the breach-of-promise context. Generally, one party to a contract could discharge the other party thereto from his contractual obligations by demonstrating an evident intention to renounce the claim. No particular form of words was required.[121] A good illustration of how the defence of release operated in general is provided by a breach-of-promise case that was brought by a *man*.[122] In this case, Miss Harvey was defendant and a Mr Bull, who had been her drawing master, plaintiff. Following what appears to have been a particularly nasty disagreement about money matters, Miss Harvey had written: 'I forgive..., but I cannot forget... With wishes that you may still have a happy life before you, yours sincerely, Edith.' And Mr Bull had answered in the following terms: 'I accept the alternative, although to me it is clear that you either did not hear or did not understand what I really said.' Counsel for the female defendant submitted that this exchange amounted to a discharge of the contract by mutual consent, and Mr Justice Lawrence upheld the submission. However, where a *male* defendant claimed that his fiancée had discharged him from his promise to marry her, the courts' attitude was very different. It appeared that, in such a case, virtually no form of words, however express, and virtually no conduct, however unequivocal, would rise to the level of a release. In *Williams v Haines*,[123] the defendant had informed the plaintiff by letter that he had been advised by his doctor to relinquish all hope of marrying for the present. To this letter, the plaintiff replied, expressing a wish 'that they might part as Christians, and be for the future like brother and sister'. Although the plaintiff's answer could very well have been argued to evidence her intention to release the defendant from his obligation to make her his wife, the question of discharge was not even addressed. In another case,[124] the defendant, Henry Pretty, had told Cecilia Bay that he could not marry her for another two years. Whereupon she said that he had better not see her again and, a few days later, returned the ring. Although Cecilia Bay's conduct clearly proclaimed that, under the circumstances, she did not want to continue the engagement, Pretty's defence of release failed. This tightening up of the defence of release in the breach-of-promise context to the point where, although it was theoretically available, no male defendant could hope to benefit by it (my sample discloses no nineteenth-century case of a male defendant's defence of release being successful), appears all the more incongruous when

---

[121] Chitty, *Practical Treatise*, 4th edn 668.
[122] *Bull v Harvey, News of the World* 11 March 1906: 9.
[123] *The Times* 2 April 1875: 11.
[124] *Bay v Pretty, News of the World* 19 March 1916: 11.

we reflect back on how little would suffice to found a woman's acceptance and counter-promise. According to *Daniel v Bowles* anything—short of an out-right rejection—would do. If one takes *Daniel v Bowles*, *Williams v Haines*, and *Bay v Pretty* together, the following curious situation presents itself. The most complete inactivity on the woman's part—Mr Chief Justice Best's 'being present, and making no objection'—would conclude the 'contract'. And the greatest activity on her part—such as Miss Williams's express words or Miss Bay's unequivocal conduct—could not terminate it. In other words, the 'contract' to marry came into being without any act on the part of the woman at all, and, once in existence, it could not be eradicated by any act of hers either. The plaintiff woman was thus virtually powerless to affect the 'contractual' relationship to which she was, ostensibly, a party.

The final defence I should like to discuss in this context is, in fact, no defence at all. The courts never recognized it. However, I have decided to include it in my consideration of the ways in which a breach-of-promise defendant might set about the task of defending the suit, because the occasional defendant did try to put it forward (two defendants in my sample did) and because its consistent failure to impress the courts is a feature of the action that supports my claim—which forms the subject matter of the fourth and final section of this chapter—that the nineteenth-century breach-of-promise action was the legal codification of the ideal of true womanhood. This final defence, or lack of one, was what I might term the plaintiff's want of demonstrativeness towards her fiancé. It was raised as an excuse for non-performance by the defendant in *Ward v Foxall*.[125] Mr Foxall complained of the cool way Miss Ward had had of evincing her affection for him. Undemonstrativeness in a fiancée, he effectively argued, should excuse a man from the obligation to make her his wife. The court failed to agree, and Mr Foxall eventually thought it best to settle the case for £300, rather than risk the fury of a jury of his countrymen.

(c) *The assessment of damages: 'what the woman ought to receive'*[126]

The award of damages was the last stage in a breach-of-promise suit and peculiarly the province of the jury. It will be recalled that, according to the contractual measure of damages, the plaintiff is entitled to the value of his lost expectations. The plaintiff is to be placed, so far as money can do so, in the position in which he would have been if the contract had been performed. If the plaintiff cannot prove the value of his expectations, he will usually be awarded his actual out-of-pocket loss. The seventeenth-century action for breach of the marriage

---

[125] *News of the World* 2 April 1876: 7.
[126] *Report of the Proceedings in the Cause of Mary Alice Orford* 71. The quotation is taken from the judge's instruction to the jury on damages.

contract, as we have seen, followed these contractual rules on the measure of damages. The plaintiff was compensated for his or her lost settlement in life or, in default, for the expenses incurred in preparing for a marriage that never came off.

By the early nineteenth century, by contrast, damages awards were no longer, primarily, about the economic injury entailed by a broken engagement. To be sure, a plaintiff might still claim for her lost settlement (ie the pecuniary value of the lost marriage) or her actual out-of-pocket loss, but these no longer formed the only, or even the most important, heads of damage. Instead, emotional distress—variously described as injured feelings, wounded affections, or loss of honour—and the physical debility consequent thereon displaced the conventional economics of contract as the most significant aspect of damages. The subordinate role the economics of contract came to play to the emotionalism of a woman's disappointed love in the nineteenth century is evident from Wharton's definition of the breach-of-promise action, quoted at the start of the first section of this chapter. According to Wharton, damages for breach of promise are meant to compensate 'for loss of health, or loss of happiness, . . . or loss of hitherto unimpeachable honor (that full measure of a woman's ruin), *and, sometimes, in addition to all these*, loss of property in the disappointment of a settlement for life'.[127] The economic injury—the lost expectation of a settlement for life—has become a mere afterthought, utterly eclipsed by the all-important injury to the plaintiff's emotions. As one American commentator remarked:

The expense occasioned in preparation for fulfillment of the contract is now simply an item to be considered by the jury in their estimate of damages, the larger portion of which is made up of mangled feelings, humiliation, or a falling off in social position.[128]

In *Jones v Yeend*, Mr Serjeant Allen, in stating Miss Jones's case in a manner typical of the period, described her as 'a slighted thing, injured in reputation, health, and spirits, and reduced to a state from which she would probably never recover' and trusted the jury 'would give the amplest compensation which money could supply for the injury thus coldly, cruelly, and heartlessly inflicted on her health, hopes, and prospects'.[129] It is probably the prominence accorded to these emotional damages in nineteenth-century breach-of-promise suits that has led some nineteenth- and twentieth-century legal commentators to classify

---

[127] Wharton 213 (emphasis added).
[128] Lawyer 274.
[129] *The Times* 27 March 1850: 7.

the cause of action as tortious, rather than contractual.[130] The centrality of this head of damage certainly does mark a striking departure from conventional contract law: 'in no other action for breach of a contract,' MacColla remarked, 'is a pecuniary *solatium* awarded for wounded feelings'.[131] These emotional damages—for psychological (and resultant physical) distress as well as for the humiliation and public disgrace attendant on the broken engagement—were classed as general damages. General damages, unlike special damages, are damages that the law implies from the cause of action itself, which necessarily arise from the facts stated in the cause of action, and which do not, therefore, have to be specifically pleaded and strictly proved. Put more succinctly, general damages are damages that go without saying.[132] In other words, that a broken engagement would break a woman's heart and physically prostrate her was, in the nineteenth century, regarded as a truth too universally acknowledged to call for especial mention. The nineteenth-century action for breach of promise thus permitted awards 'without proof of actual loss or damage sustained ... while in all other actions for breaches of contract the actual damage alone is the full measure of the award'.[133]

In addition to these emotional damages, which formed the main head of compensation in nineteenth-century breach-of-promise suits, damages could be claimed for the economic loss sustained. Damages for the pecuniary consequences of the broken engagement more closely resemble the contract theory of recovery, but here, too, nineteenth-century courts were not wholly consistent. In the area of purely economic injury, no less than in the extension of the cognizable heads of damage beyond the economic realm legitimated by contract, nineteenth-century courts were guilty of an intermingling of the contractual and tortious bases of recovery. A good illustration of this is provided by the 1870 case of *Sidebottom v Buckley*. The plaintiff, Elizabeth Sidebottom, had been, quite literally, deserted on her wedding day. In addition to her emotional distress, Sidebottom claimed damages for the lost marriage to the defendant, her out-of-pocket expenses in preparing for the wedding to the point where the 'tables were set, and the wedding guests met', and her lost

---

[130] See, for instance, F O Arnold, *The Law of Damages and Compensation*, 2nd edn (London: Butterworths, 1919) 221 ('the principles governing the measure of damages ... are ... much more akin to those relating to tort than those relating to contracts') and Frank Gahan, *The Law of Damages* (London: Sweet & Maxwell, 1936) 18. Arnold's and Gahan's view is echoed by American textbook authors Wadlington and Paulsen 92.

[131] MacColla 28. On the recoverability of damages for non-pecuniary loss in breach-of-promise actions, see also Harry Street, *Principles of the Law of Damages* (London: Sweet & Maxwell, 1962) 238.

[132] The terms 'general' and 'special' damage are used in a variety of different meanings (concerning liability, proof, and pleading) that need to be kept distinct. See Harvey McGregor, *McGregor on Damages*, 17th edn (London: Sweet & Maxwell, 2003) 19–22.

[133] Lawyer 272.

opportunity to marry someone else: 'it was an aggravation of the wrong done to the plaintiff that shortly before the breach of promise a gentleman had made her "an offer," and would have married her but for the interference of the defendant. The gentleman had since married.'[134] These three heads of damage are, however, logically inconsistent and could not, therefore, have been combined in one action. A plaintiff in a contract action, as we saw above, can recover reliance damages where she cannot prove the value of her expectations. But she cannot, logically, recover *both* expectation *and* reliance damages at the same time. This is because, where a plaintiff recovers expectation damages (the usual contractual measure of recovery), she is being placed in the position in which she would have been if the contract had been performed. This is inconsistent with the purpose of reliance damages (the usual tortious measure of recovery), which is to place the plaintiff in the position in which she would have been if the contract had never been made. In Miss Sidebottom's case, if the contract had been performed, she would have married Mr Buckley (expectation damages). In that case, however, she would still have incurred the wedding expenses and she would still have lost her opportunity of marrying Mr Buckley's rival (reliance damages). She has lost the marriage, and if the jury gives her its value, it should not, logically, also give her the value she gave up for it. Nineteenth-century breach-of-promise courts were, however, not necessarily logical or consistent in this area, and many a plaintiff may have ended up having her cake and eating it, too. Even Cousens, who argues that the ordinary contractual rules on damages were applied to breach-of-promise actions, admits that the different kinds of pecuniary damage were 'treated by the courts with exceedingly little discrimination'.[135]

Various factors could aggravate or mitigate the damages a breach-of-promise defendant had to pay. Where aggravating factors were present, the jury might award exemplary or punitive damages. The availability of exemplary and punitive damages marks yet another respect in which the nineteenth-century breach-of-promise action departed from the contractual mainstream, as it was in fact the only contractual action to admit them.[136] Exemplary damages are usually given for the defendant's bad faith or malice,[137] and they might, for instance, be awarded where the defendant put forward a defence of unchastity, which he could not subsequently substantiate. Another significant aggravating circumstance, which I briefly referred to above, was seduction under promise of marriage. The increase in damages where seduction was present

---

[134] *Lancaster Gazette* 19 March 1870: 3.
[135] Cousens 381.
[136] Atiyah, *Introduction* 439.
[137] Brown 486.

is statistically measurable. In my sample, the average damages recovered by a plaintiff who had been seduced under promise of marriage were £377. The average where seduction had not occurred, by contrast, was only £244. This significant differential persists when we look at average damages as a percentage of the defendant's annual income. Where seduction operated as an aggravating factor, plaintiffs were awarded 75 per cent of the defendant's annual income as opposed to 54 per cent, where it did not. This second set of figures is significant, because it rules out an explanation of the difference in the average absolute awards by the argument that seducers tended to be high-class rakes, made to pay higher damages simply by virtue of the fact that they had more money to pay them with. In fact, in my sample, the majority of seducers were lower middle-class.[138]

There were two more factors that were said to operate to increase the award, after the fashion of aggravating circumstances. Interestingly, however, these two factors, in open conflict with the general principle underlying the award of exemplary and punitive damages—ie that they are given for the defendant's outrageous conduct—were entirely independent of any conduct of the defendant's. Rather, these aggravating factors related wholly to matters intrinsic to the plaintiff, namely to her youth and to her beauty:

A nice-looking plaintiff can aggravate the damages greatly ... If she be pretty, she will secure a very handsome verdict from twelve gallant men, who are empannelled [sic] in the box to decide ... the amount of damages she should receive. ... Where the lady-plaintiff does not possess that captivating beauty which such a jury is ever ready to reward ... neither she nor her legal advisers can hope for the wringing damages which are given to a *belle*.[139]

In *Davies v Cleator*,[140] Mr Temple, QC, made much of Elizabeth Davies's personal attractions and even submitted a photograph of her to the jury to allow them to form an opinion of her beauty. Mr Temple's way of proceeding was not exceptional, but seems to have been common practice among plaintiff counsel.

---

[138] For statistical purposes, I assigned every defendant in my sample a class status, based on income, profession, and the terms used by counsel in describing him. The lowest status group is class 1, which would include day labourers and others with a very tenuous hold on respectability. The highest class (6) is reserved to the nobility. Class groups 3–5 are given over to the middle classes, with class 3 describing the lower middle class. Seduction tended to occur most often with defendants in classes 2–4 (87.7 per cent), with class 3 alone accounting for nearly half of all seducers (45.6 per cent).

[139] MacColla 59 (emphasis in original). See also 'Breaches of Promise' *News of the World* 9 April 1871: 2, where it was said: 'Supposing the plaintiff possessed of a more than ordinary amount of personal charms, which the jury are graciously permitted to have a sight of in court, and that the latter are, let us say, only ordinarily impressible, there is at least a possibility that their indignation at the desertion of the fair would assume a vaster proportion than if she had been destitute of those personal fascinations.'

[140] *The Times* 22 March 1865: 12.

This is evident from Mr Chief Justice Harrison's remark in *Morrison v Shaw*[141] that attorneys, 'where clients are young or good-looking, generally conceive it to be their duty... to endeavour by the presence of the young woman to strengthen the favourable impression which the jurors are asked to take of the evidence'. An attorney who played the youth-and-beauty card might, however, get caught out. In *Howard v Scudder*, the plaintiff was described as 'a fine-looking girl'. The presiding judge, Mr Baron Alderson, desired to know how old she was. The answer—'Thirty-two'—was received with hoots of laughter, and Mr Baron Alderson exclaimed: 'Girl! a young woman, you mean.' The 'young woman' was awarded a mere £20 against a defendant who had been described as 'a corn merchant and baker carrying on an extensive business'.[142]

The presence of other factors, by contrast, could reduce the damages the defendant would be made to pay. The most significant mitigating factor, frequently operating to reduce damages to contemptuous levels, was improper or simply unfeminine conduct on the part of the plaintiff. In *Pratt v Bennett*,[143] for instance, a juror was withdrawn when it appeared that the plaintiff had had two strings to her bow and kept up an affectionate correspondence with the defendant and his brother at the same time. Two-timing, it seems, was regarded with disapprobation in the nineteenth century, and this is a moral judgement most of us would still endorse today. However, there was also other conduct on the plaintiff's part which would go in reduction of damages, conduct which nowadays would almost certainly not be regarded as improper and which, even in the nineteenth century, would perhaps not have earned any more opprobrious an epithet than that of 'unfeminine' or 'unmaidenly'. In *Burrows v Bagshaw*,[144] an action by the daughter of a sweetshop-keeper against a gentleman farmer, the fact that 'all the courting was done by the plaintiff and her mother' was probably determinative of the outcome of the case. With contemptuous damages of one shilling and deprived of her costs, Miss Burrows's unmaidenly forwardness effectively lost her her breach-of-promise action. *White v Fergusson* provides another illustration of the mitigating effects of female initiative. Alice Louisa White, the plaintiff, first met Mr Fergusson in 1887, at a ball in aid of the Chelsea Hospital. They danced a great deal, and on St Valentine's Day of the following year, Mr Fergusson sent her a little something. Nothing further passed between them until Christmas of that year, when Miss White decided to send Mr Fergusson a Christmas card. Some letters passed, but Fergusson's, never more than mildly affectionate, waxed cool, and the correspondence

[141] (1877) 40 UCQB 403, quoted in Coombe 103.
[142] *Morning Chronicle* 7 March 1845: 7.
[143] *Lancaster Gazette* 24 May 1845: 2.
[144] *News of the World* 8 March 1891: 4.

petered out. On going over her box of treasures five and a half years later, Miss White came across old letters of the defendant's and took the unusual step of writing to him, confessing that it 'is ages since I least heard from you. I have been wondering if I should ever hear again. I would like to so much. I have hoped to meet you at the Caledonian balls, &c., and so I have at last summoned up enough courage to write to you...I shall be so pleased if you will write me a line.'[145] This unorthodox lead-up to their eventual 'engagement' (the defendant was, in fact, a married man) was used as a rod to beat Miss White with when her action came up in court. Mr Gill, for the defendant, thought that nothing about this case was 'more astounding than the circumstances under which she came to write to defendant in December, 1893, after 5½ years' silence',[146] clearly implying that it was not the female role to precipitate a relationship. Miss White's unfeminine initiative was reflected in her damages, which were not high, even for the 1890s period, given the wealth and standing of the man she was suing and the presence of significant aggravating circumstances in the case.[147] A woman's age and physical appearance as well as her deportment during the affair could thus have a huge impact on the amount of damages deemed necessary to compensate her for her suffering. The principle underpinning the award of damages in nineteenth-century breach-of-promise cases was that if the girl be young, pretty, and properly behaved, she should be handsomely recompensed; and that her older, plainer, or more unorthodox sisters should receive less or, in an extreme case, be sent away empty-handed.

3. Survival of actions: the rule in *Chamberlain v Williamson* (1814)

Everything looked set for a Christmas wedding. Ann Chamberlain would give up her boarding school, and, in the winter of 1812, she would walk down the aisle with Mr Williamson, her affianced lover. But Ann Chamberlain's life did not follow the storybook pattern. She never did get married—either to Williamson or to anyone else. Williamson broke off all intercourse in November of 1812, and by the following May, Ann was dead.

---

[145] *The Times* 19 March 1895: 14.

[146] *The Times* 21 March 1895: 14.

[147] The jury awarded Alice White £500. Mr Fergusson was a gentleman in the iron trade, had £30,000 invested in some Spanish mines, a yacht, and a wife whom he maintained in luxury. He had cast aspersions on Miss White's character by suggesting that she was a common flirt and had always known that he was married. The circumstances of the break-up had also been more than usually heartless.

The facts of *Chamberlain, Administrator of Ann Chamberlain, Deceased v Williamson*[148] may have more genuine pathos in them than those of the average breach-of-promise case, but today the case is only remembered for the legal precedent it set. *Chamberlain v Williamson* established that the action for breach of promise of marriage is caught by the principle *actio personalis moritur cum persona*. In other words, it held that Ann's right of action had died with Ann and that the action for Williamson's breach of promise to her could not be maintained by Ann's personal representative.[149] Thus, although Williamson's desertion may have wrought the ultimate havoc in Ann's life (we can, of course, not be sure that she died of a broken heart), he did not have to pay any compensation for it.

For the purposes of this study, a consideration of *Chamberlain v Williamson* is rewarding for two reasons. For one thing, the court's decision seems to remove the nineteenth-century action for breach of promise of marriage yet one step further from conventional contract law, where survival of actions is the norm. As one twentieth-century American critic complained: 'In this respect also the suit seems to be unique among so-called contract actions.'[150] Secondly, and even more importantly, *Chamberlain v Williamson* is instructive for what it tells us about how nineteenth-century courts conceptualized the breach-of-promise action. The legal conception of the action saw the plaintiff as so central to the injury that, if she died, the whole point of the action had vanished with her.

The court's reasoning on why the *actio personalis* principle, conventionally believed to be confined to actions in tort, should be applied to the action for breach of promise is highly convoluted and, as a piece of legal logic, ultimately not convincing. It has to rely on a distinction between marriage as a temporal advantage (which, as we saw in *Holcroft v Dickenson*, is what legitimates the common law action for breach of promise in the first place) and marriage as a benefit to the personal estate (this, rather than being increased, is extinguished by it[151]). The distinction between a temporal advantage, on the one hand, and a benefit to the estate, on the other, is, one suspects, a distinction without a

---

[148]   (1814) 2 M & S 408.

[149]   The decision in fact held that the right of action would not survive 'unless there be laid in the declaration, and proved, some special damage affecting the personal estate of the deceased' (Chitty, *Practical Treatise*, 3rd edn 541). Special damage might be wedding expenses or other specific pecuniary loss. However, the special damage exception was extremely narrowly applied. For instance, expenditure on clothing bought in anticipation of marriage did not qualify in *Finlay v Chirney* (1887) 20 QBD 494.

[150]   Brown 476.

[151]   This is a result of the common law doctrine of unity of persons or coverture, briefly considered in the Introduction. When a woman married, she was, to a large extent, divested of her property, real and personal, in favour of her husband. Thus, marriage, rather than increasing her 'estate' in fact came close to extinguishing it. See Greenberg 174.

difference (are not the two, in fact, synonymous?). Indeed, in Ontario, where the action for breach of promise remained more clearly contractual in ethos during the nineteenth century, the decision on survival of actions, unsurprisingly, went the other way.[152]

Although the legal foundations of the rule in *Chamberlain v Williamson* are therefore shaky, the case, like no other, brings out the deep connection, in the court's conceptualization, between the nineteenth-century action for breach of promise of marriage and the plaintiff woman. The plaintiff was so central to the suit that the right of action itself abated once she was gone. There simply could not be a breach-of-promise suit without the woman in it.[153] The nineteenth-century breach-of-promise action clearly placed the plaintiff woman at its centre. It was preoccupied with her. It was about her and little else: 'what *the woman* ought to receive, and... *her conduct* throughout the transaction'[154] were the guiding principles of the law of breach of promise, stealing a march over the 'contractual' issues of existence of the contract and its breach. This makes it tempting to consider whether the woman, or rather her womanhood, her essential femininity, so to speak, might not provide a unifying construct to account for the 'HETEROGENEOUS mass'[155] of rules that we have just considered.

IV. A Unifying Construct: The Nineteenth-Century Action for Breach of Promise of Marriage as the Legal Codification of the Ideal of True Womanhood

Why there should be one rule... for... all contracts but one and a separate and distinct rule in the case of that one, has never been satisfactorily explained.[156]

---

[152] Coombe 72. The Ontario case on the question of survival of actions is *Davey v Myers*, Taylor 89, decided 10 years after *Chamberlain v Williamson*. In *Davey*, all of the judges affirmed the classification of the breach-of-promise suit as a contract action and upheld Miss Davey's verdict of £500 on the ground that, in actions arising *ex contractu*, the action survives the death of the testator for the benefit of and against the executors.

[153] That it was the woman (and not, equally, the male defendant) who was essential to the breach-of-promise action is revealed by the fact that the application of the *actio personalis* principle in the breach-of-promise context was decidedly one-sided at first. Usually, where the principle applies, the right of action abates with the death of either party. *Chamberlain v Williamson* had decided that the right of action abated on the *plaintiff's* death. It had left open the question of whether it would survive the defendant's. Throughout most of the nineteenth century, damages for breach of promise could, in fact, be awarded against the estates of dead defendants (MacColla 23, 65), and it was only the late nineteenth-century case of *Finlay v Chirney* (1887) 20 QBD 494, that finally ensured equality in the application of the *actio personalis* principle in the breach-of-promise context.

[154] *Report of the Proceedings in the Cause of Mary Alice Orford* 71 (emphases added).

[155] See n 30.

[156] Lawyer 273.

In the final section of this chapter, I hope to account for the idiosyncratic complex of rules that governed the nineteenth-century action for breach of promise. The unifying construct that I shall put forward is the nineteenth-century ideal of the virtuous, delicate, and submissive woman. The thesis advanced being that the emergence of the ideal of true womanhood at the turn of the nineteenth century caused the simultaneous hybridization of the breach-of-promise action and that it was the feminine ideal that moulded the action into its distinctive nineteenth-century shape.

I am not the first to undertake the search for the cause of the transformation of the breach-of-promise action at the turn of the nineteenth century and for a common denominator to explain the action's seemingly incongruous rules. Susie Steinbach's 1996 dissertation on breach of promise is a piece of scholarship with which all writers on the subject must reckon. Steinbach sets out to explain the emergence of the breach-of-promise action as a powerful action in the late eighteenth century, its near century-long reign, and its post-1870 decline in terms of two conceptual structures that were important from the late eighteenth to the late nineteenth centuries: contract and sentiment.[157] The very fact that Steinbach relies on two conceptual apparatuses, rather than just one unifying construct means, of course, that she cannot truly integrate all of the action's features. Instead, for Steinbach, the features of the action remain 'at base *either* contractual *or* sentimental'.[158] This does not seem to me a great advance on saying that the action's features are all at base either contractual or tortious, which is something legal scholars have been arguing since the nineteenth century.[159] The drawback of Steinbach's two-pronged approach to the subject is that it fails to provide an integrated account of the law of breach of promise. The other shortcoming that I perceive with Steinbach's thesis is its emphasis on the explanatory force, with respect to the make-up of the nineteenth-century breach-of-promise action, of late eighteenth- and early nineteenth-century developments in the wider law of contract. Espousing the Atiyah and Horwitz argument that the period from 1780 to 1870 represented the age of contract,[160] Steinbach maintains that 'it is impossible to comprehend the history of the breach of promise action without appreciating the role of contract ideology in the suit's rise and fall'.[161] Steinbach's reliance on contemporaneous

---

[157] Steinbach, 'Promises' 23–30. For a similar argument see Stone, *Road to Divorce* 92, where the rise of breach of promise is linked to 'the climax of romantic moralism about the plight of seduced and abandoned maidens from respectable homes'.

[158] Ibid, 3 (emphases added).

[159] See, for instance, MacColla vii. See also Lawyer 272.

[160] Atiyah calls the period from 1780–1870 the age of freedom of contract and devotes the second part of his book to this argument (*Rise and Fall* 219–568).

[161] Steinbach, 'Promises' 203.

trends within the wider law of contract is, it seems to me, highly problematic. A glance at the wider contractual landscape makes the departure of the breach-of-promise action from the contractual fold at precisely this time period appear, if anything, even more mystifying. The late eighteenth century marked the beginning of the so-called classical period in contract law, a period character-ized by the formulation of a *unitary* law of contract. It became common to gen-eralize from particular types of contract to universal principles of contract law, which could be stated at a high level of abstraction and applied indifferently to all kinds of contracts, irrespective of details of person and subject matter. Even contracts concerning land—which, involving, as they did, the Englishman's most cherished possession, had long claimed a special place—became, in the classical period, contracts like any other, subject to the general rules.[162] The American legal historian Lawrence Friedman has maintained that, while there was never any point in time at which the law of contract was entirely pure and abstract, it came closest to being so during the nineteenth century.[163] Yet it was precisely during the nineteenth century when the law of contract, by all accounts, reached this apogee of purity, abstractness, and universality that the breach-of-promise action, as we have seen, lost its contractual moorings. The late eighteenth- and early nineteenth-century developments in the wider law of contract, therefore, far from, as Steinbach seems to suggest, accounting for the contemporaneous transformation of the breach-of-promise action, might rather be expected to have counteracted it.

I would suggest that there is nothing in legal logic or practice itself that accounts for the restructuring of the breach-of-promise action at the turn of the nineteenth century. Instead, one has to look beyond law to the socio-cultural context and the reigning feminine ideal. I argue that the nineteenth-century breach-of-promise action was nothing more and nothing less than the legal codification of a powerful cultural ideal: the ideal of the true woman. If one relates the various features of the cause of action to the constitutive elem-ents of the nineteenth-century feminine ideal, the former's peculiar *sui generis* cast appears as a translation into legal terms of the prevailing myth of true womanhood. Notions of female domesticity, modesty, chastity, physical frailty, passionlessness, emotionality, and child-like dependence, even of youth and beauty, are revealed as having their counterparts in the complex of 'rules', both legal and practical, that governed the nineteenth-century action for breach of promise. The feminine ideal becomes the unifying construct to account for all the features of a cause of action, which has defied attempts at systematic legal categorization.

---

[162] Atiyah, *Rise and Fall* 398–405.
[163] Friedman 20–1.

The origins of the 'true woman' ideal, like the origins of the hybrid breach-of-promise action, lie in the late eighteenth and early nineteenth centuries. In England, the late eighteenth and nineteenth centuries were a period of rapid economic growth. Industrialization transformed agriculture and manufacturing by mechanizing production and concentrating the labour force. With economic expansion and the resultant great increase in material wealth came a change in social organization, with status based on ability, rather than inheritance and birth. The nineteenth century became the great age of a new and self-confident middle class, the century when a specifically middle-class culture welded together the middling ranks of society, whilst simultaneously separating them off from the nobility above and the labouring classes below them. It was the century that witnessed the rise of the middle class to numerical, political, and, above all, cultural pre-eminence.

At the same time as being a modernizing age of progress and wealth, presided over by a powerful middle class, the nineteenth century was an age ridden with doubts and anxieties.[164] Having created industrial capitalism, with its twin gods of social mobility and cut-throat competition, the Victorians sought to get away from it. The home, as a private sanctuary, a haven or refuge from the rigours of the public world of commerce and the market, assumed prime importance. Home and the family were idealized in a veritable cult of domesticity.[165] An ideology of separate spheres—with capitalist values assigned to the public sphere of work and Christian values to the private sphere of home—became the Victorian coping strategy. The emergence of a sharp division between the private world of home and the public world of the market, the professions, and politics had a profound impact on the Victorian perception of women and of their appropriate (or ideal) social role. Women, it was felt, were made for the calm of the private sphere of home, and their proper role was the guardianship of the domestic virtues. '[P]laces and activities seen as tainted by [… the] public world were increasingly barred to women, while the sacred duties of maintaining the virtuous home and raising children to embrace middle-class values and practices were elevated.'[166] The Victorian[167] conception of femininity is epitomized

---

[164] Walter E Houghton, *The Victorian Frame of Mind, 1830–1870* (New Haven: Yale University Press; London: Oxford University Press, 1957) 54–89.

[165] Gorham 4. See also Davidoff and Hall, who argue that domesticity was seen as a refuge from the sordid worldliness and corruption of the market (27–8).

[166] See Leonore Davidoff, Megan Doolittle, Janet Fink, and Catherine Holden, *The Family Story: Blood, Contract and Intimacy, 1830–1960*, Women and Men in History (London: Longman, 1999) 27.

[167] The origins of the constraining norms of feminine deportment, which I refer to by the shorthand label of 'ideal of true womanhood', can in fact be traced back to the mid- to late eighteenth century, where they find expression in the novels of Samuel Richardson and Frances Burney, among others. The ideal is, however, most powerfully associated with the nineteenth century and, in particular,

by a mid-nineteenth-century poem by Coventry Patmore, the title of which expresses its essence: 'The Angel in the House' (1854–56). To the Victorians, the dream of Patmore's domestic angel in human form lent much-needed stability to a rapidly changing world, and the poem sold better than any other poetic work except Tennyson's 'Idylls of the King'.[168] Patmore's 'Angel in the House' contains a very full expression of the ideal of true womanhood, and we can look to it as a source for the distillation of the ideal's cardinal attributes.[169]

To Patmore and his contemporaries, the ideal woman was an angel *in the house*. Woman, it was believed, was by nature domestic, formed for the calm of home, ordained by God to be the priestess of a 'vestal temple',[170] the temple of the hearth. Such was woman's mission. Man would toil in the open world, and the experience would leave him hardened. Woman, by contrast, had to be sheltered from the rough and tumble of the public sphere. Her rightful place was the domestic fireside, her destiny domesticity and marriage.

The ideal woman's 'chiefest grace',[171] according to Patmore, was her modesty. A belief that female modesty was the quintessential virtue is also reflected in the etiquette manuals of the period, such as John Gregory's *A Father's Legacy to His Daughters*. The leading prescriptive writer of the nineteenth century, Sarah Stickney Ellis, thought that an 'agreeable, modest, and dignified bearing is, in the younger period of a woman's existence, almost like a portion to her'.[172] The modest woman was demure, retiring, and quintessentially passive. She submitted to man as her intellectual superior, and any (moral) influence she exercised was not exercised directly, but only indirectly *through* men.[173] In courtship, especially, the ideal woman existed to be pursued, not to

the Victorian age. See generally Martha Vicinus (ed), *Suffer and Be Still: Women in the Victorian Age* (Bloomington: Indiana University Press, 1973) ix–x.

[168] Erna Olafson Hellerstein, Leslie Parker Hume, and Karen M Offen, *Victorian Women: A Documentary Account of Women's Lives in Nineteenth-Century England, France, and the United States* (Brighton: Harvester Press, 1981) 134.

[169] American historian Barbara Welter, in her seminal article on the expression of sexual stereotypes in antebellum America, divides the 'attributes of True Womanhood, by which a woman judged herself and was judged by her husband, her neighbors and society ... into four cardinal virtues— piety, purity, submissiveness and domesticity'. See Barbara Welter, 'The Cult of True Womanhood: 1820–1860' (1966) 18 *American Quarterly* 152. Although these may also be regarded as the most important elements of the ideal as it applied in England, the list is by no means exhaustive or, at any rate, not detailed enough for my purposes. I prefer to distinguish nine attributes of the ideal woman: domesticity, modesty, chastity, physical frailty, passionlessness, emotionality, youth, beauty, and childlike dependence.

[170] John Ruskin, *Of Queens' Gardens*, Norbert Thomé (ed), Schöninghs Englische Lesebogen (Paderborn: Ferdinand Schöningh, 1947) 11.

[171] Patmore 52.

[172] Quoted in Hellerstein, Hume, and Offen 98.

[173] Vicinus xiv.

do the pursuing, to wait to be chosen, rather than to choose. Mate-selection, for the ideal nineteenth-century woman, was essentially negative: 'we have the liberty of refusing those we don't like, but not of selecting those we do', one nineteenth-century American girl summed up the ritual.[174]

If a woman's chiefest grace was modesty, her chiefest treasure was her chastity. Chastity, in the Victorian period, was 'the essence of female virtue' and its absence, for a woman, a 'matter of the utmost gravity'.[175] Female chastity was, according to Patmore, a 'priceless gift',[176] and a woman was expected to guard it with the greatest care, even to lay down her life in its preservation. In the nineteenth century, it was proper to believe that the punishment for loss of female chastity was damnation,[177] and, if the attitude of Angel Clare in Thomas Hardy's *Tess of the D'Urbervilles* is anything to go by, the average Victorian male was wholly unable to contemplate the idea of marriage to a woman who had experienced, however involuntarily and innocently, a sexual relationship with another man. The woman who had lost the priceless pearl of chastity was culturally expected to sink into prostitution[178] or, like Richardson's Clarissa, decline and die.

While the ideal woman would thus preserve her chastity with the unflinching determination of a Pamela, she would, at the same time, be physically frail.[179] Indeed, in Pamela's case, it is her physical delicacy that proves her salvation, her very frailty that preserves her chastity. Trudgill has noted that Victorian conventions, 'which deprived women of healthy diet, exercise, and dress', and made many real-life women positively feeble, 'were no accident of custom but the product of a widespread masculine predilection for a doll-like physical fragility in women'.[180]

---

[174] Eliza Southgate to Moses Porter, 1800, quoted in Nancy F Cott, 'Passionlessness: An Interpretation of Victorian Sexual Ideology, 1790–1850' (1978) 4(2) *Signs* 229.

[175] Keith Thomas, 'The Double Standard' (1959) 20 *Journal of the History of Ideas* 214, 195. Ian Watt has argued that the nineteenth century witnessed a 'redefinition of virtue in primarily sexual terms'. A woman who had lost her chastity had, by that token, also lost her virtue and her claim to social respectability. See Ian Watt, 'The New Woman: Samuel Richardson's Pamela' in *The Family: Its Structure and Functions*, Rose L Coser (ed) (New York: St Martin's Press, 1964) 281–2.

[176] Patmore 46.

[177] Cyril Pearl, *The Girl with the Swansdown Seat* (London: Frederick Muller, 1955) 66.

[178] Ibid, 62–4.

[179] The Victorians regarded physical frailty as a sign of respectable femininity. Lynda Nead, *Myths of Sexuality: Representations of Women in Victorian Britain* (Oxford: Basil Blackwell, 1988) 29. This marked preference for fragility or even downright physical debility in women has led Lorna Duffin to label the perfect Victorian lady a 'conspicuous consumptive'. Lorna Duffin, 'The Conspicuous Consumptive: Woman as Invalid' in *The Nineteenth Century Woman: Her Cultural and Physical World*, S Delamont and Lorna Duffin (eds) (London: Croom Helm; New York: Barnes & Noble, 1978) 26–56.

[180] Trudgill 67.

The ideal woman's attitude to affection and its demonstration, especially its physical demonstration, has been aptly described as 'passionlessness'.[181] The late eighteenth and early nineteenth centuries witnessed the triumph of the desexualized ideal woman. She was innocent of all sexual knowledge, fainted at the first advance, and had no feelings for her admirer until he had avowed his feelings for her or until, in Coventry Patmore's phrase, her love had been 'loosen'd by/Her suitor's faith declared and gaged'.[182] In women, desire was believed to be 'dormant, if not non-existent, till excited; always till excited by undue familiarities; almost always till excited by actual intercourse',[183] and the leading medical authority on sexual matters in Victorian England declared that 'happily for society' the supposition that women possessed sexual feelings could be put aside as 'a vile aspersion'.[184] The ideal woman's deportment towards her lover would therefore be, certainly until after the marriage knot was tied, no more than mildly demonstrative. As one conduct-book writer editorialized: 'who would not rather that English women should be guarded by a wall of scruples, than allowed to degenerate into less worthy and less efficient supporters of their country's moral worth'.[185] In fact, for a young woman from the comfortable middle class, nothing short of an entire absence of sexual experience before her engagement would do.[186]

To say that the ideal woman was passionless was not to say that she was incapable of deep and lasting emotion. On the contrary, love, according to Byron, was 'woman's whole existence'.[187] The Victorians simply had a slow-burn view of female emotionality. The ideal woman's love was not easily awakened (it would certainly, as we have seen, require her lover's avowal of his); but once in love, she loved 'with love that cannot tire'.[188] The ideal woman was constant in her affections—her love endured through death and through desertion. In contrast to men, who, as Anne Elliot observed in *Persuasion*, loved 'so long as you have an object . . . while the woman you love lives, and lives for

---

[181] See Steinbach, *Women in England* 112 ('nineteenth-century doctrine of passionlessness'). The term 'passionlessness' was coined by American historian Nancy Cott to describe the belief that 'women lacked sexual aggressiveness, that their sexual appetites contributed a very minor part (if any at all) to their motivations, that lustfulness was simply uncharacteristic' (220).

[182] Patmore 121.

[183] William Rathbone Greg, 'Prostitution' (1850) 53 *Westminster Review* 457.

[184] William Acton, quoted in Henry Havelock Ellis, *The Erotic Rights of Women, and the Objects of Marriage* (London: British Society for the Study of Sex Psychology, 1918) 9.

[185] Sarah Stickney Ellis, *The Women of England: Their Social Duties and Domestic Habits* (New York, 1843) 25. Sarah Stickney Ellis was the leading prescriptive writer of the nineteenth century.

[186] Steinbach, *Women in England* 112.

[187] Lord Byron, *Don Juan*, T G Steffan, E Steffan, and W W Pratt (eds) (Harmondsworth: Penguin, 1973) 1.194.

[188] Patmore 83.

you,' women loved the longest, 'when existence or when hope is gone'.[189] A woman's love, once won, was deep and ineradicable. Fiction decreed that a woman disappointed in love would never love again. If strong-minded, like Lily Dale in Anthony Trollope's *The Last Chronicle of Barset*, she might graduate 'O. M.',[190] but more usually, the ideal woman would ' "go into a decline" from disappointment in love or, if the shock [. . . was] severe, lie for weeks at the point of death from "brain fever".'[191]

The ideal nineteenth-century woman displayed childlike simplicity and a trusting dependence on men. Ruskin described her as possessed of a 'majestic childishness',[192] and Patmore had his angel prattling away to her 'dear despot . . . like a child at play':[193] 'the mature angel-figure was expected to be child-like. She was expected, through the ennobling experience of love, to show her lover the radiance and innocence of a child.'[194] This cultural expectation is revealed in the letters of two great Victorian men, William Makepiece Thackeray and Charles Dickens, to their respective future wives. Each woman was treated, as Trudgill has noted, as though she were 'some endearing but refractory child'.[195] In the Victorian period, female independence was discouraged, its lack encouraged. A grown-up independence in a woman was scorned as unfeminine, and every self-respecting Victorian man felt intuitive repugnance towards masculine ladies. 'An unwomanly woman [. . .] was] always avoided; a masculine woman [. . . was] more repulsive than an effeminate man.'[196] By contrast, the more dependent and child-like they became, women were told, the more they would be cherished. '[F]or there is a peculiarity in men . . . which inclines them to offer the benefit of their protection to the most helpless and dependent of the female sex.'[197]

The ideal woman was young. Deborah Gorham has pointed out that, because of her youth and her sexual purity, a young girl could in fact represent the quintessential child-like angel much more successfully than her mother or

[189] Jane Austen, *Persuasion,* 1818 (London: Penguin, 1994) 236–7; ch 23.

[190] Lily Dale jokingly refers to herself as graduating 'O. M.', the initials standing for old maid. Anthony Trollope, *The Last Chronicle of Barset*, Stephen Gill (ed), 1867 (Oxford: Oxford University Press, 2001) 817; ch 76.

[191] Robert Palfrey Utter and Gwendolyn Bridges Needham, *Pamela's Daughters* (New York: Russell & Russell, 1972) 94.

[192] Ruskin 14.

[193] Patmore 161.

[194] Trudgill 99.

[195] Ibid, 100.

[196] Anti-feminist novelist Anna Maria Hall in her husband's *Book of Memories*, quoted in Janet Dunbar, *The Early Victorian Woman: Some Aspects of Her Life (1837–57)* (Westport: Hyperion Press, 1979) 172.

[197] Ellis, *Women of England* 32.

an older woman.[198] The young child-wife was the ideal in Victorian fiction, songs, and poetry, and also in real life, as is proved by the growing practice among Victorian men of marrying women much younger than themselves. Davidoff and Hall have shown that the age gap between the Victorian husband and his wife widened with the man's status and wealth and, by implication, his degree of marital choice.[199]

Finally, the ideal woman was beautiful. Interestingly, the beauty of the ideal woman was not described in crude physical language, but, as befits an angelic ideal, cast in almost spiritual terms. Patmore apostrophizes his angel as the 'Rose of the World' and sings paeans in praise of her celestial loveliness:

> He [God] form'd the woman; nor might less
>   Than Sabbath such a work succeed.
> And still with favour singled out,
>   Marr'd less than man by mortal fall,
> Her disposition is devout,
>   Her countenance angelical;
> The best things that the best believe
>   Are in her face so kindly writ
> The faithless, seeing her, conceive
>   Not only heaven, but hope of it ... [200]

Such was the ideal of the true woman. In the nineteenth century, the attributes were believed to spring from female nature itself. The feminine ideal was seen as having its origin in the innate disposition of the female sex and to be descriptive of (rather than merely prescriptive for) womanhood.[201] Of course, the temporal specificity of the ideal—the fact that, after the Victorian period, it became culturally obsolete—and the fact that its practical realization was probably very much confined to the middle and upper classes[202] prove that the attributes assigned to the ideal woman did not lie in the nature of things,

---

[198] Gorham 7.

[199] Davidoff and Hall 346.

[200] Patmore 51.

[201] Sachs and Wilson have pointed out that it was natural to assume that femininity was biological rather than socially constructed, so as to need no logical argument for the maintenance of the highly sex-specific code of conduct that was applied to women. Albie Sachs and Joan Hoff Wilson, *Sexism and the Law: A Study of Male Beliefs and Legal Bias in Britain and the United States*, Law in Society Series (Oxford: Martin Robertson, 1978) 9. How relations between the sexes came to be enshrined in natural laws is the subject of Marina Benjamin (ed), *Science and Sensibility: Gender and Scientific Inquiry, 1780–1945* (Oxford: Basil Blackwell, 1991).

[202] Vicinus notes that while the ideal of the perfect lady was omnipresent throughout the Victorian period, it was in fact far removed from the objective situations of most Victorian women. She

but were a product of nineteenth-century social circumstances and cultural expectations. The fact that the ideal of true womanhood was an ideological construct, generated by nineteenth-century middle-class morality, is an indication that, despite its being cast in almost spiritual terms, it had a very material basis. There was what I should like to call a 'seamy side' to the poetry of the nineteenth-century feminine ideal. With the nineteenth-century separation of private from public and home from the workplace, the domestic woman had lost all productive function. Instead, the Victorian woman was turned into an article of conspicuous consumption, a showcase for her husband's ability to pay. The ideal woman of the nineteenth century was thus the ultimate status symbol: 'a treasure herself, an ornament of his [man's] material acquisitions, [. . . made] secure from loss or theft by her immaculate sexual purity'.[203]

Against the background of these beliefs about femininity, the transformation that occurred in the action for breach of promise of marriage at the turn of the nineteenth century is not at all surprising. The practical restriction of the right of action to female plaintiffs is but a reflection of the fact that the ideal woman's life (but not the ideal man's) was similarly restricted. The ideal woman, as we have seen, was an angel *in the house*, confined to the private sphere of marriage and wedded domesticity. Marriage was her mission, her one and only purpose in life; a man had wider options. When a woman failed 'in business' by failing to get married, she was perceived as having suffered a genuine injury. Nineteenth-century society intended women for marriage and held no place for those who failed to reach this blessed state. An unmarried woman was 'redundant'.[204] She might live off the charity of relatives or friends, languish away as a governess, or eke out a bare existence as a seamstress, a servant, or a factory-girl. In the fiction of the period, a spinster was a sympathetic figure at best; more usually, she was singled out for scorn. Accordingly, when a woman came to court to complain of her blasted hopes of matrimony, her complaint fell on open ears. Her story made cultural and ideological sense: here was a woman whose destiny had been thwarted by the defendant's breach of his promise to marry her, a woman 'who in place of completing, sweetening and embellishing the existence of others [. . . was] compelled to lead an independent and incomplete [even unnatural] existence of [. . . her] own'.[205] By contrast, when a man came forward in such a case, the court would ask indignantly: 'What injury had the

writes: 'Few women could afford to pursue the course laid out for them, either economically, socially or psychologically' (x).

[203] Trudgill 16.

[204] The nineteenth-century social critic William Rathbone Greg coined the expression 'redundant woman' for the woman not fortunate enough to marry. William Rathbone Greg, *Literary and Social Judgments* (Boston, 1873) 276.

[205] Greg, *Literary and Social Judgments* 282–3.

plaintiff sustained? How was he damaged? . . . Surely the plaintiff did not mean to come into court to complain that he could not be a pensioner on [. . . a] woman for the remainder of his life?'[206] In the Victorian period, this much was incontrovertible. It was for man to provide, for woman to be provided for; he was the oak, she was the vine. Nineteenth-century judges accordingly had no patience with the topsy-turvy vision of proper gender relations put forward by male breach-of-promise plaintiffs. In addition to reflecting the feminine attributes of domesticity and dependence, the practical one-sidedness of the right of action is also in a high degree expressive of the nineteenth-century conception of the ideal woman as a somewhat overgrown child. The legal effect of the restriction to female plaintiffs was, in substance, the following: a woman might sue for breach of promise of marriage, but she could not, in her turn, be sued for it. This parallels the legal position of a contracting infant. A child may, at his discretion, enforce a contract entered into by him, but the other party cannot enforce it against him. Anthony Kronman has explained the limit on a person's capacity to make contracts that are enforceable against him or her as a paternalistic restraint, 'primarily concerned with defects in the promisor's reasoning process'.[207] This explanation of the one-sided right of action well fits the nineteenth-century conception of the ideal woman as intellectually inferior to man. With 'a head . . . too small for intellect but just big enough for love',[208] a woman was liable to be taken advantage of when contracting away her hand and heart. At least in the sensitive context of love, courtship, and marriage, she was therefore not to be treated as a fully competent contracting individual. Like a child, she was paternalistically allowed a second opinion about the matrimonial promises she had made. A man, by contrast, was kept to his contract or made to pay damages for its breach.

The idiosyncrasies of the action as far as the plaintiff's task of making out a case were concerned can be accounted for in terms of the supposed modesty and passivity of the ideal woman. The ideal woman was too blushingly delicate to require her lover to commit his offer to paper, pronounce it in front of witnesses, or couch it in any set phrase. His whisperings of love would make their way to her heart no less surely for being discreetly told. Indeed, too great a formality in the evidence adduced in support of the man's promise might be regarded as an indication that the plaintiff was possessed of shrewd business sense or, worse still, a masculine intellect. This would tell against her. In both *Orford v Cole* and *White v Fergusson*, the plaintiffs had some explaining

---

[206] Counsel for the female defendant in *Kershaw v Cass, The Times* 21 March 1849: 7.

[207] Anthony T Kronman, 'Paternalism and the Law of Contracts,' (1983) 92(5) *Yale Law Journal* 786.

[208] *Lecture on Some of the Distinctive Characteristics of the Female*, delivered before the class of the Jefferson Medical College, January 1847 (Philadelphia, 1847) 17, quoted in Welter 160.

to do when it appeared that they had kept 'drafts' of their own letters to the defendant. In *White v Fergusson*, counsel for the defendant thought it 'astounding ... to find a young lady making "drafts" of her letters',[209] as though she were engaged in a business correspondence, and in *Orford v Cole*, Miss Orford's drafts were actively suppressed by her counsel and sought to be got over as 'very imperfect scraps of paper'.[210] Mr Scarlett, for the defendant, nevertheless insinuated that the reason Miss Orford's lawyers were unwilling to produce her drafts was that 'for a young lady to keep a copy of a love-letter, was rather a proof of her prudence and circumspection than the warmth of her passion'.[211] The courts' positive encouragement of an absence of formality in the proof of the man's promise can thus be accounted for by the perceived delicacy of the ideal woman.

A belief in female modesty and passivity, especially in the courtship context, also explains why the nineteenth-century courts virtually dispensed with the need for a counter-promise by the woman herself. The ideal woman's role in courtship, as we have seen, was essentially negative. She exercised no active choice in mate-selection. Her only power was a negative one: the power of refusal. A woman, who, like Miss Daniel in *Daniel v Bowles*, merely stood by without making any objection would thus be perceived as playing her part in the courtship ritual to perfection. Anything more would be unfeminine, less than ideal. As Mr Chief Justice Best so revealingly remarked in the case itself: 'It would be *indelicate* to expect that she should consent in words.'[212]

The true woman, we have seen, was essentially passive. She did not act directly, but only indirectly through men and through her influence over them. The rule in *Gough v Farr* that family and friends could act as channels of communication between the woman and her erstwhile lover is but the logical corollary of this perception of ideal femininity. The passive ideal woman could not very well confront her errant fiancé and demand to know his intentions. Such directly confrontational action was culturally expected to come from the woman's father or some other male protector.

What would and what would not act as a bar to the plaintiff's action also reflects the attributes of true womanhood. Clearly, no man was required to marry a woman who had lost that crowning jewel in the constellation of feminine virtues—her chastity. The unchaste woman was, effectively, unmarriageable. However, a man, who had known of her unchastity at the time of the promise and shown himself able to contemplate the idea of marriage to a Magdalen, did

---

[209] *The Times* 21 March 1895: 14.
[210] *Report of the Proceedings in the Cause of Mary Alice Orford* 24.
[211] Ibid, 55.
[212] (1826) 2 Car & P 553 (554); 172 ER 251 (emphasis added).

not deserve to be protected by this cultural and legal standard. He had shown how lightly he regarded it. The fact that female chastity was so highly prized in the Victorian period that a woman who had lost it was effectively unmarriageable also explains why her debaucher would be treated with indignation by the court and, as we have seen, made to pay higher damages. Since the ideal woman was dependent, trusting, and intellectually inferior to man, seduction, especially where it occurred under promise of marriage, was not seen as something the woman could help. Seduction was redefined as exploitation that sprang from the passion and deceit of men. Women were always the victims of male desire, never willing participants. Accordingly, where unchastity had occurred with the defendant and under promise of marriage, society and the law sided with the woman. Far from barring the action, seduction under promise of marriage would go in aggravation of damages, reflecting the fact that the defendant had, in what society considered an abuse of his superior position, deprived the plaintiff of her marriageability and conclusively debarred her from fulfilling her woman's mission of being someone's angel in the house.

Given that the ideal woman was distinguished by her physical frailty, it comes as no surprise that a nineteenth-century breach-of-promise defendant, unlike his predecessors in the eighteenth century, could not defend the suit by pleading the plaintiff's ill health. The ideal woman of the Victorian era was no longer expected to be the hard-working, capable helpmeet of previous centuries, whose physical robustness would allow her to provide a large variety of essential productive services and to contribute her share to the household's wealth.[213]

The practical unavailability of the defence of release to male defendants reflects—like the absence of the need for a woman's counter-promise—the overriding belief in female passivity. Engagements, especially, were something that happened *to* a woman, not something *between* the man and the woman. To deny the woman any power to affect the 'contractual' relationship, either as regards its formation (counter-promise) or its termination (release), was but the application of the belief in female passivity to the breach-of-promise context. The woman was conceptualized as completely peripheral to the 'contract' to marry, rather than an active participant in its formation and termination.

Finally, the nineteenth-century ideal of female passionlessness explains why defendants could not excuse their breaches of promise with a want of demonstrativeness on the part of their chosen ones. Indeed, a man who complained of a want of physically demonstrated affection in his fiancée almost certainly laid

---

[213] On the late eighteenth-century transition from the ideal of the perfect wife (who was an active partner in the family, fulfilling a number of vital tasks) to that of the perfect lady, see Vicinus ix.

himself open to the suspicion that he had intended her for seduction, rather than marriage. This would make a very unfavourable impression on a court and might even increase the damages he had to pay. The concept of female passionlessness has often been criticized as a denial of female sexual self-expression and its abandonment as a result of the sexual revolution of the 1920s and 1930s hailed as a great advance in female liberation.[214] However, the nineteenth-century breach-of-promise action demonstrates that the concept of female passionlessness was not exclusively a tool for the sexual oppression of women by men.[215] It could also work to a woman's advantage. An engaged woman's resistance to her fiancé's call for more openly manifested passion would not prejudice her chances in a breach-of-promise suit. On the contrary, such a woman could tell the culturally highly acceptable story of virtue tried and triumphant and win even larger damages.[216]

The influence of the ideal on the nineteenth-century breach-of-promise action is probably most clearly revealed in the rules on the award of damages. The plaintiff woman was central to the question of damages: 'what *the woman* ought to receive, and ... *her conduct* throughout the transaction'[217] were the guiding principles of breach of promise. The feminine ideal assumed that women were possessed of delicate emotions and deep feelings that would be irreparably damaged by a courtship gone awry. This explains why the emotional injury sustained by the deserted woman, rather than the purely economic one, was the focal point of damages. Since the attributes making up the ideal were believed to arise from womanly nature itself and to be an innate quality of the female sex, deep and lasting emotions were believed to be *natural* to women. In light of this perception, it was only logical to class damages for the emotional injury as general damages, arising *naturally* from the breach of promise. That a woman, who had 'in all its warmth and purity, [given] her virgin heart and affections',[218] would suffer acutely in mind and spirit on being cruelly disappointed by the object of her regard, seemed, in light of the nineteenth-century conception of the

---

[214] Edwards, for instance, has argued that the concept of sexual passionlessness was a denial of a very basic element of a woman's self-identity and tantamount to a denial of her very existence (*Female Sexuality and the Law* 48).

[215] For an argument that the concept of female passionlessness could be manipulated by nineteenth-century women to advance their own ends, such as by resisting sexual intercourse and thus limiting family size, see Cott 228, 233–6.

[216] A similar claim is put forward by VanderVelde, albeit not for the breach-of-promise context. VanderVelde argues that in nineteenth-century American seduction actions 'the woman [who] could tell the culturally more acceptable story of the heroic escape' and 'publicly assert her continued virtue' stood in a better position to get hefty damages (867).

[217] *Report of the Proceedings in the Cause of Mary Alice Orford* 71 (emphases added).

[218] *Cummins v Willisford, Morning Chronicle* 24 March 1845: 7.

emotionality of womanhood, too obvious for words and did not have to be specifically pleaded and strictly proved. Since the ideal woman's spirit and body were connected, her spiritual anguish was culturally expected to manifest itself in physical debility.[219] In the breach-of-promise context, accordingly, injury to health was seen as but a corollary of injury to the plaintiff's feelings, an injury, which, like the latter injury, arose naturally from the cause of action itself. This explains why no medical evidence of the plaintiff's physical decline was usually adduced or, indeed, thought necessary. The plaintiff's counsel was taken merely to make express the inevitable when he stated that the defendant's desertion had severely affected the plaintiff's health. A breach of promise, to the ideal woman, was always and automatically 'a blow which bid fair to blanch her damasked cheek, and dull the lustre of her lovely eye'.[220] Although injury to feelings and to health were therefore classed as general damages arising in the ordinary course of events, where an *absence* of such injury could be proved, the plaintiff would feel the consequences in her purse. In *Hurst v Greathead*,[221] for instance, the plaintiff claimed that the breach had pained her very much and that she did not think she had got over it yet. This allegation followed the cultural script and required no evidence to support it. However, the defendant's side were able to show that, within a year of the engagement ending, Miss Hurst was writing love letters to one Tom Agar and had given him her portrait in exchange for his; that she had been courted by different men before; and been engaged a number of times. This clearly proved that Miss Hurst's romantic sensibilities were made of sterner stuff than the ideal woman's, and she recovered a mere £10 in her action, a very small sum to be awarded in a breach-of-promise case. The 'emotional' damages awarded for breach of promise, as we have seen, did not just consist of damages for injury to feelings and to health. They also comprised compensation for the loss of honour—the public disgrace and humiliation—suffered as a result of the broken engagement. This aspect of the emotional damages available in breach-of-promise actions does not seem to have been linked to the plaintiff's perceived emotionality. Instead, it was a reflection of what I have termed the 'seamy side' of the nineteenth-century feminine ideal. In the nineteenth century, when a man's wife was the prime signifier of his social status, the 'marriage value' of a woman who had been rejected, for whatever reason, was seriously depreciated. In a particularly graphic case cited by Steinbach, a jilted woman is almost cannibalistically

---

[219] John Mullan, *Sentiment and Sociability: The Language of Feeling in the Eighteenth Century* (Oxford: Clarendon Press, 1988) 110.

[220] *Cummins v Willisford, Morning Chronicle* 24 March 1845: 7.

[221] *News of the World* 9 April 1876: 1.

compared to a 'half-eaten roast', the thought of tasting it being disgusting to all and sundry:

Men do not like that which other people have recently been refusing. Every man does not like to sit down to meat from which another man has risen. And many women have lost the best situations in life, from being jilted.[222]

In contradistinction to these emotional damages, which, as we have seen, were an idiosyncrasy of the breach-of-promise action, the rules on damages for the economic injury sustained did not, in the main, depart from conventional contract law. The need for an alternative explanation in terms of the feminine ideal is correspondingly less great. However, it will be recalled that there was one feature that distinguished the nineteenth-century action even in this contractually legitimated realm of damages for purely economic loss: the fact that the indiscriminate intermingling of what are generally thought incompatible heads of damage seemed to lead to a double recovery. A breach-of-promise plaintiff, as we have seen, could claim the value of the lost marriage *and at the same time* claim the value she gave up for it (namely her lost opportunity to marry some specific third person and/or her actual out-of-pocket loss), although a combination of these items should have been ruled out on the grounds of logical inconsistency. I should like to argue that these different heads of damage, while, contractually speaking, inconsistent, nevertheless represent distinct and mutually compatible items of damage if we apply the features of the feminine ideal. Applying the feminine ideal, it will appear that these so-called 'economic' losses are, in fact, economic only in part. Thus, while the damages for the value of the lost marriage can be understood as compensating the plaintiff for her economic injury, the other two heads of damage have their rationale not in economics, but in the domesticity and emotionalism as well as the 'seamy side' of the feminine ideal. Damages for the lost marriage compensated the plaintiff for the loss of the economic provision that would have attended the marriage. This head of damage thus picks up on the dependence feature of the feminine ideal: the loss of a domestic establishment was a grievous one for the ideal woman, destined by God and nature for domestic and, above all, male-supported life. The size of a breach-of-promise award was accordingly linked to the defendant's material wealth. For the American context, Charles McCormick has suggested that evidence of the defendant's fortune had a more potent effect on the amount of the verdict than any instruction on damages.[223] McCormick's claim would seem to be borne out by my own sample of cases, which has successful

---

[222] Steinbach, 'Promises' 144 (quoting from the 1792 case of *Palmer v Bernard*). In a similar (if less graphic vein), Lily Dale is referred to as her jilting fiancé's 'leavings' in Anthony Trollope's *The Small House at Allington*, 1862–64 (London: Oxford University Press, 1963) 297; ch 51.

[223] Charles T McCormick, *Handbook on the Law of Damages*, Hornbook Series (St Paul: West Publishing, 1935) 399.

plaintiffs routinely recovering damages equal to the defendant's annual income, at least in the first half of the nineteenth century. Compensation for the value of the lost marriage was rooted in hard-nosed economics, unadulterated by emotional considerations. This is apparent from the fact that the defendant's emotional undesirability as a husband, unlike his economic desirability (which, as we have just seen, was the single most potent influence on award size), was not taken account of when computing damages under this particular head. The value of the lost marriage, as a head of damage, only referenced the *economic* (as opposed to the emotional) value of that marriage:

The injury the lady has received is this—that instead of being, as she expected, the wife of the defendant for life, with the fortune that the defendant possesses, to support her and maintain her rank through life—she is as she was before, in a state of celibacy.[224]

Given that the courts only compensated the plaintiff for the economic value of the lost marriage under this head, it was *not*, in fact, logically inconsistent to combine the claim with an additional one for the lost opportunity of contracting an *emotionally satisfying* marriage with a specified third person. The plaintiff, who was wooed by another pretender to her affections and would have married him had it not been for the defendant's interference, had lost more than just the *economic* benefits of marriage. In her case, there was a further injury: the loss of the *emotional* benefits of a happy domestic life and a congenial partner. In the case of a true woman, by nature domestic and emotional, this loss was grave. It was an aggravating circumstance, which could properly enhance the award.

The true underpinning of a claim for out-of-pocket loss was, I would suggest, also not economic. Typically, out-of-pocket expenses would be incurred in the run-up to the wedding, ie in buying the dress, ordering the cake, or sending out invitations. The presence of out-of-pocket loss is thus a reliable indicator of the parties' proximity to the altar. Where a marriage was imminent, a woman's feelings would usually be especially bound up in her prospective husband. A breach of promise, under these circumstances, was therefore likely to be particularly emotionally damaging. Also, the proposed nuptials would have become public knowledge. The breach of promise would therefore be a *public* breach. This would increase her humiliation and the injury to her honour, a species of emotional damage, which, as we have seen, reflected the 'seamy side' of the nineteenth-century feminine ideal. Accordingly, where the plaintiff laid in evidence her actual out-of-pocket expenses, the true basis of recovery was not economics, but a combination of the perceived emotionality of the ideal woman, on the one hand, twinned with the seamy side of the feminine ideal, on the other: a woman's love would grow and deepen with the approach of her

[224] *Report of the Proceedings in the Cause of Mary Alice Orford* 61.

wedding day, and the further along the desertion happened, the more emotionally scarring it would be; at the same time, the Victorian woman was a status symbol, and she would have lost 'marriage value' once her rejection became publicly *known*.

Finally, the aggravating and mitigating factors that operated in breach-of-promise suits are an expression of the feminine ideal insofar as they tied the size of a plaintiff's award to the degree of her approximation to that ideal. Everything that brought the plaintiff closer to the ideal of the angelic child-woman would enhance, everything that separated her from it, detract from the damages she would receive. It is hardly surprising, therefore, that the youngest, most beautiful, and most delicate plaintiffs got the highest awards; and the unmaidenly or downright immodest the lowest.

This chapter has argued that the nineteenth-century action for breach of promise of marriage was shaped by the reigning myth of the ideal woman. The legal conception of the action saw the plaintiff as central to the injury (and the question of damages), but as peripheral to the contract (and its formation and termination). This conceptualization of the action reproduces the nineteenth-century feminine ideal. Being injured is purely passive, whereas contracting is an agentic activity. In an application of the ideal of the passive woman, the breach-of-promise plaintiff was thus conceptualized as central in a passive, and all but non-existent in an active way. The action for breach of promise of marriage was *about* the woman (and little else); but it was not *hers*, except in the very literal sense of proceeding in her name. The plaintiff woman was the object, but not the subject of the action.

2

A Structural Inconsistency: The True Woman and the Breach-of-Promise Plaintiff

[A true woman's] highest duty is so often to suffer and be still.

Sarah Stickney Ellis, English prescriptive writer (1845)[1]

You have cast me off like an old glove. I will not endure it. . . . I am determined to make public through my solicitor all I have suffered at your hands.

Annie Pendred, plaintiff in *Pendred v Smith* (1906)[2]

The preceding chapter has argued that the nineteenth-century action for breach of promise of marriage was shaped by the simultaneously emerging ideal of femininity. It was a cause of action created in the image of and designed to protect the true woman. In this chapter, I should like to begin my consideration of the implications of this feminine infusion for the law, in particular for the position of plaintiffs. I shall seek to demonstrate that the feminizing process imported a contradiction to the centre of the breach-of-promise action and lodged an inconsistency right at the very heart of the plaintiff. The nineteenth-century breach-of-promise suit was a Janus-faced cause of action, an uneasy marriage of contradictory ideas, and the person of the plaintiff was at the centre of these inconsistencies.

The feminine ideal, which gave the nineteenth-century action its distinctive shape, was, as we have seen, made up of affiliative attributes. The true woman was a passive, domestic, and submissive, in short, an angelic creature, incapable of independent action, unfitted for the public sphere, and a stranger to all vindictive and mercenary feeling. Paradoxically, the structural position of the breach-of-promise plaintiff put her in open conflict with the very attributes around which the cause of action was built. By virtue of her very position as a breach-of-promise plaintiff—having come to a public court of law to take legal

---

[1] Sarah Stickney Ellis, *The Daughters of England* (London, 1845) 73. 'Suffer and Be Still' is also the title of Martha Vicinus's anthology on women in the Victorian age.

[2] *News of the World* 8 April 1906: 6.

action about and obtain pecuniary damages for a romantic grievance—the woman concerned flouted the ideological script for proper feminine behaviour. In instituting proceedings, she asserted her legal identity, claimed agency over her life, ventured onto a platform outside the domestic sphere, showed a lack of meek submission in refusing to 'suffer and be still', and, in the eyes of some, demonstrated a (mercenary) capacity to have her heartache soothed by a monetary compensation. She moved beyond normal spheres of action for a woman in the Victorian age: from private to public space, from silence to speech, from love to lucre. In short, by the very fact of instituting an action, she put herself directly at odds with the central values of ideal femininity. The breach-of-promise plaintiff, therefore, was structurally very ill fitted to act as a standard-bearer for true womanhood.

In her study of American breach-of-promise plaintiffs, Mary Coombs has pointed out that 'bringing such a suit is itself an unorthodox action for women'.[3] Going to law to assert one's legal rights is a highly agentic activity. Indeed, instituting legal proceedings is perhaps the most highly developed form of agency of all. It bespeaks self-empowerment, a determination to be and stay in charge of one's life. It is a total abdication of passivity and victimhood: 'To file a suit is to say, first, I will not accept the harm done to me as something natural and unchangeable, and, second, I will take action to reallocate responsibility to those who caused that harm.'[4] Many of the women who brought breach-of-promise suits seem to have perceived doing so as an act of agency and self-empowerment. One plaintiff told her fiancé that if he 'turned her on the world she would put him in the Court',[5] a threat sufficiently impressive at the time to make him kiss and make up. And Annie Pendred wrote to Mervyn Smith that she would not lie down under his treatment of her: 'You have cast me off like an old glove. I will not endure it. . . . I am determined to make public through my solicitor all I have suffered at your hands.'[6] By declining meekly to bear with her disappointment, a woman who resorted to a breach-of-promise action declined to fulfil what was, according to the prescriptive writer Sarah Stickney Ellis, the true woman's highest duty: to suffer and be still under life's vicissitudes. The breach-of-promise plaintiff openly defied this cultural script. The refusal to be the passive victim and to submit to the desertion as her cruel,

---

[3] Mary Coombs, 'Agency and Partnership: A Study of Breach of Promise Plaintiffs' (1989) 2(1) *Yale Journal of Law and Feminism* 3. Unlike me, Coombs does not see the opportunity for agency that the breach-of-promise action offered female plaintiffs as leading to a destructive internal inconsistency. Rather, Coombs thinks that the agency, the empowering aspect of bringing suit to right a wrong, was so effectively obscured by the cause of action's dependency-based rationale that early twentieth-century feminist critics of the action failed to perceive it, leading them to attack their 'sisters'.

[4] Ibid, 18.

[5] *Wisker v Beeby*, *News of the World* 19 March 1876: 5.

[6] See n 2.

but unalterable, fate was written into her very position as plaintiff. As such, the position of the breach-of-promise plaintiff was fundamentally at odds with the ideal of the passive and long-suffering angel-woman, in whose image the cause of action was built.

Women who brought breach-of-promise suits did not just offend against the constraining feminine norms of passivity and submissiveness. They also transgressed the boundary lines between the public and the private sphere, and in a particularly egregious way: 'by bringing her private life into a public forum, [. . . the breach-of-promise plaintiff] threatened to merge and dissolve those cultural categories altogether'.[7] The feminine virtues of domesticity and modesty seemed to be given the lie by the woman's voluntary recourse to a public legal forum and by her readiness to shine an intrusive light on what should have been the most intimate recesses of her personal life. Modesty and self-effacement contradicted themselves to a significant extent by their very articulation and publication. Indeed, coming to court could be seen as a contribution to dishonour, in attracting or at least intensifying the glare of publicity. This internal contradiction was made express by counsel for the defendant in *Orford v Cole*, when he asked rhetorically: 'why [sic] was this ever made the subject of public discussion? why has it been brought here [to a public court of law] to entertain the whole county of Lancaster? why make public a transaction that might have been locked up in the breasts of two or three individuals to whom it was known?'[8]

Finally, a woman who took a former fiancé to court for damages for breach of promise seemed to be actuated by vindictiveness or, worse still, mercenary considerations. Getting her own back was clearly Ruth Evans's motivation for suing her faithless suitor. She brought her breach-of-promise action with revengeful relish: 'You have shown me up by having the banns called over here; I will now show you up. You will hear of it before many days. And I hope you will enjoy it and sleep well on it.'[9] A true woman, by contrast, could not entertain feelings of anger and resentment for a former sweetheart. She was constitutionally incapable of desiring revenge. Rather, 'betrayed, abandoned, insulted, she love[d] the traitor still, as only a woman can love. . . . Her heart, her peace, her life itself a patient sacrifice; living out her sorrow without complaint, dying with forgiveness on her blue lips [. . .].'[10] Also, a woman who would contemplate a pecuniary salve for her broken heart seemed to be treating money as a substance to be weighed in the scales with love. Thus, she

---

[7] Coombe 100–1.

[8] *Report of the Proceedings in the Cause of Mary Alice Orford* 48.

[9] *Evans v Lillywhite, News of the World* 12 March 1911: 5.

[10] *Lady's Own Paper* 9.299 (19 August 1872): 459, quoted in Steinbach, 'Promises' 246.

was impliedly commodifying what Victorian separate spheres ideology insisted should remain untouched by the corrupting taint of commerce and the market: the private realm of wedded domesticity.

Her structural position as a breach-of-promise plaintiff, then, seemed to put the woman concerned in flagrant opposition to key elements of the feminine ideal, in accordance with which the nineteenth-century cause of action was shaped. Thus, we can see the action as from the very start Janus-faced, an uneasy marriage of contradictory, if not incompatible, elements. As both the legal embodiment of true womanhood and a platform for not so very true women, the feminized breach-of-promise action carried within it from its inception the seeds of its own destruction.[11]

Given the centrality of the doctrine of separate spheres and of the ideal of true womanhood to nineteenth-century culture, the transgressions of the breach-of-promise plaintiff were by no means minor or venial. Rather, the plaintiff woman was contradicting the most fundamental tenets of nineteenth-century ideology. Mary Douglas, in her excellent examination of concepts of pollution and taboo, has argued that any confusion or contradiction of culturally cherished classifications constitutes a social pollution, which will invoke 'pollution behaviour' in the form of sanctions, contempt, ostracism, or gossip.[12] A nineteenth-century woman who came to court to sue her former lover for his breach of promise, as we have seen, by virtue of her very position as a breach-of-promise plaintiff, transgressed, in fundamental ways, the internal lines of the Victorian social system. The crossing of a cherished social barrier, according to Douglas, is a dangerous social pollution, and the polluter might be expected to be treated as 'a doubly wicked object of reprobation, first because [s]he crossed the line and second because [s]he endangered the social order'.[13] The breach-of-promise plaintiff, as a dangerous polluter, who flouted the divinely ordained order of things, should therefore have been a social pariah and the target of flourishing pollution behaviour. Yet the cause of action and the women who made use of it stood, in the first half of the nineteenth century, virtually unimpeached. In the early nineteenth century, the breach-of-promise action was almost uniformly seen as a protection for virtuous womanhood, and plaintiffs were routinely awarded a competency for life. It was only in the second half of

---

[11] Frost has also noted the inconsistency in the plaintiff's position: Ginger S Frost, 'I Shall Not Sit Down and Crie' 224–45, esp at 226, 238. See also Coombs 1–23.

[12] Mary Douglas, *Purity and Danger: An Analysis of Concepts of Pollution and Taboo* (London: Routledge, 1966) 36, 73. Julia Kristeva makes the same argument. According to her, abjection is caused by 'what disturbs identity, system, order [. . . and] does not respect borders, positions, rules'. Julia Kristeva, *Powers of Horror: An Essay on Abjection*, Leon S Roudiez (trans), European Perspectives (New York: Columbia University Press, 1982) 4.

[13] Douglas 139.

the nineteenth century that the action and the women at its centre became the target of hostile attack in legal and social commentary[14] and that the success rate and awards of plaintiffs declined. The initial absence of the expected pollution behaviour indicates that the structural inconsistency at the heart of the nineteenth-century action and in the position of plaintiffs was not at first perceived. This would seem to be due to the fact that the breach-of-promise action, as enacted in the courts in the early nineteenth century, successfully concealed its fatally discordant nature. Helped by a legal framework, which silenced his client (by denying her the right to testify on her own behalf), and employing various strategies of containment, counsel for the plaintiff initially managed to obscure the suit-immanent challenges to the plaintiff's true womanhood and to reassert the structurally threatened feminine virtues of passivity, domesticity, modesty, and meek submission. It was only in the high Victorian period that a series of apparently minor changes in in-court procedure—whether a matter of law, such as the Evidence (Further) Amendment Act of 1869,[15] or purely of tactics, such as the growing practice of counsel to parade the plaintiff at the trial or of the plaintiff to parade herself, sometimes in full wedding apparel—crudely exposed the structural inconsistency and provoked virulent 'pollution behaviour'.

In the following three chapters, I shall survey three consecutive periods, the early nineteenth century (1800–50), the high (1850–1900), and the post-Victorian (1900–40) periods. In each chapter, my focus will be on the internal inconsistency that we have just considered: the fatal flaw at the heart of the nineteenth-century breach-of-promise action. My aim is to tease out the longer-term implications of shaping a cause of action in accordance with an ideal at odds with the very notion of women going to law, and I shall do so, for each period, by means of my two tools of analysis—empirical case study, on the one hand, followed by literary investigation, on the other. By this process of a sustained dual interest in legal (and cultural) context and fictional text, I hope also to expose the subtle yet unmistakable ways in which what happened and what changed in the breach-of-promise courtroom influenced the changing use made of the breach-of-promise action in nineteenth- and early twentieth-century literature and film.

---

[14] The anxieties invoked by the breach-of-promise action in nineteenth-century legal and social commentary are extensively discussed in the works of Steinbach and Kellogg, among others. See Steinbach, 'Promises' esp at 241–9. See also Kellogg 4–36 and Stone, *Road to Divorce* 92–3.

[15] 32 & 33 Vict, c 68.

3

Breach of Promise in the Early Nineteenth Century (1800–50): Strategies of Containment, a Created Inconsistency, and the Aesthetic of the Grotesque

In this chapter, I would like to consider the in-court processing and the literary depiction of breach-of-promise cases in the early nineteenth century. The chapter opens with a case study of *Orford v Cole*, one of the first 'big' nineteenth-century breach-of-promise suits, tried at Lancaster before the Honourable Sir John Bailey, Knight, and a special jury in 1818. Section I considers *Orford v Cole* as an illustration of the argument made in the first chapter that the nineteenth-century cause of action for breach of promise of marriage gravitated around the plaintiff woman and her true womanhood. The argumentative structure of early breach-of-promise cases, as typified by *Orford v Cole*, was built around personal arguments, with each side striving to convince the jury of the individual plaintiff's conformity or non-conformity, as the case may be, with the mutually accepted standards of true womanhood. Section II of this chapter addresses the problem of the structural inconsistency. The outcome of *Orford v Cole*—a glittering verdict for Miss Orford—is accounted for as the result of the successful deployment of strategies of containment by counsel for the plaintiff. The strategies of containment employed by or on behalf of breach-of-promise plaintiffs, as we shall see, resembled those practised by other nineteenth-century women similarly positioned on the outskirts of domesticity, on the dangerous interface between the public and the private, so to speak: women writers and women scientists. With the action's in-built contradictory potential defused, the breach-of-promise plaintiffs of the early nineteenth century, helped by the privileges thought due to their femininity, usually had the best of the action and emerged victorious. But it is not predominantly in the success rate of actual plaintiffs that one sees the fruits of the strategies of containment. Their success is also implicit in the nature of the fictional accounts of breach of promise that date from this period. As section III reveals, there is not, in that first period, any fictional exploitation of the structural inconsistency at the heart of the ladies' action. Rather than exploiting the suit-immanent inconsistency, there is a marked tendency in the early period to *create* an inconsistency by inverting the feminine ideal and casting that inversion in the plaintiff role. Until *The Pickwick Papers,* the breach-of-promise plaintiff is a widow and hence sexually experienced rather than 'pure', mature in years, unprepossessing in aspect, the energetic head and self-sufficient manageress of either a large family or a business. The comic attack throughout is not on the woman *as a breach-of-promise plaintiff,* but as the embodiment of a type of woman (the mannish woman, the lusty widow) who, as the very opposite of the dominant feminine ideal, was much maligned throughout the nineteenth century, in all sorts of fictional roles. The comedy, too, derives not so much from the breach-of-promise element per se as from the cutting down to size of the female character in question and, usually, her subjugation under male authority. It is not surprising, therefore, that the majority of these early accounts fall into category B ('out-of-court involvement') of my systematization—the breach-of-promise element is relegated to the sidelines, the trial takes place off-stage, and the plaintiff is never seen in a mock-feminine role. The exception is, of course, *Pickwick,* where the earthy widow Bardell is deliberately miscast by Dickens as the female romantic lead of the in-court breach-of-promise drama. The artistic effects of this studied 'miscasting' are both ludicrous and faintly nauseating. In this disharmony in both the depiction and the reaction it evokes, there is an element of the grotesque, which, to my mind, constitutes the dominant aesthetic of the early period.

The early nineteenth century then, this chapter argues, is characterized by the successful defusing of the contradictory potential *in law* and the direct consequence of this *in art,* namely breach of promise as the site of a *created* inconsistency, reflected either in the 'sidelining' of the breach-of-promise element or, where it does take centre stage, in the dominance of the aesthetic of the grotesque.

I. The Making of a Perfect Nineteenth-Century Lady: Contending Plaintiff Constructions in the Case of Mary Alice Orford versus Thomas Butler Cole (1818)[1]

Orford v Cole was a breach-of-promise case tried in the first quarter of the nineteenth century. It was brought by Mary Alice Orford, the 29-year-old daughter of a surgeon from Liverpool, against Thomas Butler Cole, a gentleman of

---

[1] *Report of the Proceedings in the Cause of Mary Alice Orford.* See also *Lancaster Gazette* 28 March 1818: 4; 11 April 1818: 4; *The Times* 6 April 1818: 3.

fortune, seven years younger than herself. The engagement had lasted a mere two months, being formed in late March of 1817 and dissolved by early June of the same year. During the entire period, the parties had only thrice been in each other's company and their correspondence, which consisted of only a handful of letters, was prudent and restrained to the point of coldness. Yet Mary Orford was quite successful in her breach-of-promise suit. Not only did she win, she 'obtained the greatest damages ever given, by any jury, in a case of this nature':[2] £7,000.[3]

Mary Orford's brilliant success may surprise us. Older and (it was argued) wiser than her youthful fiancé, she does not seem to have been a perfect approximation to the ideal of the dependent child-woman in whose image the cause of action was built and against whom a breach-of-promise plaintiff (and the amount of damages thought due to her) fell to be judged. The engagement had been a short one and the parties' acquaintance with each other and, by implication, their opportunity for forming a deep and unalterable attachment slight. If injured affections were the issue, therefore, Miss Orford's would not immediately strike one as the most compelling case. Yet Miss Orford survives as perhaps the most successful breach-of-promise plaintiff of all time. Mr Justice Bailey, on refusing to grant a new trial on the ground of excessive damages, said that if he had been one of the jury, he might himself have been inclined to have awarded even larger damages.[4]

A detailed examination of *Orford v Cole* reveals that whether Miss Orford was a true woman who deserved to be handsomely compensated was indeed the central issue of the case. The suit revolved around the question of 'what the woman ought to receive', a question to be answered 'by reference to her conduct throughout the transaction'.[5] The transcript of *Orford v Cole* contains two competing constructions of Miss Orford, two contending interpretations of the same fact situation. On the one hand, there is the version presented by Miss Orford's side (the version eventually accepted by the judge and, as evidenced by their verdict, the jury); and, on the other hand, that presented by Mr Cole's. Counsel for the plaintiff sought to construct Miss Orford as a model breach-of-promise plaintiff, as every inch the true woman. Counsel for Mr Cole, by contrast, put forward a version of Mary Orford as a mature,

---

[2] *Report of the Proceedings in the Cause of Mary Alice Orford* 69 (per Mr Scarlett, counsel for Mr Cole).

[3] The award in *Orford v Cole* seems to be the highest English jury award of the nineteenth century—that is, at least the highest one to have survived a subsequent application for a new trial on the ground of excessive damages. In the 1936 case of *Beyers v Green, News of the World* 15 March 1936: 10, the jury awarded £8,000, but, of course, £8,000 in 1936 can hardly compare with £7,000 in 1818.

[4] *Report of the Proceedings in the Cause of Mary Alice Orford* 71.

[5] Ibid.

calculating woman, who had got engaged not from love, but from pecuniary motives. The two sides competed ferociously to present the more compelling interpretation of the same facts, to convince the jury of Miss Orford's conformity or non-conformity, as the case may be, to the mutually accepted standards of true womanhood.

The case of Mary Alice Orford was formally commenced before the Court of Common Pleas in London, but the trial of the action took place on Monday, 30 March 1818, in Lancaster before Mr Justice Bailey, one of the two Commissioners of Assize appointed to conduct civil and criminal trials in the Lancashire Assizes:

This trial had been the subject of general conversation throughout the county of Lancaster, for several months past, and persons of all ranks appeared to be interested in the result.... It may therefore easily be imagined what an immense concourse of auditors were pressing for admittance. Crowds were collected at every avenue, and the doors were scarcely thrown open than the court, spacious as it is, and capable of containing 3000 persons, was instantly filled.[6]

The case was reported on in the local *Lancaster Gazette* and even the national *Times* newspaper. The printing-house of J Gore, in Castle Street, Liverpool, was sufficiently inspired to publish the full 71-page transcript of the proceedings, which would soon be sold by all the principal booksellers in the country.

The immense interest excited by the case must in part have been due to the elevated condition of the parties at its centre. With an assured income of at least £5,000 per annum and two mansion houses to his name,[7] the defendant, Thomas Butler Cole, was a member of the upper crust of nineteenth-century society—the 0.3 per cent or so of the population made up of the aristocracy and the landed gentry[8]—and easily one of the richest men in the county. He had come into a large fortune seven years previously, by the death of an uncle, in gratitude to whom (rather like Frank Churchill in Jane Austen's *Emma*) he had taken the last name of Cole. And although Miss Orford might not have been Mr Cole's equal in point of fortune, she, too, was a member of a family very respectably connected in society. Her late father, who had died at about

---

[6] Ibid, 68.

[7] Cole owned Kirkland Hall and Nateby Hall, for the latter of which alone he had paid £30,000.

[8] Norman Gash estimates that the governing elite of society, the landed gentry and the aristocracy, was made up of around 4,000 families in 1815, a time when the total population stood at approximately 13.5 million. Gash puts £1,000 per annum as the lower limit of income for that exclusive class. At £5,000 a year, Cole comes very comfortably within it. In fact, £5,000 per annum represents the beginning of the very pinnacle of the income scale, as is evidenced by the fact that the revenue commissioners, for the purposes of income tax, did not think it necessary to specify any further categories after £5,000. See Norman Gash, *Aristocracy and People: Britain 1815–1865,* The New History of England 8 (London: Edward Arnold, 1979) 18, 21, 22.

the same time that Mr Cole had had his accession of fortune, had been a surgeon in a very extensive practice. The legal teams retained by both sides (and
the fact that the case was tried before a special jury of seven esquires and five
gentlemen) reflected the high standing of the parties. Miss Orford and Mr
Cole each retained teams of three barristers (as well as, of course, instructing
solicitors). Miss Orford's legal team was led by Mr Topping, then the Attorney-
General, and Mr Cole had managed to retain the services of the redoubtable
James Scarlett,[9] a future Attorney-General who would later represent another
high-profile breach-of-promise defendant in the 1824 *cause célèbre* of *Foote v
Hayne*.

Although the condition of the parties and, in consequence, that of their
counsel might therefore have been somewhat more elevated than was usual for
breach-of-promise cases, even in the early part of the nineteenth century, the
case was played out on the same stage: a court that heard *nisi prius*[10] cases for
the locality.

Orford v Cole followed the standard format for a breach-of-promise trial.
Counsel for the plaintiff, the Attorney-General Mr Topping, told his story,
punctuated by letters written by Mr Cole to Miss Orford, which the Attorney-
General read aloud in court. After an impassioned address to the jury on the
question of damages, Mr Topping called his witnesses and asked them questions, which elicited narratives in support of his own. Mr Topping could not
call Miss Orford herself, since, according to pre-1869 rules of evidence, the parties to a breach-of-promise action were not competent witnesses. Indeed, Miss
Orford does not even seem to have been present at the trial. Witnesses were,
however, called to prove that the letters that had been read were in the defendant's handwriting and to prove his pecuniary circumstances. There were also
character witnesses (one Miss Orford's trustee under her father's will, the other
a magistrate) for Miss Orford. The main witness, however, was Miss Orford's
older brother Thomas, who deposed to the existence of the engagement and the

---

[9] James Scarlett, afterwards Lord Abinger, was one of the best known and most successful advo-
cates of his day. He received a knighthood in 1827 and was made Attorney-General in 1829. His
peerage and elevation to the Bench followed under the Peel administration in 1834. See *The Bench and
the Bar* (London, 1837) 210–23; G F R Barker, 'James Scarlett, first Baron Abinger (1769–1844)', rev
Elisabeth A Cawthon, *Oxford Dictionary of National Biography*, Oxford University Press, 2004; online
edn, Jan 2009 <http://www.oxforddnb.com/view/article/24783>, accessed 12 October 2009.

[10] *Nisi prius* was the term used to refer to the civil side of the assizes. Assize courts were courts that
travelled throughout the country on various circuits to try cases: '[J]uries were always summoned to
appear on a certain day at Westminster, or before the king himself, ... "unless before then (*nisi prius*)
the king's justices would come" into the county' (Baker, *Introduction* 21). Civil cases were commenced
before one of the three Courts of Common Law in London—the Common Pleas, King's Bench, and
the Exchequer. If the plaintiff won a jury verdict at the trial out on the assize circuit, the final judgment
still had to be entered before the court in London, and it was possible at this late stage for legal issues
arising out of the trial to be ventilated before the multi-judge London court.

fact that it had been broken, with no reason given, by the defendant. Thomas Orford was then cross-examined by Mr Scarlett for the defence, in an effort to discredit the plaintiff's case. At the close of the evidence, the case for the plaintiff rested.

Mr Scarlett stated the case for the defendant. Like his colleague on the other side, he related the facts of the case to the court. However, his interpretation of the events in general and of Miss Orford in particular sounded quite different from Mr Topping's. Mr Scarlett's declared strategy was to strip the case of the colouring which the Attorney-General's 'imagination and passion ha[d] cast about it', and to reveal it as in fact a 'barren' one, a case that 'gives birth to scarce any feeling'.[11] Although Scarlett called no witnesses, he, too, quoted from the couple's correspondence, but the inferences he drew, as we shall see, were quite different from those deduced by the Attorney-General.

Finally, Mr Justice Bailey summed up the evidence to the jury. He imposed his own interpretation on the facts that had been discussed, gave the jury some instructions relative to the law, and encouraged them to be 'liberal rather than penurious'[12] in the assessment of damages. The jury then retired for a quarter of an hour and, returning into court, pronounced their verdict for the plaintiff—damages of £7,000.

1. Miss Orford's story

> [W]hat is the condition . . . of a woman so situated? I cannot describe it to you in proper terms, for I am a man.—I cannot express the poignancy of female feelings, but as a man and a father, I hope I can feel for one of a different sex.—I know the delicacy and fineness of those feelings.— Here is a lady, and she is deserted by the man who vowed he would be her protector, and taught her to believe that his happiness was connected with hers—that he wished only to be her protector and guardian—he has deserted her . . .
>
> Mr Topping, counsel for Miss Orford[13]

Mr Topping's task in presenting the case for the plaintiff was quite a daunting one. He had to put forward a version of Miss Orford that would fit the feminine ideal written into the very cause of action that she was using, and the materials he had to work with were far from ideal for the purpose. Not only was his client pushing 30, a time when 'the roses will begin to fade',[14] she was also substantially older than her ex-fiancé, quite a serious matter in the nineteenth century, when the age disparity was supposed to be the other way.

---

[11] *Report of the Proceedings in the Cause of Mary Alice Orford* 46.
[12] Ibid, 67.   [13] Ibid, 19.   [14] Ibid, 52.

The courtship and engagement had been short, and most of the correspondence was so dry that the *Lancaster Gazette*, in reporting the case for its readers, declined to reproduce it, commenting that 'it was only a dry letter of business, interesting only to the parties concerned; and it would be worse than impertinent to intrude it upon the public'.[15] (This journalistic restraint speaks volumes really, as newspapers normally loved to give their readers the parties' love letters in full.) Worst of all, Miss Orford was in the habit of preserving copies of her letters, a characteristic which might be read as a sign of 'unfeminine' prudence and circumspection, premeditation even, by the other side (as indeed it was). From these facts, Mr Topping had to construct the image of a lovely, trusting, and dependent woman, whose affections, health, and very existence had been blighted by the defendant's breach of promise. Not an easy task by anyone's standards.

Mr Topping began by introducing his *dramatis personae*. Enter, Miss Orford, the daughter of a surgeon, who had been a man of 'great respectability and character' and 'in very great and extensive business'[16] in the county of Lancashire. Unfortunately for Miss Orford, this thriving personage had died in 1810, leaving her fatherless. Not only that. It next appeared that Miss Orford's mother was also in a very precarious state of health. In fact, the Attorney-General was 'extremely sorry to say that at this day it is doubtful whether she is in existence'.[17] With a few skilful strokes of his oratorical brush, Mr Topping thus painted the moving picture of an all but orphaned Miss Orford, practically alone in the world, dependent and defenceless as a result of the absence of strong parents to protect her, a veritable babe in arms sure to appeal to the paternal instincts of a compassionate all-male jury. Next, Mr Topping introduced the defendant, Thomas Butler Cole, the son of a gentleman of the name of Butler and the successor, by the death of an uncle, to a very large fortune and the mansion house of Kirkland Hall. Though young in years, Cole, on Mr Topping's characterization, was old in spirit. He was a worldly, calculating man, who had acted with cool deliberation—first in forming, then in breaking his engagement. This much, the Attorney-General argued, transpired from the letters Cole had written, letters which showed him to be restrained, careful, and calculating, even to the declared object of his affection. The letters, as far as Topping was concerned, clearly proved that Cole had the brains and only wanted the heart of a man. His letters were 'full of matter, honorable to the head, but most disgraceful and dishonorable to the heart'.[18] If Miss Orford had the advantage of Mr Cole in point of actual age,

---

[15] *Lancaster Gazette* 11 April 1818: 4.
[16] *Report of the Proceedings in the Cause of Mary Alice Orford* 4.
[17] Ibid, 5.   [18] Ibid, 21.

therefore, the Attorney-General implied, this advantage was more apparent than real. It was more than made up for by the far greater contrast between Miss Orford's orphan helplessness and the calculation of the emotionally detached Mr Cole.

Kirkland Hall, the defendant's property in the neighbourhood of Garstang about 40 miles from Liverpool, had provided the scene of Cole's courtship of Miss Orford. In March of 1817, Mrs and Miss Orford had finally yielded to what, on Mr Topping's version of events, appeared to have been veritable importunings on the part of Mr Cole's mother,[19] who had the superintendence of his household, to come and stay at Kirkland Hall. Miss Orford being 'what nobody could deny . . . well educated, accomplished, sensible, prudent, and . . . a lady of considerable beauty', the inevitable happened. The defendant, who had known of Miss Orford for years and, as the Attorney-General insinuated, been secretly cherishing feelings for her or even contemplating a proposal for some time, now 'availed himself of the opportunity of disclosing his sentiments'.[20] Miss Orford demurred, he pressed, she accepted, and when Miss Orford left Kirkland Hall at the end of March 1817, it was to prepare for a speedy wedding.

Miss Orford, according to the Attorney-General, had placed the utmost trust in the integrity of her fiancé and the sincerity of his professions. He had vowed that 'through life, you will find me a steady and a warm friend— one that will exert every nerve for your comfort and peace of mind—my happiness is to see you happy'[21]—and she had believed him. When he came to Liverpool, he was accordingly 'received *in confidence*, that these proposals were to be carried into effect, and that he would soon become the legal husband of Miss Orford'.[22] Mr Topping stressed that trusting her fiancé and depending on his future honour, Miss Orford had ordered her wedding clothes, chosen liveries for the servants, and engaged the services of a lady's maid.

Next, the Attorney-General extolled Miss Orford for her feminine propriety of conduct. Her deportment throughout had been most passive, modest, delicate, and chaste. There was nothing in her demeanour that could have been faulted by an all too censorious world. Miss Orford had betrayed 'the most delicate affection' for her fiancé, an affection, which did 'equal honour to the

---

[19] Miss Orford's and Mr Cole's mothers were distantly related by marriage, and a degree of intimacy had subsisted between the families even after Mr Orford's death. Mrs Butler had sent express and repeated invitations to Mrs and Miss Orford on behalf of herself and her son before these two ladies finally complied with the request to come and stay at Kirkland Hall.

[20] *Report of the Proceedings in the Cause of Mary Alice Orford* 5.

[21] Ibid, 11.

[22] Ibid, 9 (emphasis added).

head and heart of the lady'.[23] The extreme delicacy of Miss Orford's feminine sensibilities, her passionlessness so to speak, was, according to the Attorney-General, put in evidence by a little episode which had occurred in May of 1817. Mr Cole had invited Miss Orford to Kirkland Hall for the purpose of meeting his aunt, who was the head of the family. This invitation Miss Orford had initially declined, the reason being, according to Mr Topping, that the invitation did not include her mother. Miss Orford, 'with a degree of delicacy which does her honour, and distinguishes every part of her conduct... suggested to the defendant that she had a variety of things to attend to; thus, putting off the invitation without appearing to reject it'.[24] Miss Orford's reluctance to accede to her fiancé's wishes, on the Attorney-General's interpretation, proceeded not from coldness of feeling or from a lack of appreciation of what was due to Mr Cole as her future husband. Rather, it stemmed from Miss Orford's perception of the indelicacy of going alone and unchaperoned.[25]

Despite her flawless character and conduct, Mr Topping went on to lament, Miss Orford's faith in Mr Cole, whom she had looked up to as her future 'protector and guardian',[26] was cruelly disappointed. Without one word of explanation or one circumstance in extenuation of his decision, Mr Cole 'withdrew himself from the family, ... closed his correspondence',[27] and, adding insult to injury, on 29 August of the same year entered into the marriage state with a Louisa Grimshaw, an attorney's daughter from Preston.

According to the Attorney-General, it was only '*natural* to suppose that the distress of [...Miss Orford, on being thus deserted] would be excessive'.[28] Although Mr Topping called a total of five witnesses in support of his story, he did not think it necessary to call one to support his claim as to Miss Orford's distress. Rather, knowing 'the poignancy of female feelings', the Attorney-General *simply knew* and could state as an incontrovertible fact that Miss Orford 'must be content to bear through life "a wounded spirit"':

It has been said that the spirit of man will sustain his infirmity, but, 'a wounded spirit who can bear?' and yet the plaintiff must bear this through life...[29]

Further, Mr Topping *knew* that Miss Orford, having wasted her affections on the defendant, would probably never love again:

---

[23] Ibid, 17.

[24] Ibid, 14.

[25] Mr Topping's interpretation of events drew strength from the fact that Miss Orford had complied with Mr Cole's request when the cause of her objection was removed. Thus, she accepted Mr Cole's third invitation, which included her mother.

[26] *Report of the Proceedings in the Cause of Mary Alice Orford* 19.

[27] Ibid, 17.

[28] Ibid (emphasis added).

[29] Ibid, 20.

Who can tell that the fine movements of the female heart, which had produced her affection towards the man who has slighted her love, may not still actuate her breast—who can tell that even time can extinguish the pure flame, which in some female minds is unextinguishable [sic].[30]

Descending from the spiritual heights of idealized female emotionality to the feminine ideal's sordid material basis, Mr Topping went on to opine that, in any case, a woman who, like Miss Orford, was known to the world to have had a prior attachment and to have been rejected by its object, had by that very fact lost her emotional virginity[31] along with her 'saleability' in the marriage market:

[W]ho is the person who after this transaction has become notorious—after it is generally known that she has been the object of one gentleman's affection, and that her intimacy with him had proceeded nearly to marriage, who, I ask, will be found inclined to form a connection with a lady so situated?—will not every man pause before he pays his addresses to such a woman—he will see she is lovely, sensible, accomplished, prudent, every thing a man can desire, but he will know that she has had an attachment to another man, and that the object of her attachment has deserted her.[32]

In light of these facts, Mr Topping felt justified in calling for heavy damages on the part of his injured client, whose conduct through life in general and through this unfortunate transaction in particular, had been 'in a very high degree exemplary'.[33] His story, he claimed, revealed that Miss Orford had been 'the most artless girl'[34] in the world and that her feminine inexperience, her dependence, and her trust had been cruelly abused by the defendant, a man proved to be worth £5,000 a year. Although the jury could and would, he trusted, make the defendant provide such monetary atonement as he could to Miss Orford, Mr Topping was quick to point out that this true woman's real loss was in fact incalculable. Her life would never be the same again:

Your verdict can only afford her a pecuniary compensation; but the wounded feelings, and the agitations of a female mind, your verdict cannot heal.[35]

---

[30] Ibid.

[31] A woman would be emotionally virgin if she had never loved before. The concept of emotional virginity may have struck a chord with some Victorian men. Frank Stanley in *The Breach of Promise*, for instance, regards it as a *sine qua non* that the lady he will one day marry is someone whose '*first* love he can win'. See Harriet Maria Smythies, *The Breach of Promise*, 3 vols (London, 1845) 1: 95 (emphasis added).

[32] *Report of the Proceedings in the Cause of Mary Alice Orford* 20.

[33] Ibid, 44.

[34] Ibid, 45.

[35] Ibid, 22.

2. Mr Cole's story

> It is not to be supposed that a woman of the age of 28, full of discretion, who writes no important letters of which she does not keep copies, could have gone upon a transitory visit to Kirkland-hall, and all at once have conceived so deep an affection as is represented. . . . Do you think I am not right in conjecturing that if . . . there was no splendid fortune, the heart of Miss Orford would ever have been smitten in the manner it was?
>
> Mr Scarlett, counsel for Mr Cole[36]

Mr Scarlett presented the (much shorter) case for the defendant. He began by submitting that the 'greatest part of this case lies not in the evidence, but in the impressive and able address which has been made to you by my learned friend'. Counsel for the plaintiff, Mr Scarlett claimed, had clothed what was in fact a naked case with his fanciful 'imagination and passion'. Now, by contrast, the jury would get the unvarnished truth, stripped of Mr Topping's histrionics. He, Scarlett, would present the case for what it was: a 'barren' one that 'gives birth to scarce any feeling'.[37]

In Scarlett's narrative, the position of the parties was reversed. It was Mr Cole, who was 'young and heedless', and who, though 21, 'had not come to years of discretion'.[38] And Miss Orford, who was mature, acquainted with the ways of the world, and emotionally detached enough for calculation. She was no helpless orphan (her mother, he told the jury, was in fact alive and well enough to come into the drawing room), but a woman quite capable of looking after herself. The parties' age difference, in Scarlett's story, came close to being a generation gap: 'I find a lady of the age of 28, who in the year 1810, had seen this schoolboy occasionally going, with satchel in hand, "unwillingly to school" . . .'.[39] 'Nature,' Scarlett informed his auditors, 'did not intend such [disproportionate] matches'[40] between mature ladies and mere schoolboys. 'Nature bids the woman look up to the man as her superior in point of age'.[41] A mature lady, like Miss Orford, Scarlett inferred from this decree of nature, could not have fallen in love with a puppy like Mr Cole, and in so short a space of time:

It is an imputation upon a woman of her [Miss Orford's] understanding and good sense, to suppose that her affections should have been engaged in so short a time. [. . . A]nd though the case may occur, where a woman eight years older than a man, may form an attachment for him, yet these are rare cases, only calculated for novel and romance.[42]

---

[36] Ibid, 51, 59.   [37] Ibid, 46.   [38] Ibid, 49.   [39] Ibid, 50.
[40] Ibid, 52.   [41] Ibid, 51.   [42] Ibid.

But if it was not love for this schoolboy, Mr Scarlett went on to argue, that had caused Miss Orford to look favourably on Mr Cole's proposals, it must have been the young man's estate that had appealed to her. 'Do you think I am not right in conjecturing,' he rhetorically asked the jury, 'that if... there was no splendid fortune, the heart of Miss Orford would ever have been smitten in the manner it was?'[43]

For Scarlett, it was Miss Orford, 'a woman full of attractions',[44] who, anxious for the defendant's money, had used her allure and charms to entrap the hapless Mr Cole. 'I can easily conceive that a young man who is beginning life, and whose passions are warm, might, in the presence of a beautiful woman, mistake his feelings for love.'[45] Luckily, Mr Cole had recovered his senses when no longer under the entrancing influence of 'the lady's beautiful countenance and attractive person'.[46]

Mr Scarlett supported his construction of a worldly-wise Miss Orford—a prudent lady 'full of discretion'[47]—with the fact that she had kept copies of her love letters to Mr Cole, a circumstance, which 'was rather a proof of her prudence and circumspection than the warmth of her passion'.[48] In the case of such a mature, businesslike, and, quite frankly, 'unfeminine' woman as Miss Orford, it was not *natural* to suppose that her affections and health would be injured by the defendant's breach of promise. Rather, according to Scarlett, it required a considerable stretch of the imagination to picture 'Miss Orford on her bed of grief—her eyes bathed in tears—her hair dishevelled and deploring the loss of this young man of twenty-one;... her friends watching round her to prevent the dagger or the cup from doing its fatal work'.[49]

Having stripped the case of what he claimed was only the Attorney-General's unsubstantiated fancywork, Scarlett closed his address to the jury with a summation of the reasons why, in his estimation, this case was one that seemed 'least to invite large damages'.[50] His reasons boiled down to what was, in essence, just one. Miss Orford, according to Scarlett, did not deserve large damages because she did not fit the ideal. She departed too far from the standards of true womanhood. She was mature, not child-like; 'acquainted with the world',[51] not domestic and dependent; and she had never loved, as a true woman must, disinterestedly. Her solicitude had been, not for that boy, Mr Cole, but for the

---

[43] Ibid, 59.   [44] Ibid, 52.   [45] Ibid, 51.
[46] Ibid, 53.   [47] Ibid, 51.
[48] Ibid, 55. Miss Orford's lawyers were clearly unhappy about the fact that she had kept copies of her letters to Mr Cole. They first sought to suppress their existence, and when Mr Scarlett brought the matter up in his cross-examination of Miss Orford's brother Thomas, they sought to gloss over the copies as 'very imperfect scraps of paper' (24). Mr Scarlett's preferred term for them, by contrast, was the official-sounding 'documents' (25).
[49] Ibid, 59.   [50] Ibid, 60.   [51] Ibid.

boy's estate. Therefore, Mr Scarlett told the jury, 'the least sum of money that you can give will be quite as much as she could require, or ought to have, at your hands'.[52]

3. Mr Justice Bailey's story

> [L]ooking at the case in every point of view, I can see nothing upon which to cast blame on the lady's conduct. She has been invited from the quarter from which such an invitation as she has received ought to come; she has gone to the defendant's house on an invitation from his mother; she has conducted herself with prudence and judgment. [. . . S]he has . . . not conducted herself hastily. I can see nothing that argues the slightest degree of levity, want of prudence or caution; and I cannot take upon myself to say, that the damages were vindictive.
>
> Sir John Bailey, judge in *Orford v Cole*[53]

When both sides had been heard, Mr Justice Bailey summed up the case for the jury. His summation, like the stories that had preceded it, was not neutral. Rather, Mr Justice Bailey imposed his own interpretation on the events that had been discussed and told his own story.

Bailey began by concentrating the minds of the jurors on the question before them. This question, he told them, was 'one of great difficulty and great magnitude'. It was: 'what is the proper compensation in damages which such a plaintiff under such circumstances ought to receive'.[54] In other words, the jury had to ask themselves 'what the woman ought to receive', and for that, they had to look at 'her conduct throughout the transaction.'[55] There was, Bailey told the jury, 'a great deal of difference in cases of this kind'. This difference, it appeared, lay in the character and conduct of the woman at the centre. First, there were the cases where it seemed that 'a woman of more advanced age lays traps for a young man and draws him into a promise of marriage'. Such unfeminine agency, Bailey pointed out, should not recommend itself to a British jury. Then, there were the cases where the engagement 'does not seem to have been sought for by the woman'.[56] *These cases*, where the plaintiff woman had shown proper feminine passivity in allowing herself to be pursued rather than doing the pursuing, called for heavy damages.

To help the jury in their task of deciding what category of case they had before them, Mr Justice Bailey next reviewed the 'facts'. The story he told bore a strong resemblance to the one that had been put forward by Mr Topping for the plaintiff. Bailey accepted the Attorney-General's characterization of

---

52 Ibid, 61.   53 Ibid, 70.   54 Ibid, 61.
55 Ibid, 71.   56 Ibid, 62.

the parties. Miss Orford was, once again, 'a young lady', Mr Cole 'a young man rather more than 22',[57] whose 'cool, considerate, and calculating' letters showed him possessed of 'an understanding beyond his years'.[58] As far as the plaintiff's conduct was concerned, the case, according to Bailey, clearly fell within his second category. It was Mr Cole and his mother who had sought out Miss Orford by sending several pressing invitations: 'there does not seem any extraordinary haste on the part of [...Mrs Orford] and the plaintiff to go to Kirkland-hall'.[59] During the engagement, Miss Orford had been properly passionless and acted with 'becoming prudence' in declining to do 'so imprudent and precipitate a thing as to go to the house of her expected future husband, without the presence and the sanction of so near a relation as her mother'.[60] Thus far, Miss Orford's deportment appeared a model of feminine passivity, passionlessness, and delicacy. Mr Bailey next addressed the contentious subject of the copies of the love letters. Mr Scarlett, for the defendant, had described these copies as 'documents',[61] and insinuated that the plaintiff had artfully preserved them for future use as evidence in an anticipated breach-of-promise suit. For Scarlett, the copies had been proof that Miss Orford fell short of the standards of true womanhood. According to him, they showed her to be prudent, calculating, and masculine. Mr Justice Bailey, by contrast, construed the copies very differently. For him, the copies did not confirm the absence of feminine virtue, but were evidence of its very presence. According to Mr Justice Bailey, Miss Orford, in keeping the 'rough copy', was not collecting evidence. Rather, she was preserving a woman's 'treasure'. Miss Orford, on his interpretation, had innocently and artlessly, in true woman fashion, 'treasured...up' the rough draft of a letter to the object of her adoration, 'without having any view to her ultimate disappointment'.[62] Miss Orford's love, according to Bailey, had been as disinterested as it was delicate. He did not think her mercenary; quite the opposite. He felt inclined to believe that Miss Orford would 'have chosen to have accepted him [Mr Cole] rather than damages to...any...amount'.[63]

Miss Orford then was a true woman, wronged by a 'cool calculating [sic], discriminate man', who had 'draw[n]' her to Kirkland Hall and 'gone on amusing her for a period of two or three months, under the expectation that she was to be the mistress of his establishment',[64] only to ultimately abuse her confidence. Since Miss Orford's conduct so clearly proved her every inch the true woman, Mr Justice Bailey had no hesitation in giving her the benefit of the presumption of a true woman's emotionality: 'I can...easily imagine that the mind of such a woman may be for ever unsettled, by the loss of what she may

---

57 Ibid, 61.   58 Ibid, 64.   59 Ibid, 63.   60 Ibid, 65.
61 Ibid, 25.   62 Ibid, 64–5.   63 Ibid, 70.   64 Ibid, 67.

have set her heart upon.'[65] Mr Justice Bailey accordingly advised the jury to be 'liberal rather than penurious'[66] in the assessment of the damages.

4. The true story, or, why she won

The true 'facts' of *Orford v Cole* will of course never be known. We will never *really* know whether Miss Orford was virtuous or calculating, whether she truly loved Cole (or only his money), and why she kept those copies. We will never know even how Mr Cole's breach of promise affected her subsequent life. Whether she married, had children, and when and how she died. We do not know what became of her. Miss Orford simply appears out of the shadows of nineteenth-century domesticity into the glare of a breach-of-promise courtroom, briefly struts out a failed courtship upon the public stage, and then disappears again, to leave no further trace of her existence in recorded history. The true story, therefore, is that there is no true story.

What we do know is that the jury gave Miss Orford £7,000 in damages—a staggeringly high award. This tells us that the 12 esquires and gentlemen who were empanelled to decide on the pecuniary consequences of Mr Cole's breach of promise shared Mr Topping and Mr Justice Bailey's interpretation of the 'facts': they *believed* Miss Orford virtuous and in love with the man, not his money.

If we accept that we do not (and never will) know the real facts as to Miss Orford's true womanhood and that convincing arguments could be made either way, then one way of accounting for the verdict and its size would be to say that Mr Topping (and Mr Justice Bailey) were the better orators. After all, they had their particular version of the 'facts' accepted. Mr Scarlett did not. But this answer is surely disingenuous. Scarlett was one of the most able of his contemporary counsel and perhaps 'the most successful lawyer of his time, as regarded the number of cases he gained'.[67] Scarlett, therefore, would not have failed, and failed so completely, if there had been a true equality of arms. But the arms in this case and indeed in any breach-of-promise case, I would contend, were not in fact equal. Rather, an early-nineteenth-century breach-of-promise jury, I would argue, was culturally predisposed to accept the plaintiff's construction of the 'facts' in general and of herself in particular.

A statistical analysis of 242 breach-of-promise cases reveals that female plaintiffs had a success rate of 95.3 per cent over the whole period from 1800 to 1940 and of over 97.5 per cent in the early nineteenth century before 1850. Miss Orford's victory, therefore, while perhaps a particularly resounding one,

---

[65] Ibid, 71.   [66] Ibid, 67.
[67] *The Bench and the Bar* 211.

was not in itself exceptional. Rather, once Miss Orford's case or, for that matter, the case of any female breach-of-promise plaintiff got to court, victory was, statistically speaking, almost a foregone conclusion.

What accounts for the high success rate of female breach-of-promise plaintiffs? Steinbach has argued that the plaintiff women were buoyed up by the cult of sentimentality, which was strong in the late eighteenth and nineteenth centuries and which could be manipulated by breach-of-promise plaintiffs for their own benefit. Breach of promise, according to Steinbach, worked because it was good melodrama. Everybody, high and low, wanted to see the good girl win. 'Women were depicted in court as heart-broken maidens, of pure heart if not spotless reputation, virtually destroyed by unfeeling cads, and these sentimental depictions, no matter how unlikely, usually worked to the plaintiffs' advantage.'[68] While Steinbach's interpretation carries conviction and fits with her overall analysis of the breach-of-promise action in terms of the twin concepts of contract and sentiment, I should like to put forward an alternative explanation in terms of what I take to be the unifying construct behind the nineteenth-century action: the nineteenth-century ideology of femininity. We have already seen that when the feminine ideal was written into the cause of action at the turn of the century, women plaintiffs were given considerable legal advantages in the form of (effectively) exclusive rights of action, eased evidentiary requirements, and additional heads of damage. I would now like to go further and suggest that the nineteenth-century conceptualization of this feminine ideal as biologically determined rather than socially constructed additionally privileged female plaintiffs by making it easy for them to present themselves as answering the ideal, as in fact true women, thus paving their way to resounding victories over the men that opposed them.

Although these days it is commonplace to state that the nineteenth-century concept of true womanhood was an ideological veneer, produced by middle-class interests and masking social and economic service whose benefits were unevenly shared,[69] this is not how true womanhood was conceived of in the nineteenth century. In the nineteenth century, the feminine ideal was seen as springing from the fundamental attributes of female nature itself. True womanhood was understood as biologically determined, tied to the innate quality of the female sex, to the point where the adjectives 'female' and 'feminine' became

---

[68] Steinbach, 'Promises' 103.

[69] See, for instance, Janet Sayers, *Biological Politics: Feminist and Anti-Feminist Perspectives* (London: Tavistock Publications, 1982), who is concerned 'to demonstrate the historical and social roots of some of the avowedly purely biological analyses of sexual inequality advanced in support of conservative antifeminism during the [… nineteenth] century' (2).

virtually interchangeable.[70] This concept of true womanhood as biologically determined, as we have already seen, gave women plaintiffs the evidentiary advantage of not having to prove their emotional injuries. Such damage was 'natural' and did not have to be strictly proved. By the same token, I would argue, the concept of natural femininity privileged the plaintiff's version of herself as a true woman (who deserved compensation) over the defendant's version of her as someone who was devoid of the attributes of true womanhood.

Intertextual correspondence, the matching of courtroom stories to ideological narratives, is a significant factor in determining legal outcomes. Recent empirical studies of jury trials have confirmed that 'people carry around with them a stock of socially-constructed narratives' and that the plausibility of a newly communicated story is enhanced in proportion as 'it fits a narrative which already exists within this stock of social knowledge'.[71] The plaintiff's version of herself as a true woman clearly fitted the nineteenth-century ideological narrative of biological femininity. It would therefore be perceived as a 'natural' and plausible and hence a probable courtroom story by a nineteenth-century jury. As a result of their cultural 'priming', nineteenth-century jurors would be predisposed to accept the plaintiff's version of herself as 'natural' and true. Thus, when Mr Justice Bailey interpreted Miss Orford's copied love letters as a woman's treasured-up mementos, his story must have made cultural sense to the jury he was addressing. The jury, hearing a story that fitted a narrative of innate femininity that they had been exposed to throughout their lives, must have been pre-inclined to accept it for truth. Mr Scarlett, by contrast, in arguing that the copies proved masculine business sense on Miss Orford's part, must have been perceived as putting forward an 'unnatural', hence unlikely, story. His version of Miss Orford as an unfeminine lady, who was devoid of the *innate* attributes of true womanhood, was a courtroom story that tilted at cultural windmills. Scarlett, therefore, as indeed any defence counsel, did not find himself on a level playing field. It was not just Miss Orford's impressive legal team that was arrayed against him. It was cultural ideology as well: a cultural ideology that was all the more powerful for not being perceived as ideological.

Thus far, I have discussed the ways in which the femininity concept at the centre of the nineteenth-century breach-of-promise action favoured the female plaintiff. For one thing, it gave her the legal advantages discussed in Chapter 1. And because the ideal of true womanhood was believed to have its origin in

---

[70] For a discussion of how relations between the sexes came to be enshrined in natural laws and how gender relations were scientized, see Benjamin's *Science and Sensibility*.

[71] Bernard S Jackson, 'Narrative Models in Legal Proof', *Narrative and the Legal Discourse: A Reader in Storytelling and the Law*, David Ray Papke (ed), Legal Semiotics Monographs (Liverpool: Deborah Charles, 1991) 163. Jackson bases himself on research by W Lance Bennett and Martha S Feldman in their *Reconstructing Reality in the Courtroom* (London: Tavistock Publications, 1981).

female biology, rather than the needs and pressures of society, it also privileged the plaintiff's presentation of herself as in fact a true woman who deserved protection. However, as we saw in Chapter 2, the feminization of the action also imported a fatal structural inconsistency. The action's marriage with the feminine ideal cut both ways. It was both source of the action's popularity and cause of its ultimate disintegration. It favoured the plaintiff at the same time as it destabilized her position. However, the fatal contradictions in the action's structure were, in the early nineteenth century, significantly mediated or even obscured by the rules of evidence then existing and by four strategies of containment routinely employed by counsel for the plaintiff. It is to these that we must now turn.

II. 'How can you be a woman and be out here at the same time?':[72] Strategies of Containment in the Early Nineteenth Century

The position of a nineteenth-century breach-of-promise plaintiff, as we saw in Chapter 2, was a vexed one. She was putting herself forward as the nineteenth-century dream of an angel in the house at the same time as she was actively pursuing a contractual claim in a public legal forum with the ultimate object of obtaining a pecuniary award. Her structural position as plaintiff in a contract action thus threatened to undermine her claim to the cardinal feminine attributes of passivity, domesticity, modesty, and a true woman's emotionality. Her problem was how to reconcile her representation of herself as a virtuous woman with her insubordinate position 'out here', on the dangerous interface between the public and the private, in an age when prescriptive writers like More and Gisbourne took pains to stress that a woman's virtue was a function of her exclusion from the public sphere and of her submission to men.[73] The breach-of-promise plaintiff, by actively throwing herself and the innermost recesses of her private life open to public inspection for the sake of a monetary compensation, was, in a sense, voluntarily rendering herself public property and at risk of being classed a 'public woman'—at a time when that term was a euphemism applied to the least virtuous among the female sex: the prostitute.

The position of the prostitute, that quintessential 'public woman' of the Victorian period, does not, however, offer the most striking parallel to the

---

[72] Luce Irigaray, *This Sex Which Is Not One*, (trans) Catherine Porter and Carolyn Burke (Ithaca: Cornell University Press, 1985) 145.

[73] Benjamin 38.

position of the breach-of-promise plaintiff.[74] Since she had given up all claims to feminine virtue, a prostitute did not confront the breach-of-promise plaintiff's problem of how to reconcile virtuous womanhood with an unsettlingly improper 'public' position. A closer approximation to the position of the breach-of-promise plaintiff—as a 'proper' private woman seeking to negotiate a space for herself in an 'improper' public sphere—can be found in that of other nineteenth-century women similarly positioned on the outskirts of domesticity and uneasy about being so: the position of women writers and women scientists. 'I always consider a female author,' Mathew Gregory Lewis, author of *The Monk*, wrote to his mother, 'as a sort of half-man.'[75] As this extreme example of a pervasive cultural attitude shows, 'border women' like female writers and scientists, faced the same problem of being perceived as assertive, immodest, 'public'—half-men, in short. Their activities catapulted them directly into the public arena, where attention was fought for and an ethic of competition reigned. Yet they, too, wished to preserve intact their social reputations as private and modest women. In much the same way as breach-of-promise plaintiffs were anxious to paint pictures of themselves as true women worthy of the protection the nineteenth-century action offered, these professional women, as Benjamin has noted, were overwhelmingly reluctant to forego the ideals of true womanhood.[76] Rather, women writers and scientists strove to remain within the bounds of proper femininity and, in pursuance of that goal, 'relied on attitudes to the acquirement, display and transference of knowledge that were consistent with the ideals of womanliness'.[77] These 'attitudes' or 'artistic strategies'[78] relied on by nineteenth-century women professionals to resolve debilitating ideological contradictions, as we shall see, strongly resembled what I describe as 'strategies of containment' practised on behalf of breach-of-promise plaintiffs in the early nineteenth century.

[74] Since the figure of the prostitute stands for the total breakdown between the public and the private, rather than a delicate attempt to reconcile forays into the public arena with a reputation for privacy, I find comparisons between prostitutes and breach-of-promise plaintiffs, as made, for instance, by Kellogg (9), fundamentally misconceived, at least as regards the early nineteenth century. The equation between the breach-of-promise plaintiff and the prostitute, as I shall go on to argue in Chapter 4, becomes more appropriate for the high Victorian period.

[75] Quoted in Margaret Oliphant, *The Literary History of England in the End of the Eighteenth and the Beginning of the Nineteenth Century*, 3 vols, 1882 (New York: AMS Press, 1970) 3: 169. In writing thus, Monk Lewis was desperately trying to persuade his mother to refrain from publishing a novel she had just written.

[76] Benjamin 40.

[77] Ibid, 44.

[78] Mary Poovey, *The Proper Lady and the Woman Writer: Ideology as Style in the Works of Mary Wollstonecraft, Mary Shelley, and Jane Austen*, Women in Culture and Society (Chicago: University of Chicago Press, 1984) xvii.

Before examining these strategies of containment, which were a matter of tactics, I would like to consider a matter of *law*, which, if not an outright condition of the strategies' practicability, at least helped to maximize their effect. This legal matter is a feature of the early nineteenth-century law of evidence. According to pre-1869 rules of evidence,[79] the parties to a breach-of-promise suit were not competent to give evidence at trial. They could not act as witnesses in their own cause. While such a party-witness disqualification had been general to all classes of action before 1843 and the passage of Lord Denman's Evidence Act of that year,[80] thereafter, it became a restriction increasingly special to the breach-of-promise context.[81] The effect of the pre-1869 rules of evidence—the fact that party testimony was excluded in breach-of-promise cases—was a kind of 'system-enjoined muting' of the parties. The plaintiff (and, of course, the defendant) to the suit could not speak. While this muting applied equally to both parties, its structural effect was more striking in the plaintiff's case. The woman, not being able to speak at her trial, was rendered a silent observer of her own case. She had to rely on others, her counsel and witnesses, to speak for her. The plaintiff woman's position was thus sub-ordinal. Hers was not an active legal role. She did not (at least not visibly) control the litigation. Rather, she had to be spoken and acted for by others, usually men, and had little outward connection with the breach-of-promise action beyond the fact that it proceeded in her name. It is easy to see how this system-enjoined muting would have eased concerns about the plaintiff woman's agency. The silent plaintiff, central to the investigation, but sub-ordinal to the litigation, was object examined, rather than examiner. She was properly passive, rather than improperly active.

In addition to assuaging misgivings about plaintiff agency, the system-enjoined muting, by relegating the plaintiff woman to the sidelines of the action, made for an arena where further (voluntary rather than system-enjoined) strategies of containment could flourish. We have already seen that one consequence of the evidentiary rules was that the woman had to be spoken and acted for by others. In other words, she had to be represented. This strategy of plaintiff representation is the first I would like to consider. I am taking this strategy first, because, of the four strategies to be discussed, it is the one that

---

[79] A sea change in the law of evidence relating to breach of promise, making the parties to the suit competent to give evidence at trial, was wrought by the Evidence (Further) Amendment Act of 9 August 1869, 32 & 33 Vict, c 68.

[80] 6 & 7 Vict, c 85. This Act was the major evidence amendment act of the nineteenth century.

[81] An 1851 amendment to Lord Denman's Act made all parties in all cases competent witnesses except those involved in adultery or breach-of-promise cases, and a further amendment of 1853 allowed the spouses of involved parties to give evidence as well. See Steinbach, 'Promises' 236. Breach-of-promise suits, by contrast, were not assimilated into this evidentiary mainstream until 1869.

is least a matter of voluntary tactics. As representation was rendered necessary by the system-enjoined muting of the plaintiff, this is a strategy that in fact comes close to being system-imposed. Plaintiff representation functioned on two levels: in court and out of court. In its in-court version, it took the form of representation by counsel. As legally configured and acted out in the courtroom, the action for breach of promise was not an action the plaintiff woman brought, controlled, dismissed, or settled for herself. Rather, it was the plaintiff's barrister, as a male figure of authority, who publicly exacted retaliation for her. Counsel for the plaintiff in breach-of-promise cases would often use language that implied an almost paternal relation to the woman they were representing. In *Orford v Cole*, for instance, Mr Topping said that he felt for Miss Orford 'as a man *and a father*'.[82] This in-court representation by male counsel prevented the plaintiff woman from becoming, symbolically, her own agent, her own 'man', so to speak. It stopped her being perceived as autonomous, as subjective, rather than subjected. In-court representation thus fitted the plaintiff's structural position to the cultural paradigm of men maintaining women and maintaining suits for women and, in the process, reasserted her structurally compromised claim to the virtue of feminine passivity. In its out-of-court version, plaintiff representation took the form of representation by (usually male) family members. Stories of out-of-court representation would filter back into the courtroom through witness narratives. In the 1824 case of *Rose v Ollier*,[83] for instance, it appeared from witness accounts that the plaintiff, Sarah Rose, had not acted herself, but only through her influence over a veritable chain of male intermediaries. Her cousin, given that she had no brother, had felt it his duty to call on the defendant to ask his intentions respecting her. The cousin had then communicated the (unfavourable) answer he received to Sarah's brother-in-law. And it was only the brother-in-law who had eventually passed on the answer to Sarah herself. This quite obviously made Sarah, although the plaintiff in the subsequent case, the last and most inactive link in a chain of male initiative. Similarly, in *Orford v Cole*, it appeared from Thomas Orford's statements that he had represented his sister in her pre-trial dealings with Cole. When Cole broke off all contact, Thomas Orford had tried to 'get an answer from him'.[84] These witness narratives of out-of-court plaintiff representation served to reinforce the jury's mental image of the plaintiff as passive in symbolic and actual ways and to obscure her structural position as in fact an active party to the suit.

---

[82]   *Report of the Proceedings in the Cause of Mary Alice Orford* 19 (emphasis added).

[83]   *Report of a Trial, Rose v Ollier, for a Breach of Promise of Marriage, Tried at Lancaster Lent Assizes, Saturday, March 13, 1824* (Manchester, 1824).

[84]   *Report of the Proceedings in the Cause of Mary Alice Orford* 35.

A similar tactic of representation was employed by nineteenth-century professional women. When Elizabeth Gaskell was trying to negotiate a space for herself as a writer of 'domestic' fiction in the mid-nineteenth century, she, rather like a breach-of-promise plaintiff, chose to come before the public not directly, but under the aegis of a male authority figure: Charles Dickens. Gaskell chose to publish through Dickens's periodical *Household Words*, because she believed that the magazine's anonymity and male figurehead would preserve her from the taint of an unmediated exposure to the public sphere.[85] Unlike many of Dickens's male contributors, who complained about not getting enough recognition for their work,[86] Gaskell was quite happy to pay the price of having her work appropriated by Dickens,[87] and of being kept in 'leading strings'[88] by him, if interposing Dickens as a buffer between herself and the public sphere gave her an indirect, disguised entrée into the arena of literary publication and meant that she could escape being classed as a scandalously public woman.

If the strategy of representation was employed to reassert the plaintiff's claim to feminine passivity and a proper submission to men, a strategy of detachment was used to protect her claim to domesticity. This strategy, like the strategy of representation, functioned on two levels. In its milder version, it was a physical separation of the plaintiff from the courtroom. In its more extreme version, it took the form of a cognitive detachment between the plaintiff and her legal counsel. In the early nineteenth century, when the breach-of-promise plaintiff was not an eligible witness, there was no need for her to come into court. Accordingly, it appears to have been the norm for plaintiffs not to be physically present at the trial or, if present, to remain *incognito*. Although the newspaper reports never explicitly note the plaintiff's absence from court, the fact that express mention of a plaintiff's open attendance was made in *Green v Ramwell*[89] renders eloquent the newspapers' more usual silence on the subject. Also, it is unlikely that the same newspapers that indulged in minute descriptions of the

---

[85] For this argument see for instance Elsie B Michie, *Outside the Pale: Cultural Exclusion, Gender Difference, and the Victorian Woman Writer*, Reading Women Writing (Ithaca: Cornell University Press, 1993) 79–112.

[86] When Dickens approached Douglas Jerrold for contributions to *Household Words*, for example, asserting that the periodical was anonymous throughout, Jerrold pointed to the phrase, 'Conducted by Charles Dickens', which appeared at the top of every page of the magazine, and described it instead as '*mono*nymous throughout'. Quoted in Edgar Johnson, *Charles Dickens: His Tragedy and Triumph*, 2 vols (New York: Simon and Schuster, 1952) 2: 704 (emphasis in original). Jerrold refused to publish through Dickens, choosing to run his own periodical instead. Another male writer who complained about the lack of recognition he got publishing through Dickens and took successful action about it was Wilkie Collins (Michie 88–9).

[87] Michie has claimed that, in publishing through Dickens, 'Gaskell finally finds little or no way for her stories to remain her own property' (92).

[88] Winifred Gérin, *Elizabeth Gaskell: A Biography* (Oxford: Clarendon Press, 1976) 126.

[89] *News of the World* 8 April 1866: 2.

plaintiff's physique and dress once her presence became more or less *de rigueur* after 1869 would have failed to seize every opportunity for doing so in the early period. In some instances, the plaintiff's absence can be inferred. In *Davies v Cleator*,[90] for instance, counsel for the plaintiff submitted a photograph of her to the jury, to give them an idea of her beauty. This gives rise to the inference that Miss Davies was not physically present at the trial, as her presence would have removed the need for a photograph.

Because she would be perceived as shrinking from the public glare of the courtroom and as preferring to stay enveloped in the softer shades of the domestic sphere, the breach-of-promise plaintiff who remained physically detached could reassert her claim to the structurally threatened virtue of domesticity. A strategy of plaintiff/court detachment would not just overcome the publicity problem. It could bring additional benefits. Leaving the plaintiff's beauty and virtue to the oratorical skill of counsel and the imagination of the jury might stand a plaintiff in better stead than physically to expose herself to critical examination. The jurors, MacColla opined, their fertile minds fired by adequate promptings from counsel, 'would picture the supposed charms... and become "inebriated with the exuberance of their own imaginations"'.[91] In *Orford v Cole*, Mr Topping took this strategy of detachment to another level. In addition to keeping Miss Orford out of the courtroom,[92] he stressed that, while intimately acquainted with her family, he had no personal knowledge of Miss Orford herself:

Of the plaintiff herself I have no personal knowledge; I never had the honor or pleasure of her acquaintance; but, from the accounts given to me, I have no doubt that she has well maintained the character and respectability of the family to which she belongs.[93]

That Mr Topping, although Miss Orford's barrister, should have no personal knowledge of his client is not in itself unusual. Under the English system, legal representation is split between solicitors and barristers, with clients normally dealing with solicitors, and solicitors, in their turn, instructing

---

[90] *The Times* 22 March 1865: 12.

[91] MacColla 60.

[92] Again, the report of the case does not contain explicit proof that Miss Orford was absent from the proceedings. Her mother, according to Thomas Orford's evidence, however, certainly was. It is very unlikely that the delicate Miss Orford, who would not even go to her betrothed husband's house without so near and dear a relation as her mother, would have braved the lion's den of a breach-of-promise courtroom without her. In fact, it takes Miss Orford's absence to make Mr Topping's version of her as a woman of great delicacy ring true. Topping would therefore almost certainly have advised that Miss Orford stay away, irrespective of her own feelings on the subject.

[93] *Report of the Proceedings in the Cause of Mary Alice Orford* 3–4.

counsel.[94] What *is* unusual, however, is that Topping should have taken the trouble to mention, indeed stress, his lack of personal knowledge. In disclaiming any personal knowledge of Mary Orford, Topping was superimposing a kind of cognitive detachment between the plaintiff and her counsel onto the physical detachment between the plaintiff and the courtroom. He thereby removed his client one step further from the corrupting influence of the public sphere. It is as though any personal contact with, indeed knowledge of, the Attorney-General, as a man of the law and an actor in the public sphere, would have had power to sully Mary Orford's spotless character as a private and domestic woman.

Just as breach-of-promise plaintiffs were at pains to preserve their reputations as private and domestic, so women writers and scientists were reluctant to forego the virtue of domesticity.[95] To guard their domesticity, these nineteenth-century professional women employed a comparable strategy of self-effacement, a kind of self-imposed detachment from their published work. The women deliberately distanced themselves from the literary or scientific product, which would be released into the public sphere. Mary Shelley, for instance, according to Mary Poovey, dealt with her dislike of female self-assertion and publicity-seeking by distancing herself from the narrative in *Frankenstein*. Poovey interprets Shelley's split of the narrative of the novel between three male characters (the monster, Frankenstein, and Walton) as a bid to avoid being labelled, as her mother had been, a monstrously improper female artist.[96] That a detachment of the private, domestic Mary from the public author-persona was indeed Shelley's goal is clear from the preface to the revised edition of the novel, where she notes rejoicingly: 'I can scarcely accuse myself of a personal intrusion.'[97] In a similar fashion, the nineteenth-century scientist Mary Somerville strove to preserve her domesticity by eliminating her identity from her work. John Hershell, on reviewing Somerville's *Mechanism of the Heavens*, in fact praised the book for this very self-effacement. Remarking on the absence of anything like female self-aggrandizement or attention-seeking in a work 'totally without ambition', he rejoiced: 'We see nothing of the author,

---

[94] In England, a barrister may not normally see or advise a client or accept a brief to appear on behalf of a client without the intervention of a solicitor. Dickens satirizes the strictness of the separation between counsel and client in *The Pickwick Papers*, when he describes Mr Pickwick's Herculean efforts to come face to face with his counsel, Serjeant Snubbin: ' "See Serjeant Snubbin, my dear Sir!" rejoined Perker, in utter amazement. "Pooh, pooh, my dear Sir, impossible. See Serjeant Snubbin! Bless you, my dear Sir, such a thing was never heard of..." ' (383; ch 31).

[95] Benjamin 40.

[96] Poovey 131.

[97] Quoted in Poovey 40. For another example of a nineteenth-century novelist eager to 'absent herself from her own text', see Hilary M Schor's study of Elizabeth Gaskell, *Scheherezade in the Marketplace: Elizabeth Gaskell and the Victorian Novel* (New York: Oxford University Press, 1992) 26.

and think only of the subject; … it is quite clear … that while she was penning this dissertation, a single thought of self never once crossed her mind.'[98] By a process of rigorously enforced detachment from any part of themselves that would be sent forth into the public sphere, nineteenth-century women were able to guard their identities as private and domestic beings.

The third strategy employed in breach-of-promise suits was a strategy of voluntary muting. We have already seen that the plaintiff was not an eligible witness, and, to that extent, she was already being muted by the system. However, counsel for the plaintiff frequently went further than was rendered necessary by the constraints of the evidentiary rules and in effect practised a kind of voluntary muting of their client. Not only would the plaintiff not speak from the witness-box, her 'voice' would not be heard at all. Thus, while the defendant would 'speak' through his letters to the plaintiff (which were always read and expatiated on at great length in court), the plaintiff's voice was eliminated from the in-court narrative. Her letters, even where they were available to her side, were almost never produced. On the contrary, counsel for the plaintiff would often profess that their client felt the greatest possible aversion to having her letters read in court and published in the newspapers. This strategy of voluntary muting was clearly designed to preserve the plaintiff's reputation for female modesty and delicacy. 'Modesty,' Dr John Gregory told the true woman, 'will naturally dispose you to be rather silent in company',[99] and, accordingly, the modest plaintiff chose not to be heard in public. In particular, she chose not to divulge the whisperings of her heart.

Women writers and scientists pursued a comparable strategy of voluntary muting in 'keeping silent' towards certain sections of the public. By only 'speaking' to other women and children[100] and never presuming to instruct men, they, too, were striving to respect the bounds of female modesty.[101]

The final and perhaps most significant strategy employed by counsel for the plaintiff was the strategy of rhetoric. Rhetoric, as a technique to handle dichotomies, is the use of language to cloud what is really going on. An obvious rhetorical device, used in almost every breach-of-promise case, was the ritual of claiming that the plaintiff had been *forced* to resort to legal redress. The

---

[98] John Hershell, 'Review of *The Mechanism of the Heavens*,' *Literary Gazette and Journal of the Belles Lettres* (1832): 807. Mary Somerville has been described as the woman who most successfully reconciled the domestic role of wife and mother with a professional career. See Valerie Sanders, *The Private Lives of Victorian Women: Autobiography in Nineteenth-Century England* (New York: St. Martin's Press, 1989) 105.

[99] Quoted in Poovey 24.

[100] Gaskell's choice of the Dickens-published *Household Words*, a magazine targeted at women and catering to housewifely interests and pursuits, might again serve as a case in point.

[101] Benjamin 43. Davidoff and Hall make the same argument that 'self-limitation' (in the form of a restriction of audience and genre) was practised by nineteenth-century women writers to contain the risk of immodest self-exposure (147).

plaintiff's fair fame, her counsel would argue, was blotted and her good name lost by the defendant's breach of promise, because such a breach always raised a presumption of some impropriety on the deserted woman's part. It followed that the plaintiff's decision to come to court was not voluntary and gratuitous, but 'forced' by the need to repudiate the implicit accusation and to investigate the public scandal which attached to her name. In *White v Fergusson*, for instance, counsel for the plaintiff claimed that the action 'would probably never have been brought if [the] defendant had not chosen to put an infamous falsehood upon the record by charging the plaintiff with knowing that he was a married man. Under these circumstances she had *no option* but to vindicate her character.'[102] And in *Orford v Cole*, Mr Justice Bailey opined that 'a consideration of what [... was] due to her own character, may make it *incumbent* on [... the woman] to bring the subject forward in a court of justice... that it may appear to the world there was no foundation for that calumny which is always the effect of a man's abrupt desertion of a lady to whom he is betrothed'.[103] This language of force was clearly rhetoric that 're-victimized' the plaintiff to ease concerns about her agency. It also provided an explanation of the plaintiff's motivation in bringing the action other than vindictive rancour or downright mercenariness. It suggested that the suit was brought to restore the plaintiff's injured reputation in the eyes of the world and that the pecuniary reward, rather than being the central concern, was merely incidental to the fact that bringing and winning the action would vindicate the plaintiff's character. It suggested that the plaintiff's true goal was a public acknowledgement of her womanly virtue and that the damages awarded were nothing more than the monetary manifestation of that public acknowledgement.[104]

Once again, a parallel for this final strategy can be found in the attitudes adopted by nineteenth-century professional women. These women also made use of language games to avoid the taint of self-aggrandizement and, more particularly, commercialism. Thus, they would not classify their occupation as 'work', preferring to describe it as 'an ornament, or an amusement'[105] to be indulged in when home duties allowed or as a 'refuge'[106] to shelter in when they became too oppressive. And they almost uniformly professed complete

---

[102] *The Times* 19 March 1895: 14 (emphasis added).

[103] *Report of the Proceedings in the Cause of Mary Alice Orford* 66 (emphasis added).

[104] This point—that a public recognition of the plaintiff's virtue was the primary goal and the pecuniary reward only secondary and evidentiary in function—is very well made and presented in more detail in Steinbach's dissertation ('Promises' 96).

[105] Quoted in Claire Tomalin, *The Life and Death of Mary Wollstonecraft* (London: Weidenfeld & Nicolson, 1974) 247.

[106] Elizabeth Gaskell thought that it was healthy for women to have the 'refuge of the hidden world of Art to shelter themselves in when too much pressed upon by daily small Lilliputian arrows of peddling cares', Elizabeth Gaskell, *The Letters of Mrs. Gaskell*, J A V Chapple and Arthur Pollard (eds) (Manchester: Manchester University Press, 1966) 106.

indifference to, if not downright ignorance of, its financial rewards. Elizabeth Gaskell, for instance, anxious to avoid the taint of commercialism, professed ignorance about her financial dealings with Dickens: 'I never fixed any price on what I did then, nor do I know at what rate he pays me.'[107] Similarly, the sisters Ann and Jane Taylor, ambivalent about their professional authorship, never stipulated a price for their work, leaving it to their 'publishing friends' to fix their remuneration.[108]

Taken together, the four strategies just considered served to obscure the inherent inconsistency at the heart of the nineteenth-century action and to reassert the plaintiff's claim to the structurally threatened virtues of passivity (representation), domesticity (detachment), modesty (voluntary muting), and a true woman's emotionality (rhetoric). With the contradictory potential defused, early-period breach-of-promise plaintiffs usually had the best of the action and emerged victorious. In the period before 1850, they had a success rate of 97.5 per cent (39 out of 40 cases) and received average awards of £454. By contrast, after mid-century, as we shall see in Chapter 4, both the overall success rate and the average awards declined, due, I would argue, to the growing abandonment of the strategies of containment. The strategies of containment helped make the breach-of-promise action strong because, in obscuring the features of the action that were antithetical to the ideal of true womanhood, they concealed the action's inherent threat to the symbolic economy and to the patriarchal order. They seemed to allow a resolution of the Irigarayan riddle of how one could be 'out here and be a woman at the same time'.[109] Paradoxically then, by striving to remain within the restrictive, even crippling bounds of proper femininity, early-period breach-of-promise plaintiffs, like women writers and scientists, were able, simultaneously, to extend them.[110]

III. '[B]e wery careful o' widders all your life':[111] Feminine Inversion and the Grotesque in Early Nineteenth-Century Breach-of-Promise Fiction

This section marks the beginning of a consideration, to be continued over the next two chapters, of the relationship between the law of breach of promise

---

[107] *Letters* 699.

[108] Davidoff and Hall 66.

[109] See n 72.

[110] Benjamin makes the same observation (that strategies of containment 'paid off') for women writers and scientists (40–2).

[111] Dickens, *Pickwick* 244; ch 20.

and its literary (and cinematic) representations throughout the nineteenth and early twentieth centuries. In the course of these chapters, I should like to demonstrate that this relationship was far more interactive and dynamic than most readers, critics or not, have realized. Hitherto, most writers on breach of promise who have related the law and the literature in this area at all—and there are, unfortunately, some who entertain and propagate the misconception that there is a 'general exclusion of breach of promise trials from fiction'[112]—have been content to compare, briefly, breach of promise as dramatized in art with the law on the books, note that the action has always been a subject for (largely undeserved) humour, and then quickly move on.[113] As a result, there has been a more or less complete failure to analyse the causes and effect of breach-of-promise comedy in any detail. While it is true that humour was never forsaken in breach-of-promise fiction, I would contend that the quality of this humour was anything but the 'strangely uniform'[114] and static variety described by previous investigators. I argue that there was in fact tremendous fluidity in breach-of-promise comedy in the three periods under investigation—in terms both of what was being laughed at and of the overall quality and tone of the audience's laughter.

To investigate breach-of-promise comedy through the decades, a theory of comedy that focuses on the laughable as well as the laughter is required. Although, millennia of effort notwithstanding, no one has yet been able to determine conclusively what makes people laugh,[115] the dominant theory as to the secret of humour is known as the incongruity theory.[116] Incongruity

---

[112] Craig 96.

[113] To my knowledge, Frost is the only writer to have considered the relationship between the breach-of-promise action in fiction and in reality. In the introductory chapter of her *Promises Broken: Courtship, Class, and Gender in Victorian England*, entitled 'The Myth of Breach of Promise', she concludes that nineteenth-century fiction yields up a 'strangely uniform representation of the people who brought such litigation' (1) and presents a comic and 'unflattering depiction' (8) of the cause of action. This comic image of the action, Frost claims, was inaccurate insofar as it ignored that breach of promise, in real life, was 'closer to tragedy than comedy' (9).

[114] Frost, *Promises Broken: Courtship, Class, and Gender in Victorian England* 1.

[115] There are, in essence, three different theories as regards the secret of humour. The dominant theory is the incongruity theory, which I espouse for the purposes of my analysis. Its competitors are the superiority theory, most famously formulated by Thomas Hobbes, and the relief theory. For an overview, see John Morreall (ed), *The Philosophy of Laughter and Humor*, Suny Series in Philosophy (Albany: State University of New York Press, 1987) 5–6.

[116] Incongruity theory can already be found in the Roman poet and satirist Horace, who wrote: 'If a painter chose to join a human head to the neck of a horse, and to spread feathers of many a hue over limbs picked up now here now there, so that what at the top is a lovely woman ends below in a black and ugly fish, could you, my friends, if favoured with a private view, refrain from laughing?' Horace, *Satires, Epistles and Ars Poetica*, (trans) H Rushton Fairclough, Loeb Classical Library 194 (London: William Heinemann; New York: G P Putnam's Sons, 1926) 451. It has attracted adherents in large numbers. See Leigh Hunt, *Wit and Humour, Selected from the English Poets; with an Illustrative Essay and Critical Comments* (London, 1846) 8–9; John Allen Paulos, *Mathematics and Humor*

theorists assume that the piece at the centre of humour is the perception, or the perception and resolution, of some incongruity in human physique or conduct. John Morreall's formulation of the theory makes a helpful point of departure: 'What amuses us is some object of perception or thought that clashes with what we would have expected in a particular set of circumstances.'[117] A fictional incongruity theorist, Jane Austen's Elizabeth Bennett, summed up the theory's central tenet even more succinctly when she acknowledged that 'inconsistencies *do* divert me,... and I laugh at them whenever I can'.[118] For the purposes of my analysis of the cause of laughter in breach-of-promise fiction, I shall adopt the incongruity theory. Consequently, I assume that to elicit readership and audience laughter, writers and playwrights had to try to present some incongruity in the physique or conduct (or both) of one or more of their characters. As previously stated, among the range of fictional characters, my prime focus is on the breach-of-promise plaintiff. Maintaining one's gaze firmly fixed on the role of the plaintiff promises to keep one close to the site of the incongruity and, by implication, to the cause or butt of laughter in breach-of-promise fiction. As Manfred Pfister has observed, female sexuality has been one of the main incentives or targets of laughter throughout the ages: 'gender roles, relations, and hierarchies—and, in particular, their transgressions!—have proved the common laughing stock of cultures otherwise far apart from each other'.[119] The fictional character cast in the role of breach-of-promise plaintiff—a role, as we have seen, inscribed with female sexuality (and beset by an internal inconsistency)—is therefore likely to constitute the fount of the humorous in breach-of-promise fiction.

To arrive at a well-rounded picture of the changing nature of breach-of-promise comedy through the decades, we have to analyse the *quality* of the laughter as well as its cause. Although we tend to employ only one term for it, 'laughter' in fact covers a wide and highly varied range of human response:[120] laughter 'can be merry or bitter, conciliatory or aggressive, disarming or provocative, pathological or remedial, foolish or wise, salacious or anguished, excessive or muted, scoffing or rollicking'[121] and much, much more. In investigating the kind of

(Chicago: University of Chicago Press, 1980) 9; Helmut Plessner, 'Lachen und Weinen' in *Ausdruck und Menschliche Natur*, Gesammelte Schriften 7, Günther Dux, Otto Marquard, and Elisabeth Stroeker (eds) (Frankfurt: n p, 1982) 210–389, esp at 234–5.

[117] Morreall 6.

[118] Jane Austen, *Pride and Prejudice*, 1813 (New York: Bantam Books, 1981) 43; ch 11.

[119] Manfred Pfister (ed), *A History of English Laughter: Laughter from Beowulf to Beckett and Beyond*, Internationale Forschungen zur Allgemeinen und Vergleichenden Literaturwissenschaft 57 (Amsterdam: Rodopi, 2002) vi.

[120] Robert L Latta, *The Basic Humor Process: A Cognitive-Shift Theory and the Case against Incongruity*, Humor Research 5 (Berlin: Mouton de Gruyter, 1999) 13.

[121] Pfister v.

laughter evoked by breach-of-promise comedy, it will obviously be impossible to reconstruct the actual responses of contemporary readers and audiences. But, as Merle Tönnies has done in her investigation of audience laughter in the nineteenth-century British theatre, one can examine what kind of readership or audience reactions were invited by the texts, always remembering, of course, to impose and interpret in light of the contemporary ideological environment, rather than in light of our own.[122]

In outline, this section and the corresponding sections of the following two chapters will argue that both the laughed-at and the laughter in breach-of-promise comedy changed from one historical period to another. In the early nineteenth century, the butt of laughter was provided by a popular fictional 'type'—that of the man-woman or lusty widow. In the high Victorian period, by contrast, the shafts of ridicule homed in on the person of the breach-of-promise plaintiff herself. And in the final, post-Victorian, period readers and movie audiences were invited to laugh at the (outmoded) nineteenth-century feminine ideal. Similarly, the quality of the laughter did not remain constant, but instead came full circle over the course of little more than a century. In the first period, what started out as a predominantly jovial laughter of superiority gradually darkened to a diffuse laughter of disgust and terror, mingled with uneasy amusement. In the second period, the quality of the laughter acquired a sharp and satirical note, inspired, I argue, by powerful reformist impulses. And in the third period, the tides of laughter turned once again, back to a good-natured laughter of superiority.

***

Breach-of-promise fiction started to appear in the early 1830s, just a few decades after the feminization of the legal cause of action.[123] In the early nineteenth century up to about 1850, there appeared what I consider to have been five major fictional renditions of the theme. The first writer to have fictionalized breach of promise seems to have been the playwright and actor John Baldwin Buckstone, whose two-act play *The Breach of Promise: Or, Second Thoughts Are Best* debuted at London's Haymarket Theatre on 4 August 1832.[124] *The Breach of Promise* was quickly followed by *The Boarding House*, a short story published

---

[122] Merle Tönnies, 'Laughter in the Nineteenth-Century British Theatre: From Genial Blending to Harsh Distinctions' in Pfister 99–119, esp at 99.

[123] Steinbach is wrong in her passing observation that 'various types of fiction about the action' only started to appear from 1869 onwards ('Promises' 278). The breach-of-promise action in fact inspired period literature from as early as the 1830s.

[124] John Baldwin Buckstone, *The Breach of Promise: Or, Second Thoughts Are Best,* 1832 (New York: O A Roorbach, n d).

by the 22-year-old Charles Dickens in the *Monthly Magazine* in May 1834.[125] In 1836, Dickens returned to and enlarged on the breach-of-promise theme in his debut novel, *The Pickwick Papers*, bestowing on his contemporaries and posterity one of the best-loved fictional trials of all time. The final two early fictional depictions of breach of promise hail from the other side of the Atlantic. The American author and humorist Joseph Clay Neal published a short story called *Duberly Doubtington: The Man Who Couldn't Make Up His Mind* in 1838.[126] Nathaniel Hawthorne's *Mrs. Bullfrog*, a short story first published in 1840, rounds off the list of early-period breach-of-promise fiction.[127]

If the wellspring of humour lies in the perception of some incongruity, the feminized breach-of-promise suit, with its inherent structural inconsistency, seemed pre-destined for comic treatment. It therefore comes as no great surprise that the four authors just considered, most of whom are best known for their humorous work, should have been attracted to it. What does, at first, come as a surprise, however, is that the early works do not seem to rely on this immanent inconsistency to make their readers and audiences laugh. Instead of exploiting the inconsistency already inhering in the structural position of the breach-of-promise plaintiff, the tactic of choice for eliciting readership and audience laughter in these early works appears to be the *creation* of an incongruity by deliberately substituting another well-known type in place of the expected true woman and to make that other type the true woman's opposite in every respect.

The sharpest contrast to the idealized nineteenth-century bourgeois image of the sexually uninitiated and socially passive true woman is provided by the mature woman of sexual experience and social masculinity—by a mannish widow, in short. Accordingly, up to and including *The Pickwick Papers*, fictional plaintiffs are widows, and hence sexually experienced rather than 'pure', mature in years, unprepossessing in aspect, energetic heads and self-sufficient manageresses of either large families—Mrs Trapper (*The Breach of Promise*) and Mrs Maplesone (*The Boarding House*)—or a business (Mrs Bardell in *The Pickwick Papers*, although it is the relatively domestic one of a landlady).[128]

[125] Charles Dickens, 'The Boarding House' in *Sketches*, 1834 (Leipzig, 1843) 283–322.

[126] Joseph Clay Neal, 'Duberly Doubtington: The Man Who Couldn't Make Up His Mind' in *Charcoal Sketches; or, Scenes in a Metropolis* (Philadelphia, 1838) 82–92.

[127] Nathaniel Hawthorne, 'Mrs. Bullfrog' in *The Centenary Edition of the Works of Nathaniel Hawthorne*, William Charvat, Roy Harvey Pearce, and Claude M Simpson (eds), vol 10 (n p: Ohio State University Press, 1974) 129–37.

[128] For another illustration of the same principle, see Frances Trollope, *The Widow Barnaby* (London, 1840), where the eponymous 'heroine'—'a widow fair, fat, and forty' (312; vol 2, ch 14)— entertains the sanguine expectation of becoming Viscountess Mucklebury and nearly sues for breach of promise when she is disappointed of that hope. Frances Trollope's novel in fact contains more than a few allusions to Dickens's *Pickwick Papers*.

In short, in the early works, a complete inversion of the feminine ideal is deliberately 'miscast' in a role unmistakably scripted for the idealized true woman.

Why this inversion, this deliberate striving to *create* an inconsistency, given that there was an inherent structural inconsistency only awaiting dramatization? I would suggest that the absence of any fictional exploitation of the inbuilt incongruity in the early nineteenth century can be accounted for in the same way as the glittering successes of real-life plaintiffs at that time: by the strategies of containment then practised. These strategies, it appears, concealed the structural inconsistency from the eyes of writers and playwrights every bit as successfully as they concealed it from the eyes of judges and juries. In fact, the strategies appear to have been so effective that the structural inconsistency escaped even Charles Dickens himself, that writer's 'incomparable...insight'[129] and boasted genius for perceiving things not generally apparent notwithstanding. It is because the strategies of containment left early writers and playwrights unconscious of any suit-immanent inconsistency then, that they had to resort to the creation of an inconsistency by means of a strategy of feminine inversion.

This strategy of inversion had two obvious advantages. For one thing, casting the opposite of what the role called for obviously created an incongruity not to be missed, sure to elicit side-splitting and sustained readership and audience laughter. Secondly, the inversion of the feminine ideal was itself a type as familiar to Victorian readers and theatre audiences as the angel it supplanted. Hostility to the man-woman and the lusty widow quite literally shrieks down the ages and came to a crescendo in the Victorian period. Aggressively sexualized and masculine women had borne the brunt of both classical and Renaissance scorn,[130] and in the nineteenth century, characterized, as it was, by an 'intuitive repugnance toward masculine ladies'[131] as well as oversexed ones, strong and libidinous women became prime targets of ridicule, emblems of socially demonized female dominance and deviance, respectively, sought to be exorcized through laughter.[132] In early-period breach-of-promise fiction, these two stock types of traditional anti-woman commentary—the virago-figure, on the one hand, and the lusty widow, on the other—were combined in the single character of the breach-of-promise plaintiff. One half or the other of the

---

[129] Grahame Smith, *Dickens, Money, and Society* (Berkeley: University of California Press, 1968) 79.

[130] In the classical period, Juvenal and Aristophanes produced mocking portraits of the man-woman. Renaissance criticism of the 'androgyne' is most powerfully embedded in the works of Jonson. See Grace Tiffany, *Erotic Beasts and Social Monsters: Shakespeare, Jonson, and Comic Androgyny* (London: Associated University Presses, 1995), esp at 14, 15, 23.

[131] Wise 84.

[132] Tönnies 105.

literary ancestry usually preponderates in any given case. Mrs Trapper, for instance, is almost devoid of sexual passion, while Mrs Bardell is more lusty widow than formidable virago. But whether strong or lusty, the early fictional plaintiffs are united in their widowhood.

Since at least the sixteenth century, but probably since long before then,[133] widows have been distrusted for their financial independence and for the 'sexual legacy' left them by a prior marriage. On a husband's death, his widow became legally, socially, and financially independent. She recovered her own property, received her widow's dower, and acquired the right to carry on her late husband's business, complete with full trading privileges and even guild membership, where applicable. Her position, legally and socially, thus approximated that of a man.[134] Further, according to Paulian[135] and popular analysis, a widow was a creature of immense sexual appetites. Awakened to sexual experience by prior intercourse, libidinous impulses were believed to govern virtually every aspect of a widow's social relations.[136] A widow, assertive and athirst for sexual pleasures, therefore brought together all that was worst in women and all that men most feared. A widow could never be married for love, but only, if at all, as 'a most desirable addition to a limited income'.[137]

It is perhaps because of the very familiarity of the type cast in the early accounts and its incongruity with the socially dominant feminine identity that the butt of laughter in these early works seems to be, not the breach-of-promise plaintiff as such, but rather the stereotypical man-woman or lusty widow, who was much maligned, throughout the nineteenth century, in all sorts of fictional roles.[138] This deflection of the comic attack away from the

---

[133] Kathryn Jacobs has argued that although the anti-widow tradition only came into full swing in the sixteenth and seventeenth centuries, the negative stereotype in fact pre-dated the Middle Ages by hundreds of years. Kathryn Jacobs, *Marriage Contracts from Chaucer to the Renaissance Stage* (Gainesville: University Press of Florida, 2001) 71–4.

[134] On the legal position of widows, see Bodichon 10. See also Utter and Needham 21.

[135] Saint Paul recommended marriage, because he believed human beings to be innately lustful. Marriage was required to channel man's carnal lusts and desires. But if Saint Paul was right and regular sexual intercourse was necessary to keep partners chaste, a widow was in a sore predicament: she had no one to pay the marriage debt. According to Paulian analysis, a widow would therefore be continually 'on the prowl' for a sexual outlet.

[136] Jacobs 74.

[137] Dickens, *Pickwick* 20; ch 2. In that scene, Dr Slammer pursues 'a little old widow, whose rich dress and profusion of ornament bespoke her a most desirable addition to a limited income'. Widows, in nineteenth-century fiction, are never the object of any man's disinterested affection. Where they have any money, they might, at most, be targets for fortune-hunters.

[138] A good example of a mannish woman who is treated with unmitigated hostility is Mrs Proudie in Anthony Trollope's *The Last Chronicle of Barset* (1867). The lusty widow was, of course, a Renaissance stereotype. A famous fictional example of an amorous (and hence comic) widow, closer in time to the period studied, is Mrs Wadman in Lawrence Sterne's *Tristram Shandy*, 1760 (New York: W W Norton, 1980). Finally, as a Victorian case in point, there is Charles Dickens's Flora Finching in *Little Dorrit*,

role (breach-of-promise plaintiff) onto the type cast in that role (the mannish woman or lusty widow) seems reflected in the fact that most of the early
accounts (with the exception of *Pickwick*) fall into category B ('out-of-court
involvement') of my systematization. The writers in this period do not fit the
breach-of-promise element into the plot to the extent of allowing the trial to
take place before the audience. In *The Breach of Promise, The Boarding House*,
and *Duberly Doubtington,* for instance, the trial takes place off-stage. And in
Mrs. Bullfrog it is an accomplished fact in the background of the action, pre-
dating the time at which the story is set. As a result, the breach-of-promise
element is relegated to the sidelines. In using breach of promise, the writers
seem to be thrusting in a theme which does not really serve the plot. It is more
or less tacked onto it. Accordingly, the comedy, in the early accounts, derives
not so much from the breach-of-promise element per se, as from the cutting
down to size of the woman concerned, the expurgation of her rampant desires,
and her subjugation under male authority.

The re-establishment of the proper (patriarchal) order is clearly the main-
spring of the action in Buckstone's *The Breach of Promise*. The play opens on a
complete reversal of traditional gender relations. We meet the female protagonist, Mrs Trapper, a widow with three marriageable daughters, and are immediately struck by her masculine attributes. Her very name, Trapper, already
evokes the quintessential rustic frontiersman, and her character well fits her
name. Trapper is no domestic angel, happy to potter about the house, indulge
in the usual feminine avocations, and make love matches for her three girls.
Rather, experienced in the ways of the world and independent of any man,
Trapper scorns the occupations nineteenth-century society believed proper
for women—occupations like her daughters' album-keeping, novel-reading,
and ornament-making—as 'a species of industry so much like idleness that
I scarcely know the difference'.[139] Instead, this enterprising widow has made it
'the whole *business* of [. . . her] life'[140] to get her daughters well married, and, true
to character, she is far from desiring them to marry for love. Rather, spouting of
'the folly of mere love-matches— . . . of young people marrying without prospects—of the bickerings inseparable from poverty—of the gradual subsiding
of the supposed love as wants increase',[141] Trapper approaches match-making
in the mercenary manner of a seventeenth-century patriarch. In Trapper's marriage plans for her daughters, personal preferences are disregarded. Marriage, to

---

1857 (London: Everyman's Library, 1992). I will examine Flora and Mrs Bardell—two of Dickens's
romantic grotesques—in detail later in this section.

[139] Buckstone 6.
[140] Ibid, 7 (emphasis added).
[141] Ibid, 9.

a shrewd businessperson like herself, is a contract of material convenience, and she accordingly instils in her girls their paramount duty to play the marriage market for what they can get. Preferences for younger, better-looking, or more temperamentally congenial men are irrelevant in a world where the richer man is the better provider: in Trapper's book, if a man be wealthy, 'that atones for every... deficiency'.[142]

Just as Trapper, in her activity, self-sufficiency, and unromantic nature, is less than a woman, so her suitor, Sudden, is less than a man. Sudden has no masculine firmness of purpose. Every single one of his characteristically rash decisions is liable to be overturned on equally rash 'second thoughts'. Even his offer of marriage is entirely unpremeditated ('it's a sudden thought; I had no idea of it when I entered this house...'[143]) and a prey to second thoughts within the hour. Worse still, Sudden betrays womanish dependence in his need for someone he can recline on, someone who will manage for him. When he finds that he cannot control his household, he decides to marry Trapper and proposes to her in terms that would be better suited to the hiring of a steward or a general domestic manager:

[M]y servants impose upon me; my ward rebels against me; my animals are refractory; even my pony strives to throw me; there's not a clock in the house that strikes the hour correctly; my windows won't open; my gates won't shut; everything opposes me—and I am at length convinced that I want *an active partner* in my establishment.[144]

A role reversal along the Trapper/Sudden lines, with the woman the 'active partner' and the man the one who requires to be 'properly nursed',[145] is a characteristic of early-period breach-of-promise fiction. *The Boarding House*, for instance, pairs an 'enterprising' and 'shrewd' 'accomplished parent'[146] of two—the gender-neutral 'parent' already rendering Mrs Maplesone's gender affiliation deliciously doubtful—with 'an old boy... still on the look-out for a wife with money'.[147] In *The Pickwick Papers*, Mr Pickwick is so ignorant of the ways of the world that he needs a Sam Weller character to protect his interests; so virginal, that he has never even proposed;[148] and so un-businesslike, that he

---

[142] Ibid, 12.

[143] Ibid, 10.

[144] Ibid, 9–10 (emphasis added).

[145] Ibid, 7.

[146] Dickens, 'The Boarding House' 289, 286.

[147] Ibid, 288–9.

[148] Mr Pickwick emphasizes that he has no personal experience of proposing when giving courtship advice to Mr Magnus: ' "I beg your pardon, Mr Pickwick; but have you ever done this sort of thing in your time?" said Mr Magnus. "You mean proposing?" said Mr Pickwick.—"Yes."— "Never," said Mr Pickwick, with great energy, "never"' (289; ch 24). Although this exchange post-dates the Bardell episode, Mr Pickwick's emphatic denial is truthful insofar as his 'proposal' to Mrs Bardell was, of course, unintentional.

lacks method even in his charity.[149] His opposite number, Mrs Bardell, by contrast, runs her own lodging business, has a son to vouch for her sexual experience, and, like her predecessor Mrs Maplesone, is for the most part referred to in gender-neutral or even de-humanized terms ('the relict and sole executrix of a deceased custom-house officer'[150]). Male effeminacy finally reaches its apogee in the characters of Duberly Doubtington and Mr Bullfrog. The former is a vine in search of an oak ('he invariably leans his back against the nearest sustaining object'[151]), who would like to play a passive woman's role in courtship: 'He had a faint hope that he would be married, as it were, imperceptibly; that it would, like old age, steal upon him by degrees, so that he might be used to it before he found it out.'[152] And of the latter we are told that 'the ladies themselves were hardly so lady-like as Thomas Bullfrog'.[153] The characters' spheres tend to be inverted as well. Nearly all of the women display a noticeable lack of domesticity in their living arrangements. Mrs Maplesone, for instance, lives in a boarding house, and Mrs Bardell runs one.[154] Such a confusion of the public and the private—indeed, the literal integration of business and domesticity in Mrs Bardell's case—was anathema to the Victorians. The Temples, the perfect Victorian family of Harriet Smythies's mid-nineteenth-century novel *The Breach of Promise*, for instance, 'had tried boarders, too, but . . . found they reaped nothing from them but discontent and insult',[155] and Charles Dickens, Victorian par excellence, could not introduce a landlady into his fiction without putting on record his hostility towards the breed.[156] Just as the women in early-period breach-of-promise fiction are rather too at home in the public sphere, the men are a bit too fixed in the domestic one. With the exception of Mr Bullfrog, who pursues the rather ladylike occupation of 'suiting silken hose to delicate limbs, and handling satins, ribbons, chintzes, calicoes, tapes, gauze, and cambric needles',[157] none of the fictional breach-of-promise defendants

---

[149] Grahame Smith has observed that, unlike the benevolence of the Cheeryble brothers, Mr Pickwick's charity is characterized by a 'lack of method' (24). In fact, many critics have pointed out that Mr Pickwick seems so un-businesslike that it is hard to credit that he made his fortune as a businessman. Hardy's comment is typical: 'not only are we shown neither the early stage of business nor the pursuit of wealth, but Pickwick's large sweet innocence is utterly incompatible with any such experience'. Barbara Hardy, *The Moral Art of Dickens* (London: Athlone Press, 1970) 83.

[150] Dickens, *Pickwick* 137; ch 12.

[151] Neal 84.

[152] Ibid, 88.

[153] Hawthorne, 'Mrs. Bullfrog' 130. However, there is no (Ethelinda St Simon Sapsago) or at any rate only better concealed (Laura Bullfrog) 'social masculinity' in the female half of the pairing in these last two stories.

[154] On the lack of domesticity of living in lodgings, see Davidoff and Hall 358–9.

[155] Smythies 1: 8.

[156] Mrs Tibbs (*The Boarding House*) and Mrs Raddle (*The Pickwick Papers*), to name but two of the galaxy of Dickensian landladies, are both depicted in decidedly negative terms.

[157] Hawthorne, 'Mrs. Bullfrog' 130.

toil in the public world of work. Indeed, Sudden has such an aversion to publicity that he does not even go to court on the day of his breach-of-promise trial, preferring to ride out the storm at home instead.

The fictional plaintiffs' familiarity with the public sphere is but an acknowledgement of the well-known legal and social independence of the widow. Where the virago half of her mixed ancestry preponderates, the woman's business sense and legal know-how tend to be particularly marked. Mrs Trapper, for instance, is almost only virago, and her pragmatism and legalism are unsurpassed in the canon of early-period breach-of-promise fiction. The reader is alerted to Trapper's strong masculine intellect by the emphatically official, irreproachably legal, and ceremonial nature of her 'contract' to marry Sudden. The play isolates and emphasizes this contractual moment—with the exception of *Pickwick*, it is in fact the only piece in this period to show us the contractual moment at all—and, in so doing, highlights the business aspect of Trapper's character. In the proposal scene, what begins as an unpremeditated, off-the-cuff offer of marriage is systematically transformed into a written contract. The values implied are resolutely mercantile in every detail. For instance, as a general rule, contracts should be easily demonstrable in court and unambiguous, and Trapper's contract certainly cannot be faulted on that score. Not only is Trapper pragmatic enough to get Sudden's promise in writing, very readily providing that mercurial man with pen, ink, and paper, she also makes sure that there can be no mistake about her acceptance of it. When Sudden proffers his promise with the words: 'There's a written promise—take it', Trapper is quick to point out that in physically accepting the paper, she is also symbolically accepting his offer. Her taking the paper, she tells Sudden, 'will amount to an acceptance of your suit'. And as if that was not legally watertight enough, she immediately follows up her symbolic acceptance with an irreproachably express one in words: 'I—I accept your promise. (*Taking the paper and perusing it.*)'[158] Trapper's business sense, already made manifest in the proposal scene, never deserts her. Having secured the written promise, she locks it up to keep it safe; when Sudden later reneges on his promise, she instantly knows that 'there's law to be had';[159] and when he seeks to avoid judgement, she knows how to deal with that, too: 'a judge's warrant shall issue for his apprehension. Come with me, sir, to my lawyer's; you are the evidence of his intention, and must not leave me.'[160] Mrs Trapper, unlike the 'ideal' breach-of-promise plaintiff, is clearly an active party to her contract, making sure it will stand up in court,[161] and the avowed instigator of every legal measure taken against Sudden.

---

[158] Buckstone 11.   [159] Ibid, 22.   [160] Ibid, 33.

[161] In fact, Mrs Trapper clearly errs on the side of caution, given the informality of the evidence that, as we saw in Chapter 1, sufficed to make out a case.

But, ultimately, Trapper's unnatural hegemony is not long-lived. The whole point of Buckstone's play is in fact the re-establishment of the proper order of things and the subjugation of the 'unnatural' woman, as personified by Trapper, under the rightful male authority. The play is strikingly similar to Renaissance drama in its characters and plot construction. As in Renaissance drama, Trapper, in the end, turns out to be a pseudo-widow, separated from her husband, whom she believed dead, for years or maybe decades. And, just as in Renaissance drama, by the end, 'remarriage is generally averted or annulled, the family estate...restored, the family reunited, and [the] heirs of the first husband safely recognized',[162] so order is restored at the end of *The Breach of Promise*. Jacobs notes that in Renaissance drama, the husband usually arrives to reclaim his wife when the wedding is imminent.[163] This is exactly what occurs in Buckstone's play, with the slight variation that Mr Trapper returns when the wedding-substitute, namely the payment of damages for breach of promise, is imminent. At the end of *The Breach of Promise*, Mrs Trapper is literally placed under lock and key by Sudden ('I have her under lock and key—now I am at liberty, and the world is all before me...'[164]) and reduced to the quintessentially feminine role of calling for help. And although Trapper soon recovers her physical liberty, she never regains her symbolic freedom. She is released from her lock-up only to find herself under her returned husband's 'coverture'. On coming face-to-face with Mr Trapper (or Mr Hudson, as he now calls himself), Mrs Trapper is instantaneously and somewhat miraculously transformed from virago to docile wife. From that moment, she displays only proper feminine behaviour. She shrieks, faints, starts, and depends on her man. On being applied to for help by her daughters, she dutifully refers them to her husband: 'Ask it not of me—here's your father—(*pointing to HUDSON.*)'[165] Thus, although *The Breach of Promise* opened on a reversal of traditional gender roles, the curtain goes down on a reformed Mrs Trapper, playing her divinely ordained role in a 'delightful family picture'.[166]

Like the initial reversal of traditional gender roles, an eventual containment of the threat posed by the 'unnatural' woman, as in *The Breach of Promise*, is a characteristic of early-period breach-of-promise fiction. In *Pickwick*, for instance, Mrs Bardell's comeuppance is eerily reminiscent of Mrs Trapper's final moments. She is imprisoned in the Fleet and reduced to sending a begging letter to Mr Pickwick, in which she admits the error of her ways, deplores having been an instrument of vexation to him, and beseeches his assistance. And as if to convince the reader that Mrs Bardell's dangerous romantic and litigious tendencies are exorcized by this ordeal, Dickens garrulously records, at the end

---

[162] Jacobs 74.   [163] Ibid.   [164] Buckstone 37.
[165] Ibid, 39.   [166] Ibid, 40.

of the book, that this chastened widow 'never brought any more actions for a breach of promise of marriage'.[167]

In early-period breach-of-promise fiction then, the evil is clearly represented, not by the breach-of-promise plaintiff as such, but by the unnatural type cast in her role. There is little evidence of any hostility to the cause of action or to the plaintiff herself. This is borne out by the fact that where a writer casts a true woman in the plaintiff role, as Joseph Clay Neal does with Ethelinda St Simon Sapsago in *Duberly Doubtington*, there is never the slightest question: the claimant is entirely sympathetic. In Neal's text, there is no suggestion that the contract is a mistake or that holding Duberly to it would be a pedantic legalism. Rather, the author's and the reader's sympathies are with the lovely Ethelinda, who has 'comported herself so graciously to Duberly'.[168] The text plainly invites the reader to feel unalloyed satisfaction on learning that the case of *Sapsago v Doubtington* made heavy inroads upon Duberly's fortune.

In the early period, there is thus an externalization of the conflict. The conflict is not located *inside* the character of the breach-of-promise plaintiff, but imported from outside, through a casting of female 'inverts' in the plaintiff role. As a result, the criticism is deflected. The butt of laughter is an established comic type—the ridiculous strong woman or lusty widow. The representation of this type on stage, according to Merle Tönnies's analysis of the quality of audience laughter in the nineteenth-century British theatre, was sure to elicit a Hobbesian laughter of superiority.[169] In early-period breach-of-promise comedy, accordingly, the reader or theatregoer is invited to express his distance and moral superiority over the unnatural woman by laughing at her. The laughter is invoked to signal a warning, to all women, against falling out of the patriarchal system and to help exorcize the twin threats of female dominance and female sexual deviance. As order is usually restored at the end of the play or text, the laughter of superiority called forth by early-period breach-of-promise comedy is predominantly jovial and indulgent in character.

It is only in the later texts in this period—namely in *The Pickwick Papers* and in *Mrs. Bullfrog*—that this laughter of good-natured amusement becomes tinged, first, with mild disgust and then with downright terror. This darkened laughter, I would argue, is the result of a greater yoking together of two incompatible elements—the unnatural woman, on the one hand, and its opposite, the nineteenth-century feminine ideal, on the other. This greater yoking together is achieved by actually showing the unnatural woman in a mock-angelic role. *Pickwick*, as we have already seen, falls into category A ('in-court involvement')

---

[167] Dickens, *Pickwick* 718; ch 57.
[168] Neal 87.
[169] Tönnies 104.

of my systematization. The breach-of-promise trial takes centre stage, and the reader is treated to the spectacle of Mrs Bardell, cast against type, vainly striving to live up to her role as female romantic lead of Dickens's in-court breach-of-promise drama. And although *Mrs. Bullfrog* is a category-B ('out-of-court involvement') text, in its eponymous protagonist the unnatural and the angelic are also uneasily blended. Laura Bullfrog, in the course of Hawthorne's story, is transmogrified from 'young angel, just from Paradise'[170] to 'a person of grisly aspect, with a head almost bald, and sunken cheeks, apparently of the feminine gender, though hardly to be classed in the gentler sex'.[171]

Where, as in *Pickwick* and *Mrs. Bullfrog*, the feminine ideal is presented in immediate juxtaposition with its opposite, the resultant disharmonious compound has a potential for the grotesque. According to Philip Thomson, '[t]he most consistently distinguished characteristic of the grotesque has been the fundamental element of disharmony.'[172] This disharmony is a disharmony both of depiction and of the reaction evoked. Thus, Thomson identifies the classic response to the grotesque as a combination of 'amusement and disgust, laughter and horror, mirth and revulsion',[173] as the kind of darkened laughter, in short, that, as I argue, is invoked by *Pickwick* and *Mrs. Bullfrog*. Thomson's definition of the grotesque as disharmony in both depiction and reaction is echoed by other modernist theorists[174] and not in fact new. The Victorian art critic John Ruskin had already insisted that in the grotesque a ludicrous and a terrible element are almost invariably found together. According as the one or the other element predominates, Ruskin termed the grotesque either sportive or terrible.[175] This distinction between a lighter or sportive grotesque and a darker or terrible grotesque has become traditional critical discourse. The former variety is occasionally referred to as Bakhtinian and the latter as Kayserian grotesque, after Mikhail Bakhtin and Wolfgang Kayser, respectively, the two most significant writers on the grotesque in the modern period.[176]

---

[170] Hawthorne, 'Mrs. Bullfrog' 130.

[171] Ibid, 133.

[172] Philip Thomson, *The Grotesque*, The Critical Idiom 24 (London: Methuen, 1972) 20.

[173] Ibid, 24.

[174] See, for instance, Arthur Clayborough, *The Grotesque in English Literature* (Oxford: Clarendon Press, 1965) 70, 72.

[175] Quoted in Clayborough 15.

[176] The conceptions of the grotesque espoused by Bakhtin and Kayser, respectively, represent the opposite ends of the grotesque spectrum. Michael Bakhtin emphasized the good-naturedly comic aspect of the grotesque, whereas Wolfgang Kayser stressed its terrible metaphysical element. See Mikhail Bakhtin, *Rabelais and His World*, (trans) Helene Iswolsky (Bloomington: Indiana University Press, 1984); Wolfgang Kayser, *The Grotesque in Art and Literature*, (trans) Ulrich Weisstein (New York: Columbia University Press, 1981).

I have said that the disharmonious compound achieved in *Pickwick* and *Mrs. Bullfrog* as a result of the greater integration of the feminine ideal and its opposite has a *potential* for the grotesque. But this grotesque potential is *realized* only if the disharmonious compound is in fact given grotesque treatment, in particular if the author manages to elicit the mixed reader response, which, as we have just seen, is considered a necessary ingredient of grotesque art. A potential for the grotesque would certainly not go unexploited by Charles Dickens. Any grotesque feature he noticed in the world came as grist to Dickens's mill.[177] In Dickens, the imperfect[178] and, in particular, imperfect womanhood[179] are nearly always singled out for grotesque treatment. Where, as in Mrs Bardell's position, imperfect femininity comes face-to-face with its sublime opposite, the true depth of Dickens's grotesque art can be revealed. Martha Bardell is developed as a romantic grotesque[180] by Dickens, and as such, she is a literary precursor of Dickens's most famous rendition of that type, about a decade after *Pickwick*, in the character of Flora Finching in *Little Dorrit*. Of course, by the time he came to portray Flora, Dickens had a real-life model to draw on, his re-discovered former sweetheart Maria Beadnell, now woefully the worse for wear,[181] and this real-life experience may account for the artistic superiority of the later portrait. But, artistic merit apart, Martha Bardell is strikingly similar to Flora. Just as Mrs Bardell, oblivious to her age, imagines herself Mr Pickwick's love interest and casts herself in the romantic role of 'sensitive and confiding female',[182] Flora Finching grafts herself at 18 'on to the relict of the late Mr F; thus making a moral mermaid of herself, which her once boy-lover contemplated with feelings wherein his sense of the sorrowful and his sense of the comical were curiously blended'.[183] In the once boy-lover Clennam's mixed reaction to Flora's re-enactment of herself as a young and pretty girl, there is already a powerful hint at

---

[177] David Cecil, *The Fine Art of Reading and Other Literary Studies* (London: Constable, 1957) 107.

[178] Clayborough 211, 216.

[179] Nancy Hill has pointed out that androgyny, for instance, is associated with the grotesque by Dickens. Nancy K Hill, *A Reformer's Art: Dickens' Picturesque and Grotesque Imagery* (London: Ohio University Press, 1981) 109.

[180] Clayborough distinguishes different kinds of grotesque characters in Dickens. One of Clayborough's categories is the absurdly romantic grotesque. Clayborough expressly classes Flora Finching in that category, although he omits Mrs Bardell (222).

[181] Maria Beadnell had been the object of the young Dickens's all-consuming passion for a period of about four years. She inspired the character of Dora Spenlow, David Copperfield's adorable, if inept, first wife in Dickens's 1850 novel. Maria unexpectedly re-entered Dickens's life as Mrs Winter 22 years after their youthful romance, having become 'toothless, fat, old and ugly'. Dickens immortalized this sadly aged Maria in the character of the very stout, soft-headed, and garrulous Flora Finching in *Little Dorrit*. See Michael Slater, *Dickens and Women* (London: J M Dent, 1983) 49–76. Quote at page 67.

[182] Dickens, *Pickwick* 426; ch 34.

[183] Dickens, *Little Dorrit* 155; ch 13.

the grotesque. This hint is made explicit when Dickens describes Flora's self-mimicry as a '*grotesque* revival of what he [Clennam] remembered as having once been prettily natural to her'.[184] As Martha Vicinus has noted, in the nineteenth century, it was perceived as obscene and comic or, in a word, grotesque for a middle-aged woman to still want marriage; and as even more grotesque for her to imagine that any man would still want her.[185] Accordingly, both Mrs Bardell and Flora Finching are developed in true grotesque fashion. By their very introduction, they are rendered inanimate, becoming 'the relict ... of a deceased custom-house officer'[186] and 'the relict of the late Mr F'[187] respectively. Not only that: in Dickens's description, both are immense puppets. A reduction of human bodies to puppets, marionettes, and automata, as Wolfgang Kayser has noted, is one of the most persistent motifs of the grotesque.[188] In *Little Dorrit*, Flora Finching acts as her own puppeteer, 'tossing her head with a caricature of her girlish manner, such as a mummer might have presented at her own funeral, if she had lived and died in classical antiquity'.[189] And in *Pickwick*, Mrs Bardell is nothing more than a stage figure in the able hands of her wily solicitors, Dodson and Fogg.[190] Equipped with an oversized umbrella and pattens to symbolize her domesticity and deprived of any instinctual energy, she mechanically obeys the stage directions thought up by her 'capital' attorneys, with their 'excellent ideas of effect': 'At sight of her child, Mrs Bardell started; suddenly recollecting herself, she kissed him in a frantic manner; and then relapsing into a state of hysterical imbecility, the good lady requested to be informed where she was.'[191] Here, Mrs Bardell's sudden mechanical vitality, on remembering what must have been her solicitors' instructions to kiss her child, is just as grotesque as the equally abrupt relapse into morbid paralysis which follows on its heels. In the trial scene in *Pickwick*, Mrs Bardell is locked into inescapable and ineluctably grotesque self-contradiction by the disparity between her quite ordinary middle-aged

---

[184] Ibid (emphasis added).

[185] Vicinus xii.

[186] Dickens, *Pickwick* 137; ch 12.

[187] Dickens, *Little Dorrit* 155; ch 13.

[188] Kayser 183.

[189] Dickens, *Little Dorrit* 150; ch 13.

[190] Critics sometimes wrongly describe Mrs Bardell as the prime mover of the action against Pickwick. Ross Dabney, for instance, speaks of 'Mrs. Bardell's conspiracy', Ross H Dabney, *Love and Property in the Novels of Dickens* (London: Chatto & Windus, 1967) 76. The assumption of a Bardell-led conspiracy is, however, contradicted by Dickens's text itself. Thus, Mr Pickwick believes the action to be 'a base conspiracy between these two grasping attorneys, Dodson and Fogg. Mrs. Bardell would never do it;—she hasn't the heart to do it . . .' (221; ch 18). A better reflection of the textual evidence is therefore Craig's assessment that 'the heartlessness and villainy appear to reside entirely on one side—that of the legal profession' (89).

[191] Dickens, *Pickwick* 420; ch 34.

appearance, on the one hand, and the magnificence of the claims made for 'the charms and accomplishments of my client'[192] by her legal counsel, Serjeant Buzfuz, on the other. Serjeant Buzfuz's oratory only widens the gulf between the widow actress and the angelic role for which she is so woefully miscast. Mrs Bardell's feeble attempts at transcendence of her earthiness and approximation to an etherealized ideal cannot hope to succeed, and because her efforts are doomed from the outset, they are inherently ludicrous. Bound to her middle-aged 'drooping'[193] physicality, on the one hand, and committed to fulfilling a spiritual ideal, on the other, Bardell is victimized by the gap that separates her feminine reality from the action's idealization of it. Through the gap the grotesque incurs to mock, even as it renders her pathetic. Listening to counsel's high-flown language at the same time as gazing on the widow Bardell, in her drooping 'state of hysterical imbecility',[194] we physically experience the lowering of all that is high, spiritual, and ideal. We are brought down with a bump to the material level, to the sphere of earth and body. The placing of a tired, drooping, indeed a deathly ('relict'[195]) body where a blooming, youthful one should be can, in an extreme case, evoke disgust, only barely tinged with amusement. In Stanley Kubrick's adaptation of Stephen King's *The Shining*, for instance, a character is passionately kissing a beautiful young woman when he catches sight of her reflection in the mirror. The reflection shows that he is in fact holding a rotting corpse. During the initial release of the film, this immediate juxtaposition of beauty and death was 'greeted with prolonged, disgusted, soundtrack-obscuring groans'.[196] In *Pickwick*, the juxtaposition of beauty and death is, of course, much more subtle, much more a matter of careful reading and inference than in-your-face expressness. The amount of disgust that infiltrates our amusement is correspondingly milder. Accordingly, the laughter invoked by the grotesquerie of the trial scene is one predominantly of rollicking amusement, with only the odd twinge of disgust. Probably the most powerful such twinge is called forth by the 'love-letters' that, as Serjeant Buzfuz puts it, 'have passed between these parties'. The first reads: 'Dear Mrs. B.—Chops and Tomata [sic] sauce. Yours, PICKWICK', the other 'Dear Mrs. B., I shall not be at home till to-morrow [sic]. Slow coach... Dont [sic] trouble yourself about the warming-pan.'[197] On one level,

---

[192] Ibid, 425; ch 34.
[193] Ibid, 420; ch 34.
[194] Ibid.
[195] See n 186.
[196] Greg Metcalf, 'The Soul in the Meatsuit: Ivan Albright, Hannibal Lecter and the Body Grotesque', in *Literature and the Grotesque*, Michael J Meyer (ed), Rodopi Perspectives on Modern Literature 15 (Amsterdam: Rodopi, 1995) 160.
[197] Dickens, *Pickwick* 426; ch 34.

these blatantly innocuous notes are only Dickens's parody of the innocent correspondence from which an allegation of criminal conversation was sought to be raised against the then Prime Minister Lord Melbourne in *Norton v Melbourne*,[198] an 1836 *cause célèbre* which 'played the devil'[199] with Dickens, when he was reporting it for the *Morning Chronicle*. As in *Norton v Melbourne*, letters that seem to be capable of only one construction are sought to be read as bearing quite a different, amorous one. Unlike the letters in *Norton v Melbourne*, however, the first note in *Pickwick* must derive its hidden amorous meaning, if at all, from a reference to food, from 'Chops and Tomata sauce'.[200] But if this dietetic expression is read as a term of endearment, as a stand-in for the more conventional 'dearest' or 'ducky,' then it clearly is a referent to love and the loved one that emphasizes the physicality, the very carnality of both, as when we say that someone looks good enough to eat. In apostrophizing Mrs Bardell as 'Chops and Tomata sauce', this letter, read as a love letter, stresses Mrs Bardell's body not just as matter, but as meat. With its grotesque conjunction of food, love, and the loved one, it makes an obscene, almost cannibalistic gesture, occasioning, even as it amuses, a touch of 'disgusted indigestion' in the reader. But, despite this admixture of mild disgust, the laughter of *Pickwick* is predominantly one of joyous hilarity. The novel's grotesque humour, therefore, is located at the sportive or Bakhtinian end of the grotesque spectrum. The final text of this period, *Mrs. Bullfrog*, by contrast, evokes a laughter touched with terror and as such falls at the opposite, terrible or Kayserian end of the grotesque scale. Wolfgang Kayser has formulated four criteria, which, as he claims, are key characteristics of (terrible) grotesque art. Since I regard *Mrs. Bullfrog* as an example of the terrible grotesque, it is useful to examine the text in terms of Kayser's criteria. Showing that the criteria apply to *Mrs. Bullfrog* will, incidentally, bear out my classification of the quality of its grotesque humour. According to Wolfgang Kayser, in grotesque art, the world we know and love is suddenly metamorphosed into a strange and unpleasant place, and what is trusted and familiar becomes, in an instant, something alien and uncanny. The grotesque, in a word, is the familiar made strange. It is 'the

---

[198] (1836) 3 Bing NC 67; 132 ER 335; 5 LJCP 343.

[199] Charles Dickens, letter to John Macrone, 23 June 1836, *The Letters of Charles Dickens*, Madeline House and Graham Storey (eds), vol 1 (Oxford: Clarendon Press, 1965) 153. Dickens's report for the *Morning Chronicle* occupied 26½ columns on 23 June. Mr Norton's suit against Lord Melbourne for criminal conversation with Norton's wife Caroline was unsuccessful. For background on *Norton v Melbourne* and the parties involved, see Caroline Norton, *English Laws for Women in the Nineteenth Century*, (rpt edn), 1854 (Westport: Hyperion Press, 1981).

[200] Another writer to have remarked on the connection between sexuality and eating in *Pickwick* is Barbara Hardy. Hardy suggests that overt sexuality was transformed in *Pickwick* into a stress on eating and swilling to satisfy nineteenth-century censorship rules. She points to the Fat Boy as a tangible example (95).

alienated world'.[201] An alienation of the familiar is the baseline of Hawthorne's short story. In *Mrs. Bullfrog*, familiar Victorian beliefs about the innate angelic nature of women are suddenly unsettled, forcing the nineteenth-century reader to question what he thought he knew about the gentler sex.

The story opens on the world Hawthorne's Victorian readership knew and cherished. The story's first-person narrator, Thomas Bullfrog, sets out to relate his personal experience of a quest familiar to every Victorian: the quest for an angel in the house. Like the average male of his period, Thomas Bullfrog desires to marry a woman straight off the pages of Patmore and Ruskin:

> I demanded the fresh bloom of youth, pearly teeth, glossy ringlets, and the whole list of lovely items, with the utmost delicacy of habits and sentiments, a silken texture of mind, and, above all, a virgin heart. In a word, if a young angel, just from Paradise, yet dressed in earthly fashion, had come and offered me her hand, it is by no means certain that I should have taken it.[202]

Despite these somewhat exacting requirements, Thomas Bullfrog soon finds exactly what he dreams of and woos, wins, and marries his charming angel, all within a fortnight. That a female angel is easily found and, once found, easily won was, of course, consonant with familiar cultural beliefs. As we have seen, according to the nineteenth-century conception of femininity, true womanhood was inscribed into female biology and a natural quality of all women, from the lady to the factory girl. Thomas Bullfrog's almost instant and complete success in his matrimonial quest is therefore by no means something that the average male reader would have despaired of meeting with in his own case. But like Thomas Bullfrog's, the Victorian reader's complacent notions about women are about to be unsettled. 'Women,' he is about to learn, 'are not angels. If they were, they would go to Heaven for husbands—or, at least, be more difficult in their choice on earth.'[203] The sudden 'making strange' of the familiar ideal woman is brought about by an overturn of the carriage, which is bearing the couple towards what, until the accident, promised to be connubial bliss. The overturn functions as an epiphany, as a sudden showing forth of Mrs Bullfrog's true colours. When, in the tumult of the overthrow, a befuddled Mr Bullfrog again becomes conscious of his wife, or at least of a figure in 'a riding-habit like Mrs Bullfrog's, and also a green silk calash, dangling down,' the angel has become 'a fearful apparition...of grisly aspect, with a head almost bald, and sunken cheeks, apparently of the feminine gender, though hardly to be classed in the gentler sex',[204] and is inflicting pugilistic punishment on the driver for causing the overthrow. Mr Bullfrog's first reaction on coming face to

---

[201] Kayser 185.
[202] Hawthorne, 'Mrs Bullfrog' 130.
[203] Ibid, 136.   [204] Ibid, 133.

face with an ogre in his wife's clothes is to fancy that her body has been taken over by the devil himself: 'In my terror and turmoil of mind, I could imagine nothing less, than that the Old Nick, at the moment of our overturn, had annihilated my wife and jumped into her petticoats.'[205] Mr Bullfrog's reaction echoes the second of the characteristics of the terrible grotesque described by Kayser. According to Kayser, the grotesque alienation is the creation of an impersonal force: 'it is as if…an alien and inhuman spirit had entered the soul'.[206]

Kayser's final two characteristics, which can be dealt with in one, concern the purpose and effect of the grotesque. According to Kayser, the grotesque is cathartic. It is an attempt to banish and exorcize the demonic element in the world, to get rid of our fears of something hidden by dragging it into the light. By the grotesque, the 'darkness [. . . is] sighted, the ominous powers [are] discovered, the incomprehensible forces challenged'.[207] This final Kayserian hallmark of grotesque art well describes the effect on the reader of Hawthorne's short story. Outlandish, fiendishly energetic, and sexually threatening, the transformed Mrs Bullfrog brings together all the characteristics a Victorian man most feared to encounter in a woman, especially if she be his wife. In confronting the reader with his deepest fear—the fear that the wife of his bosom might turn out a hideous Gorgon—Hawthorne's text brings that fear out into the open. A hidden anxiety the reader may only have been semi-conscious of before, or kept suppressed, is at last sighted and raised to the conscious level. But if the nineteenth-century male reader smiled at all on finishing Hawthorne's tale, one would guess it to have been an uneasy smile, not unlike the smile we sometimes wear during a daylight consideration of the previous evening's nightmare.

Mrs. Bullfrog then, is a prime example of the terrible grotesque, displaying all the characteristics that Kayser has described for that aesthetic. For one thing, it far surpasses *Pickwick* in the extent to which the world is alienated. In fact, the narrative dissolves the boundary line between the fantastic and the real world. Further, in Hawthorne's text, the alienation seems the result of an impersonal force, threatening to engulf reality. In *Pickwick*, by contrast, the fictional cosmos is limited to the personal sphere, with good and evil located in the nature of Dickens's figures. And while the grotesquerie of *Pickwick* is peppered with moments of delightful ludicrousness and provokes essentially good-natured laughter in the reader, the grotesque laughter of *Mrs. Bullfrog* is dark and desperate.

As befits its position at the close of the first period, *Mrs. Bullfrog* clearly marks the high point in grotesquerie in breach-of-promise fiction. But to leave it at that would be to miss the richness of Hawthorne's multi-layered text.

---

[205] Ibid.   [206] Kayser 184.   [207] Ibid, 188.

Mrs. Bullfrog is so rich that it will not stay confined to any one period. It speaks not only to the first, but to the second and even the third period as well and will continue with us, as a recurring point of interest, over the next two chapters. All in all, I will offer three different readings of this short story—corresponding to the three developmental stages that, as I argue, can be demarcated in the history of the breach-of-promise action during the 'long nineteenth century'—to demonstrate how Hawthorne succeeded in 'layering' three fictional treatments of breach of promise (one grotesque, one satirical, and one critical of the feminine ideal itself) in a single text. At this point, I am interested in elucidating the connection the short story makes between the first and second periods. *Mrs. Bullfrog*, I would argue, serves as a connecting link between the early nineteenth century and the high Victorian period, because, at the same time as perfecting the early aesthetic of the grotesque, it points ahead to the satire, which would predominate in the period to come. This double-facedness of Hawthorne's text is a result of the fact that there are two ways of reading *Mrs. Bullfrog*.[208] As is usual with Hawthorne, we are teased with the status of Mr Bullfrog's experience at the critical moment:[209] 'What became of my wits [as a result of the carriage accident],' Mr Bullfrog reports, 'I cannot imagine; they have always had a perverse trick of deserting me, just when they were most needed.'[210] As a result of Hawthorne's blurring of the demarcation line between illusion and reality, a symbolic as well as a literal reading of the narrative is possible. If Mr Bullfrog's senses do not deceive, then we have a physical transformation of Mrs Bullfrog from lovely woman to hideous monster. On this reading, Mrs Bullfrog's 'ugliness' is on the outside as well as on the inside. This literal reading of the text is supported by some hints Hawthorne throws out prior to the accident, indicating that Mrs Bullfrog's pearly exterior is fake. Her apprehensiveness about her curls, for instance, suggests that she is wearing a wig. On a symbolic reading, by contrast, Mrs Bullfrog's outward transformation is but a projection of her husband's imagination, his mind momentarily lending physical form to her suddenly perceived hideous *inner* nature. On this reading, the ugliness is all within. Mr Bullfrog, in the critical scene, is experiencing a moment of greater psychological insight and catching a glimpse of the termagant inside his angel. In other words, a literal reading of the text makes Mrs Bullfrog a physical as

---

[208] As I said before, there are in fact not only two, but *three* ways of reading *Mrs. Bullfrog*, with the third reading, which I offer in Chapter 5 (at pp 182–4), carrying the ultimate punch and point of Hawthorne's text.

[209] In Hawthorne's much more famous short story *Young Goodman Brown*, the reader is left similarly uncertain about the status of the protagonist's nighttime experience in the woods and, by implication, about the accuracy of his resultant conviction that everybody whom he once believed in is in league with the devil. Nathaniel Hawthorne, 'Young Goodman Brown' in *Young Goodman Brown and Other Tales*, Brian Harding (ed), 1835, (Oxford: Oxford University Press, 1998) 111–24.

[210] Hawthorne, 'Mrs. Bullfrog' 132.

well as a moral monster, a symbolic reading only a moral one. A literal reading clearly aligns Hawthorne's short story with the other texts we have encountered in the early period. Mrs Bullfrog, on this reading, is just another 'monstrous' woman of the Trapper or Bardell type, her inner, moral departure from the feminine ideal finding its fitting counterpart in her outward, physical departure from it. Physiognomy, as in the other early nineteenth-century breach-of-promise narratives, would, on this reading, still be a key to character and the principle of concordance between outward appearance and inner nature adhered to. A symbolic reading, by contrast, makes Mrs Bullfrog a new type of fictional breach-of-promise plaintiff. On such a reading, Mrs Bullfrog's lovely exterior is deceptive, dangerously *un*reflective of her perverted inner nature. On a symbolic reading, there is a split between the exterior and the interior of Mrs Bullfrog, with her outward true womanhood irrevocably contaminated by the perversion inside. On such a reading, Hawthorne's concern is with false pretensions and female hypocrisy, with the disparity between Mrs Bullfrog's outward appearance and her inner reality. A discontinuity between appearances and reality, between professions of virtue and the practices that contradict them, is the wellspring of satire, precisely that mode or tone, in short, that would dominate breach-of-promise comedy in the decades to come. Read symbolically, therefore, *Mrs. Bullfrog* already ushers in the next period in breach-of-promise fiction, when the breach-of-promise courtroom becomes a world of sham and when the pathetic and largely unsuccessful female 'inverts' of the first period are forced out of the plaintiff role by angel-faced hypocrites, who successfully manoeuvre themselves into solid and respectable positions.

4

Breach of Promise in the High Victorian Period (1850–1900): The Inconsistency Unveiled, Pinchbeck Angels, and the Dominance of Satire

In this chapter, I should like to consider breach-of-promise actions and their literary representation during the high Victorian period. This period, which extended from the middle to the close of the nineteenth century, witnessed a number of changes to the law of breach of promise and the tactics employed in the handling of breach-of-promise suits. It was also a time of both mounting pressure and mounting insistence on separate spheres ideology. From the 1850s onwards, 'feminists concentrated most of their energies on increasing women's opportunities for education and employment',[1] with the inevitable consequence that the threatened feminine ideal was sought to be inscribed with redoubled force.[2]

Section I considers the impact of these contextual changes on the suit for breach of promise to marry. It argues that the tactical, legal, and social factors outlined above brought out the publicity and agency inherent in the position of the breach-of-promise plaintiff and gave unprecedented prominence to the structural inconsistency at the heart of the ladies' action. The section examines the fall-out of this exposure, drawing on the statistical evidence and the emergent legal and social criticism of the action. With the abandonment of the strategies of containment and the attendant unveiling of the structural inconsistency, the breach-of-promise courtroom became an increasingly improper space that all women with pretensions to true womanhood were expected

---

[1] Shanley 49.

[2] It is no coincidence that one of the central documents of Victorian sexual politics—Ruskin's *Of Queens' Gardens*—was presented in 1864, at a time when, as Ruskin bemoaned, 'wilder words were [never] spoken or more vain imagination permitted respecting this question [women's rights]'. Quoted in Kate Millett, 'The Debate over Women: Ruskin vs. Mill' in Vicinus 123. On the sharpened conflict over gender roles, see also Michael Meyer, 'The Pleasures of Men and the Subjection of Women' in *In the Footsteps of Queen Victoria: Wege zum Viktorianischen Zeitalter*, Christa Jansohn (ed), Studien zur englischen Literatur 15 (Münster: LIT Verlag, 2003) 186.

to (and most upper- and middle-class women in fact did) deny themselves. Involvement in a breach-of-promise suit, to the respectable woman of the high Victorian period, was, like a loss of virtue, a fate worse than death. By popular decree, a 'lady of delicate feeling would rather die than [... face] all the glaring publicity of an Assize Court, amid the scowls and sneers of an assembled county'.[3]

Section II introduces a mid-Victorian case that did much to strengthen the growing popular association of breach-of-promise actions with fallen, morally corrupted womanhood. Mary Elizabeth Smith, the youthful and, at first blush, charming girl at the centre of what was without question one of the most intriguing breach-of-promise suits of all time, the 1846 action of *Smith v The Earl Ferrers*, came to be 'a bye-word, blotted, stained'[4] for the kind of artful and subversive duplicity which was now widely believed to be a characteristic of breach-of-promise plaintiffs.

Mary Elizabeth Smith, fatally poised on a dialectical rift between personally claimed womanly worth and publicly defined fallenness, might well be put forward as the real-life prototype of the false angel figure, 'brimful with deceit and duplicity',[5] whom we see stepping into the plaintiff role in high Victorian breach-of-promise fiction. If the fictional plaintiff of the earlier period had been an inversion of the feminine ideal, the plaintiff of this period, as section III reveals, is the ideal corrupted, a pinchbeck angel. Her outwardly perfect womanhood is shown to be inwardly flawed, hollow, and vicious. Passivity is really wiliness, domesticity publicity, passionlessness mercenariness, and emotionality cloying hyperbole. The fiction of this period thrives on the inherent structural inconsistency, and, unsurprisingly given this orientation, a fair proportion of the accounts fall into category A ('in-court involvement') of my systematization. The in-court trial, where ideal and plaintiff have to be, but cannot be, fused is the centre of the action. In this second period, breach-of-promise fiction takes on the features of satire as it dramatizes the utter lack of coherence between surface appearance and reality, between professions of virtue and the practices that contradict them. While the shafts of comedy in the first period were aimed at a particular type of woman, a type of woman similarly and simultaneously vilified in any number of guises outside of breach-of-promise fiction, in the second, they penetrate the person of the breach-of-promise plaintiff herself. As the period evolves, to bring or not to bring an action for breach of promise, in fiction no

---

[3] 'The Action for Breach of Promise of Marriage' *The Times* 12 February 1878: 9.

[4] Mary Elizabeth Smith, *A Statement of Facts Respecting the Cause of* Smith v. The Earl Ferrers, *Tried before Mr. Justice Wightman, in Westminster Hall, on the 14th, 16th, 17th, and 18th Days of February, 1846; with an Examination of the Speech for the Defendant, of the Late Attorney-General Sir Frederic Thesiger* (London, 1846) 36.

[5] MacColla 65.

less than in reality, becomes the hallmark of true womanhood. However, in this second period, breach of promise also becomes an ideologically contested site. This is reflected in the fact that period literature is not unanimous in its vilification of the suit and of the women bringing it. In breach-of-promise songs of the period, probably addressed to a more working-class audience, which would have been less invested in the feminine ideal, breach-of-promise plaintiffs, as we shall see, were treated with considerably more sympathy.

The high Victorian period then, this chapter argues, is characterized by the exposure of the action's contradictory potential through a change in the legal and social context and the manifestation of this exposure in the fictional text—in the shape of a luxuriant exploitation of the inherent structural inconsistency, reflected in the increasing centrality of the breach-of-promise element to the fictional accounts of this period and in the dominance of the satiric mode.

I. 'No pure-minded woman would submit herself to such indignities':[6] The Abandonment of the Strategies of Containment and the Vulgarization of the Breach-of-Promise Suit

The feminized breach-of-promise action, a mass of contradictions that enshrined the nineteenth-century ideal of virtuous womanhood at the same time as placing the plaintiff in a position antithetical to the ideal's central values, was an extremely unstable compound, ever prone to slippages. Any change in the in-court processing of breach-of-promise suits or in the wider social context carried the risk of upsetting the delicate balance which had hitherto kept the action and the women at its centre safe from attacks upon their respectability. If this balance was lost and the contradictory potential unleashed, the action and the plaintiff might fall. From about the middle of the nineteenth century, a number of factors—practical, tactical, legal, and social—conspired to bring about just that destabilization of the breach-of-promise action.

For one thing, as a purely practical matter, breach-of-promise cases became something of a cultural phenomenon. From about mid-century, there was a sudden and dramatic surge in the number of breach-of-promise actions brought[7]

---

[6] Mabel J J Blott, 'Should Men Break Engagements?' *Womanhood* (1899–1900): 224, quoted in Steinbach, 'Promises' 263.

[7] Unfortunately, the *Civil Judicial Statistics for England and Wales* were only kept from 1859 onwards, so that there is no way of being sure that there was in fact an increase in the overall number of breach-of-promise actions after mid-century. For most of my statistical claims about breach of promise, I can only refer to my own sample of cases as well as similar samples compiled by other investigators of the subject.

and, more importantly, in the number of breach-of-promise actions reported on, at some considerable length, in the newspapers. The national *Times* newspaper, for instance, after carrying at most one breach-of-promise report per month up until 1845,[8] more than tripled its monthly breach-of-promise coverage from 1850 onwards.[9] This increased coverage satisfied a popular demand for, as *The Times* well knew, there were 'few matters of home or foreign policy, of national or local interest, that would stand a chance beside a column of a good breach of promise of marriage case'.[10] In the later nineteenth century, tabloid-style newspapers like the *News of the World* started to embellish their reports with sketches or even photographs of the principal parties involved. The *News of the World*'s write-up of the 1896 case of *Sealley v Creed*, for instance, which bore the attention-grabbing title of 'Love and Folly', was rounded off by a sketch of the plaintiff, Miss Annie Sealley, ornately dressed in a plaid cape and feathered cap, surrounded by some of the supporting characters in this particular breach-of-promise drama.[11]

The result of the intense media attention was, of course, that breach-of-promise suits were much more in the public eye than they had been in the early nineteenth century. The bringing of a breach-of-promise case now spelt publicity. One's name and private heartache would be revealed not only to a judge and jury, but, quite literally, sent forth on the wings of the press. A preservation of the true womanly virtue of domesticity was rendered well nigh impossible.

There is also evidence that the strategy of detachment, which had previously been employed to guard the plaintiff's claim to that very domesticity by keeping her out of the courtroom, was increasingly abandoned.[12] Even before her presence became more or less *de rigueur* with the passage of the Evidence (Further) Amendment Act of 1869,[13] the post-1850 breach-of-promise plaintiff was quite likely to attend court. This much may perhaps be inferred from a statement by Chief Justice Robert Alexander Hamilton in *Morrison v Shaw*,[14] a Canadian case heard before the parties to a breach-of-promise action were

---

[8] For each two-month (March and April) period, *The Times* reported a total of one or at most two cases up to and including 1845. This averages out at less than one case per month.

[9] Over the two-month period (March and April) checked, there were six in 1850, four in 1855, four in 1860, five in 1865, 11 in 1870, six in 1875, one in 1880, two in 1885, seven in 1890, and six in 1895. With the close of the high Victorian period, ie from 1900 onwards, there was a drop back to approximately pre-1850 levels.

[10] 'The Action for Breach of Promise of Marriage.'

[11] *News of the World* 26 April 1896: 4. See the image online at http://ukcatalogue.oup.com/p2p/endecaSearch.do?normalSearch=true&keyword=978-0-19-956997-7

[12] In my sample, only five out of the 133 cases tried between 1850 and 1900 made a conscious and studied use of the strategy of detachment.

[13] 32 & 33 Vict, c 68.

[14] (1877) 40 UCQB 403.

made competent witnesses in that country.[15] Jurors, according to Hamilton, 'have a natural desire to see the woman who is the real or supposed sufferer, *and this desire is generally gratified*, although sometimes most painful to the feelings of the woman principally concerned'. It is difficult to know whether the widespread abandonment of the strategy of detachment was voluntary or forced. Hamilton seems to suggest that it was a grudging concession to jury curiosity, overriding the plaintiff's natural preference for staying away. Frost, by contrast, in her account of mid-nineteenth-century breach-of-promise actions, opines that the parading of the plaintiff, 'dressed nicely, often in the clothes she had bought for the wedding',[16] was a deliberate tactic, employed to obtain higher damages. The two interpretations are not in fact mutually exclusive. The plaintiff's side may well have felt that they would maximize their chances by jollying the jurors along and indulging their whim for a first-hand view, in particular where the plaintiff had assets worth displaying. But although the decision to bring the plaintiff to court might therefore have been actuated by self-interest and as such at least semi-voluntary, it does not follow that the choice was a shrewd one. Presence in court clearly represented an abandonment of a strategy of containment, annihilated any detachment, and exposed an incompatibility with true womanhood. As such, it was bound to backfire on the plaintiff. This is exactly what happened in *Dunlop v Ferguson*.[17] In *Dunlop*, the plaintiff's mother advanced the familiar claim that the plaintiff's health had been very materially affected by the defendant's breach. Under cross-examination, however, she had to admit that her daughter had been well enough to come to court, court attendance evidently being taken to disprove any severe emotional or physical suffering. This shows that, whereas in the early nineteenth century, breach-of-promise plaintiffs had still been able to draw strength from the cultural concept of innate femininity to the point where their emotional and physical debility would be presupposed as natural and go without saying, in the high Victorian period, their claim to a true woman's emotionality was increasingly regarded as suspect.

The strategy of detachment was not the only previously employed technique of containment to fall by the wayside after mid-century. Thus, only a handful of cases between 1850 and 1900 made a studied use of the remaining strategies of representation, voluntary muting, and rhetoric.[18] That the strategy of representation, which sought to preserve the plaintiff's claim to feminine passivity by subjecting her to the tutelage of male family members and

---

[15] The Canadian equivalent to the 1869 Act was not passed until 1882. *Morrison v Shaw* was heard in 1877. See Coombe 83, 103.

[16] Frost, *Promises Broken: Courtship, Class, and Gender in Victorian England* 29.

[17] *The Times* 27 April 1855: 9.

[18] Representation (6), muting (4), rhetoric (10) out of a total of 133 cases.

legal counsel, was not extensively employed in the high Victorian period may have been due to a significant shift in plaintiff composition that set in during the middle decades of the nineteenth century. These decades witnessed a marked increase in the proportion of breach-of-promise plaintiffs falling into categories 1 and 2 of my systematization. The incidence of category-1 plaintiffs jumped from 28.9 per cent (11 out of 38 cases) for the period before 1850 to 35.9 per cent (46 out of 128 cases) for the period between 1850 and 1900, and the increase in category-2 plaintiffs was even more marked. Whereas before 1850, 18.4 per cent (7 out of 38 cases) had had a plaintiff in category 2, in the period between 1850 and 1900, 32.8 per cent (42 out of 128 cases) did so—a rise of nearly 100 per cent. Categories 1 and 2 of my systematization are given over to working-class women, with the more menial workers, the lowly general servants, barmaids, factory and shop girls, comprising category 1, and their more respectable sisters, the upper servants, small shop-keepers, landladies, and their like, making up category 2. That working-class plaintiffs made energetic use of the breach-of-promise action after mid-century is in itself noteworthy. As a general rule, private law was almost wholly irrelevant to the condition of the poorer classes until late in the nineteenth century: the poor had neither the time, nor the money, nor probably the inclination to sue.[19] Actions for breach of promise, however, seem to have constituted an exception, with women at the bottom of the social heap forming the majority of plaintiffs as early as the mid-nineteenth century.[20] In the industrialized society of the nineteenth century, finding work often meant long-distance migration. Young working women would frequently move quite far from the parental home, causing family ties to weaken.[21] As a result, working-class breach-of-promise plaintiffs were less likely to be able to call on male family members to conduct their pre-trial transactions with the defendant. The potential for employing the strategy of representation, at least in its out-of-court version of representation by family and friends, was correspondingly less great.[22] Also, the experience of working for wages outside familiar confines, of controlling one's productive

---

[19] A W Brian Simpson, *Leading Cases in the Common Law* (New York: Oxford University Press, 1995) chs 5 and 7; John P S McLaren, 'Nuisance Law and the Industrial Revolution—Some Lessons from Social History' (1983) 3 *Oxford Journal of Legal Studies* 211.

[20] Access to justice for these poorer women may have been eased by the willingness of lawyers to take on breach-of-promise cases on a contingent fee basis. See p 29 above.

[21] Theresa M McBride, 'The Long Road Home: Women's Work and Industrialization' in *Becoming Visible: Women in European History*, Renate Bridenthal and Claudia Koonz (eds) (Boston: Houghton Mifflin, 1977) 287. See also Branca 34.

[22] This is not to say that male family members and friends never stepped into the breach where a working-class plaintiff was concerned. Many working women in fact retained close links with the families they had left behind (McBride 288). In such a case, the family might be expected to get involved when the woman's courtship failed.

capacities, collecting one's own pay, and generally fending for oneself by the use of one's wits and physical strength might be expected to have instilled a spirit of independence in the Victorian working girl. Françoise Barret-Ducrocq, for instance, has noted that the nineteenth-century working women who applied to the Foundling Hospital were characterized by their physical robustness and a certain pugnacity.[23] A working-class breach-of-promise plaintiff, therefore, was likely to be more assertive, more ready to take independent action both before and after a case came to trial. Such a woman might be expected to claim and retain agency over the conduct of her case, in both symbolic and actual ways, and, by implication, not to favour an agency-*dissembling* tactic like the strategy of representation.[24]

The exposure of the features of the position of the breach-of-promise plaintiff which were inconsistent with true womanhood—an exposure which, as we have just seen, had set in at about mid-century with the widespread abandonment of the strategies of containment—came to a head in 1869, with the passage of the Evidence (Further) Amendment Act of that year.[25] The 1869 Act was the copingstone in a new civil law of evidence, concluding a reform process begun more than 20 years before.[26] Although nearly all of the evidentiary reforms were put in place in 1851—when the so-called party-witness disqualification, which prevented the parties to a suit from acting as witnesses in their own cause, was abolished for most classes of action—suits for breach of promise long remained a significant (and increasingly anomalous) exception. Despite a further amendment to the law of evidence in 1853 and two specific attempts at assimilating breach of promise into the evidentiary mainstream in the mid-1860s,[27] it was not until 1869 that the parties to breach-of-promise actions were finally given their speaking rights. As of 9 August 1869, plaintiffs and defendants in actions for breach of promise of marriage could be witnesses

---

[23] Françoise Barret-Ducrocq, *Love in the Time of Victoria: Sexuality, Class and Gender in Nineteenth-Century London* (London: Verso, 1991) 154.

[24] Annie Sealley, the class-1 plaintiff in the case referred to above (*Sealley v Creed*), for instance, got her lover, as he then was, to execute a settlement. She later had it stamped. This clear display of agency and business sense caused one witness in the case to conclude that Annie was quite capable of looking after herself. At which remark no one, in fact, laughed louder than Miss Sealley herself. Unsurprisingly, given Annie Sealley's shamelessly unfeminine deportment, the jury found for the defendant.

[25] 32 & 33 Vict, c 68.

[26] In 1843, Lord Denman's Evidence Act (6 & 7 Vict, c 85), the major evidence amendment act of the nineteenth century, was passed, allowing most interested persons in most types of action to bear witness.

[27] The first such attempt was made by Sir Fitzroy Kelly in 1865. The bill made it to the second reading, but in committee the clause dealing with breach of promise was struck out and the bill accordingly dropped. The second attempt—by the then Lord Chancellor, Lord Cranworth, in 1866—proved equally unsuccessful. See *Hansard's Parliamentary Debates*, 3rd series, vol 198 (26 July 1869) 674.

at their own trials, provided their testimony was 'corroborated by some other material evidence in support of such promise'.[28]

The Evidence (Further) Amendment Act of 1869 has been described as a watershed or 'turning point in the history of breach of promise',[29] with the time prior to the Act represented as the action's heyday and the period thereafter as that of its decline and fall. Although this sweeping claim seems to me to be somewhat overstating the significance of the Act[30] by viewing it in isolation from other contributing factors—the practical and tactical changes considered above and the changes in the wider social context, which I will turn to later—the Act was doubtless important. It removed the system-enjoined muting of the plaintiff and, in so doing, demolished a legal framework that had allowed voluntary strategies of contradiction management to flourish.[31] The Act accelerated and perhaps made irreversible the (fatal) trend, underway since mid-century,[32] of unveiling the structural inconsistency at the centre of the feminized breach-of-promise action. After mid-century, and certainly after 1869, breach-of-promise plaintiffs were widely perceived as inviting publicity and as having come to court by their own deliberate agency. The feminine virtues of domesticity, passivity, modesty, and a true woman's emotionality certainly seemed hard to claim for a plaintiff, present in public court, speaking up loudly, voluntarily directing 'the unwinking sun of legal inquiry...upon

[28] *Hansard*, vol 198 (30 July 1869) 988. This proviso was included at the suggestion of Lord Chelmsford, who, although not opposing the change as such, entertained 'very serious apprehensions as to the danger that would be incurred' by trusting to the woman's word alone. *Hansard*, vol 198 (26 July 1869) 673.

[29] Steinbach, 'Promises' 235.

[30] Steinbach distinguishes two periods, namely the period from 1780 to 1869 and the period from 1869 to 1920. She identifies the former period as the 'Golden Age' ('Promises' 105) of the breach-of-promise suit. However, I find her statistical support for labelling the entire period before 1869 the golden age problematic: Steinbach divides her data into the two periods first and then proceeds to calculate the average number of cases and the average award for each period ('Promises' 212). From differences in the results she concludes that 1869 was a highly significant year. But that conclusion does not follow. Since I find signs of an increasing awareness of the inherent structural inconsistency (and hence of a growing suspicion of the action and the women making use of it) at about mid-century, I have decided to fix 1850 as the point of transition between the first and the second period in the evolution of the ladies' action.

[31] This is not to say that strategies of containment could not be practised at all after 1869, only that they did not come as naturally. Of course, even after the Act, a plaintiff might still not come to court (detachment), not take the stand (voluntary muting), and rely heavily on representation and rhetoric, and there is some evidence that where the strategies continued to be employed, the plaintiff would reap the benefits: in *Mitchell v Hazeldine, The Times* 4 March 1870: 11, where all four strategies were used (the defendant having unsuccessfully tried to deprive the plaintiff of her detachment by compelling her attendance in court), the plaintiff recovered £2,000 by consent, one of the highest awards of the post-1850 period. One juryman said that £2,000 was the lowest sum they could possibly have given.

[32] In this claim, I have the support of the statistical evidence, which shows that there was in fact a significant drop in the success rate and in the average awards—the two indicators relied on by Steinbach to shore up her 'watershed argument' ('Promises' 204–5, 212–13)—as early as 1850.

the most secret and sacred passages in her life',[33] and holding up an itchy palm for pecuniary compensation.

The 1869 Act, explicitly designed to make it easier for women to bring and win their breach-of-promise suits,[34] in fact had the opposite effect. Plaintiffs gained next to nothing. Because of the Act's requirement of corroboration, the testimony of witnesses or written evidence continued to be necessary to make out a case. At the same time, they lost a great deal. The Act ignored that 'a young woman, good-looking, and well-dressed, who sat below her counsel, *but whose mouth was shut*, had the opportunity of producing quite as great, if not a greater, effect'[35] than one who spoke up on her own behalf. After 1869 and the plaintiff's entrée into the witness box, defence counsel had every opportunity for dramatizing her non-conformity to true womanhood. Particularly where the plaintiff was lower class, which, as we have seen, a significant proportion of plaintiffs were in the high Victorian period, cross-examinations could be used to make the woman look ridiculous. The plaintiff in *Streather v Jacques*, for instance, came across as very foolish indeed when, on being asked if she was a staunch Protestant, she rejoined: 'No, I belong to the Church of England.'[36] Her solecism caused roars of laughter in court. Additionally, counsel for the defendant increasingly came to rely on structural, rather than merely personal arguments to discredit the plaintiff's claim to true womanhood. That is, they no longer confined themselves to demonstrating the plaintiff's non-conformity to the feminine ideal on a personal level, but began to deduce her non-conformity thereto from her status as a breach-of-promise plaintiff. In *Gorst v Hodgson*,[37] for instance, the defence advanced the structural argument that Miss Gorst's decision to bring a breach-of-promise action (instead of jumping at the defendant's offer to settle the matter privately—however inadequate that offer might have been[38]) established what sort of a woman she was.

The social environment of the high Victorian period only served to quicken the general perception of the unorthodoxy of the plaintiff's position and its irreconcilability with true womanhood, for, in the second half of the nineteenth century, 'the conflict over gender roles sharpened'.[39] The

---

[33] *Law Journal* (13 January 1877): 29–30, quoted in Steinbach, 'Promises' 247.

[34] Steinbach, 'Promises' 239–40.

[35] *Hansard*, vol 195 (28 April 1869) 1801 (per Mr Denman) (emphasis added).

[36] *The Times* 21 March 1870: 11.

[37] *Lancaster Gazette* 27 March 1841: 3.

[38] The defendant had offered £150 in private settlement. His annual income, however, came to four times that amount. Given that juries frequently awarded damages equal to the defendant's annual income, Miss Gorst might well have thought that she could do better than £150 in a breach-of-promise suit.

[39] Meyer 186.

high Victorian period marked the beginning of feminist efforts to widen women's sphere beyond the precincts of the home. The 1850s and succeeding decades were a time of agitation by feminists and their male supporters for women's higher education and suffrage and for a reform of the marriage laws. Sophia Jex-Blake mounted an attack on the male exclusivism of the medical schools, Emily Davies founded Girton College, and the likes of Barbara Leigh Smith and Caroline Norton clamoured for the vote and for a change in the law on married women's property, a mother's right to custody, and divorce. The consequence of this mounting pressure on separate spheres ideology was that the domestic ideal was sought to be inscribed with redoubled force. Women who, like breach-of-promise plaintiffs, ventured beyond the confines of the Victorian home now met with unprecedented angst and resistance.

Thus, in the high Victorian period, an un-camouflaged exposure of the breach-of-promise plaintiff's structural antithesis to the feminine ideal combined with a social climate inimical as never before to departures from true womanhood. The efforts at papering over the inherent inconsistency could not have been abandoned at a more inopportune social moment. The breach-of-promise plaintiff, who, in the first period, had successfully negotiated the public/private divide, in the second—on being exposed to the more hostile high Victorian climate without the protective armour of the strategies of containment—lost her hold on respectability. A comparison I rejected for the first period therefore becomes apropos with regard to the second. While the breach-of-promise plaintiff of the early nineteenth century had her closest status approximation in respectable 'border women' like female writers and scientists, the breach-of-promise plaintiff of the second half of the century is closely aligned with the fallen woman of the Victorian period, the actress, the compulsive liar, or even the prostitute.[40] In high Victorian times, to be guilty of such an 'offence to good taste'[41] as the bringing of a breach-of-promise suit was nearly as much a matter of social life and death as a literal fall from virtue. Just as a true woman would lay down her life in the preservation of her physical chastity, so she 'would rather die than [. . . face] all the glaring publicity'[42] and indignity of a breach-of-promise action. MacColla's 1879 description of breach

---

[40] The Victorian concept of fallenness extended beyond the woman who engaged in 'nonlegitimated, or unmarried, sex', Deborah Anna Logan, *Fallenness in Victorian Women's Writing: Marry, Stitch, Die, or Do Worse* (Columbia: University of Missouri Press, 1998) 16. It was a 'wide umbrella term,' signifying 'a complex of tabooed behaviors and degraded conditions', Amanda Anderson, *Tainted Souls and Painted Faces: The Rhetoric of Fallenness in Victorian Culture*, Reading Women Writing (Ithaca: Cornell University Press, 1993) 2. It included any women who were perceived as 'disturbingly "false" (painted, melodramatic, histrionic)' (Anderson 10), in particular actresses (ibid 58).

[41] 'The Action for Breach of Promise of Marriage.'

[42] Ibid.

of promise as the 'great social question'[43] powerfully insinuates a kinship with prostitution, a phenomenon the Victorians were wont to refer to euphemistically as the 'great social evil'.[44]

The vulgarization of the breach-of-promise suit is statistically measurable (see Figure 4.1). The marked rise in the number of plaintiffs in categories 1 and 2, which occurred during the high Victorian period, is matched by an equally striking decrease in the number of plaintiffs in categories 3 and up, those categories, in short, comprising women of the middle and upper classes. Thus, the incidence of category-4 plaintiffs dropped from 23.6 per cent (9 out of 38 cases) for the period before 1850 to a mere 5.5 per cent (7 out of 128 cases) for the period between 1850 and 1900. Category-3 women followed suit a little later. They began to turn their backs on breach of promise with the passage of the Evidence (Further) Amendment Act.[45]

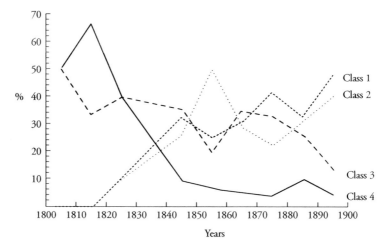

Figure 4.1 Percentage of Female Breach-of-Promise Plaintiffs According to Class, 1800–1900[46]

---

[43] For this term, see MacColla's dedication of his book to Farrer Herschell.

[44] Logan 82.

[45] There is no significant change in the incidence of class-3 plaintiffs for the periods before 1850 and between 1850 and 1900 (26.3 per cent (10 out of 38 cases) and 25.8 per cent (33 out of 128 cases) respectively). However, for the periods before 1869 and between 1869 and 1900, one observes a drop from 32.1 per cent (26 out of 81 cases) to 22.4 per cent (19 out of 85 cases).

[46] The table only covers classes 1–4. My sample disclosed too few breach-of-promise plaintiffs in class groups 5 and 6 to make any statistically meaningful claims as regards the upper echelons of society.

These statistics prove that in the high Victorian period, the breach-of-promise courtroom became a space that higher-class women tended to deny themselves.[47] Breach of promise assumed the character of 'a class action'[48] virtually unknown among the upper reaches of society. In practice no less than in prescription, true women shrank from the exposure the action entailed and the discredit of bringing it.[49]

The role of the breach-of-promise plaintiff, although originally scripted with the true woman in mind, now came to be seen as a sure means of proving the absence of true womanhood in those who chose to assume it. A breach-of-promise plaintiff, the *Law Times* thought, should be told that '[y]our presence here is proof positive that you had no true womanly feelings to be outraged...'[50]

In the high Victorian period, breach of promise became a self-stultifying procedure. When the abandonment of the strategies of containment opened up an unobstructed vista of the plaintiff's internally conflicted situation, her professions of virtue became, in the words of English philosopher John L Austin, 'infelicitous' utterances.[51] Her professions were infelicitous because they did not fit what Austin calls 'the total speech-act,'[52] ie the total situation, courtroom and all, in which they were spoken. The plaintiff, in invoking the nineteenth-century ideal of femininity by her tale of womanly worth and wounded affections, was perceived as engaging in an 'abuse'[53] of language, because what I term her structural position and what Austin would term her 'total situation'[54] belied her claim to the ideal. As a result, the breach-of-promise plaintiff of the high Victorian period met with distrust or downright incredulity. She was suspected of being 'a scheming, enterprising, and rather clever

---

[47] The statistical evidence also shows Frost's claim that 'in the nineteenth [century], breach of promise plaintiffs were most often lower middle-class and upper working-class women', (Frost, 'I Shall Not Sit Down and Crie' 225) to be too undifferentiated. There was in fact a significant downward shift in plaintiff composition that occurred *during* and not, as Frost suggests, prior to the nineteenth century.

[48] 'Breach of Promise' *The Times* 7 May 1879: 9 (per Mr Herschell).

[49] The high Victorian idea that it was somehow inappropriate for a respectable woman to litigate a broken engagement contains the seeds of a privatization of what Mary Wollstonecraft has called 'the wrongs of woman'. See Mary Wollstonecraft, *Maria, or The Wrongs of Woman,* 1798 (Mineola, NY: Dover Publications, 2005).

[50] *Law Times* 45 (5 September 1868): 340, quoted in Steinbach, 'Promises' 244.

[51] In the second of this series of lectures, originally presented at Harvard University in 1955, Austin deals with infelicities of language (occasions where the speech act is at least to some extent a failure). See John L Austin, *How to Do Things with Words* (Cambridge, MA: Harvard University Press, 1962) 12–24.

[52] Ibid, 52.

[53] Austin distinguishes three main types of infelicities: misinvocations, misexecutions, and abuses. He defines an abuse as the use of a procedure designed for persons having certain thoughts or feelings by persons who do not in fact have those thoughts or feelings (15–18).

[54] Austin 52.

woman',[55] incapable of true love, and quite ready 'to lie...about everything and everybody'.[56]

In view of the unmitigatedly negative picture entertained of breach-of-promise plaintiffs in the high Victorian period, it comes as no surprise that there were several attempts at reforming or even abolishing the cause of action between 1869 and 1900.[57] Since it was now thought that breach of promise could not, by definition, afford protection to the true woman, the action's idiosyncratic, non-contractual features came to be seen as fundamentally misconceived. Would-be reformers accordingly advocated a return to the strict law of contracts, by tightening up the evidentiary rules and restricting the measure of damages. In 1869, for instance, Mr Staveley Hill proposed that written evidence of the promise should be required,[58] and 10 years later, Farrer Hershell, MP for Durham, presented a resolution that called for the abolition of breach of promise except for restitution of pecuniary loss.[59] These proposals were not enacted into law. Only in 1879 was there any debate on the issue; subsequent bills had no discussion and were dropped after the first or second readings.[60] Nevertheless, the suspect high Victorian breach-of-promise plaintiff could not hope to rival the glittering successes of her early nineteenth-century predecessor. After 1850, the success rate of plaintiffs declined, and average awards in breach-of-promise actions sank to half their former level.[61]

II. *Smith v The Earl Ferrers*: 'this infamous attempt to forge and to fasten an engagement upon [...a noble individual]'[62]

If the high Victorians had been asked to substantiate their decidedly low opinion of breach-of-promise plaintiffs, they would probably have been unanimous in their selection of one real-life case in point. They should have cited Mary Elizabeth Smith as living proof of the aberration, degradation, and sinfulness they ascribed to that class of woman. *Smith v The Earl Ferrers* was a breach-of-promise

---

[55] 'The Action for Breach of Promise of Marriage.'

[56] *Pump Court* (March 1886): 113, quoted in Steinbach, 'Promises' 243.

[57] Between 1879 and 1890, bills for the abolition of the breach-of-promise suit were introduced on five occasions: in 1879 by Mr Hershell; in 1883 by Mr Caine; in 1884 by Colonel Makins; in 1888 and again in 1890 by Sir Roper Letherbridge (Steinbach, 'Promises' 241).

[58] *Hansard*, vol 195 (28 April 1869) 1807.

[59] MacColla 52–3. A limitation to actual out-of-pocket loss was also favoured by MacColla (61).

[60] Steinbach, 'Promises' 241, 271–2.

[61] Before 1850, average absolute damages for female plaintiffs stood at £454. For the period between 1850 and 1900, they came to £229.

[62] *Proceedings upon the Trial of the Action Brought by Mary Elizabeth Smith against the Right Hon Washington Sewallis Shirley Earl Ferrers for Breach of Promise of Marriage, before Mr Justice Wightman and a Special Jury on the 14th, 16th, 17th, and 18th of February 1846 in the Queen's Bench Westminster Hall* (London, 1846) 351.

case tried at the dawn of the high Victorian period, just before mid-century. It was brought by the 21-year-old daughter of a Warwickshire farmer in respect of a deep attachment that she claimed had taken up five years of her life. To all outward appearance, Mary Elizabeth Smith was perfect breach-of-promise material. She was young, untried, constant in her affections, and aspired to domestic bliss. She seemed to conform very closely to the accepted norms of true womanhood. But Mary Elizabeth Smith, unlike the vast majority of breach-of-promise plaintiffs, did not win her suit. Instead, after three and a half days of trial, her own counsel declared it to be 'due to the interests of truth and justice... to withdraw from the present contest'[63] and elected to be non-suited. Mary Elizabeth Smith was left to depart from court, 'unmasked' as but the hollow mockery of true womanhood: a pinchbeck imitation masquerading as true gold.

On Valentine's Day of 1846, appropriately, the Court of Queen's Bench sitting at Westminster heard the case of Mary Elizabeth Smith versus Washington Sewallis Shirley, the 9th Earl Ferrers, for a breach of promise of marriage. As the *News of the World* reported: 'Very great anxiety was manifested to hear this extraordinary case, and the Court was completely crammed.'[64] Over the course of the following week, public interest in the proceedings only continued to mount. On the second day of the trial, the court was even more crowded than on the first. By the fourth and final day, 'the interest... appeared... to have increased tenfold. The rush of the crowd at the doors was tremendous, and in a moment after they were thrown open every part of the court was filled...'.[65]

Smith v The Earl Ferrers was such a tremendous draw (the *Times* in fact compared its appeal to that of the Opera-house[66]), partly because the party constellation was atypical. As a farmer's daughter, Mary Elizabeth Smith was a member of the social stratum that, according to Frost, made up the bulk of breach-of-promise plaintiffs.[67] But she was suing a man who was further apart from her in class than the average defendant in a breach-of-promise action. Although it was quite common for plaintiffs to sue men socially superior to themselves,[68] it was something of a rarity for a member of the aristocracy to fill the defendant role.[69] Washington Shirley, however, the errant fiancé sued

---

[63] Ibid, 411.

[64] *News of the World* 22 February 1846: 2.

[65] *The Sun* 19 February 1846: 4.

[66] *The Times* 18 February 1846: 7.

[67] Frost, 'Promises Broken: Breach of Promise of Marriage in England and Wales 1753–1970' 107.

[68] In Steinbach's sample, plaintiffs sued their social superiors in 142 out of 182 cases ('Promises' 231).

[69] Out of my sample of 242 cases, only two featured a titled defendant. These two defendants, moreover, were far below the rank of earl. See *Hales v Guinness*, *Taunton Courier* 12 April 1905: 3; *The Times* 8 April 1905: 14 and *Fender v St. John-Mildmay*, *The Times* 11 April 1935: 4; 12 April 1935: 4; 13 April 1935: 4; 16 April 1935: 5.

in *Smith*, was that rare thing, an aristocratic defendant. To the audience in court, he was presented as 'a [young] Nobleman of very ancient family, and vast landed possessions in the counties of Leicester and Stafford, and some other of the midland counties'.[70] This description was hardly necessary, however, as the Earl, to his contemporaries at least, must have been a man who needed no introduction. His family could trace their history to the Norman Conquest and in the eighteenth and nineteenth centuries had won doubtful notoriety through a string of high-profile scandals: one earl was found to be of unsound mind and another, also 'of an ungovernable temper, at times almost amounting to insanity', not only justified his wife in obtaining an Act of Parliament for her separation from him (next to an impossibility in the eighteenth century, short of outrageous cruelty by the husband), but came to a premature end at Tyburn gallows, being hanged for the murder of his land steward. The defendant's immediate forbears, his father and grandfather, had scandalized the public by their decided *mésalliances*. Of the 8th Earl's second wife it was rumoured that she had previously been his mistress, and the defendant's father had married a servant girl who, until her sudden elevation to the peerage, had 'swept the walks in [...the family's] grounds at Himley'.[71] The product of this unequal union, the defendant had in fact only narrowly escaped the stain of illegitimacy, his mother being eight months pregnant when his father married her. Nobody with even the slightest interest in society news or gossip would have found it at all surprising that the 9th Earl Ferrers should now be the defendant in a breach-of-promise case. He was simply running true to family form.

Mary Elizabeth Smith, the girl who claimed the Earl had promised to make her his wife, was the eldest daughter of a numerous family of six children. Her father[72] was a tenant farmer in the Warwickshire village of Austrey. While the Smiths themselves were not wealthy, Mary was a little better connected on her

---

[70] *Proceedings upon the Trial of the Action Brought by Mary Elizabeth Smith* 2.

[71] See G E Cokayne, *The Complete Peerage of England, Scotland, Ireland, Great Britain, and the United Kingdom, Extant, Extinct, or Dormant*, Vicary Gibbs and H A Doubleday (eds), vol 5 (London: St. Catherine Press, 1926) 336.

[72] There is in fact an issue over whether Mr Smith was Mary Elizabeth's father or only her stepfather. A 1921 article in the *Weekly Dispatch* (included as part of the *Dispatch's* series on 'Real Crime and Mystery Stories') describes Mr Smith as Mary's stepfather (*Weekly Dispatch* 13 March 1921: 2). This corresponds with the *News of the World's* 1846 write-up of the trial (*News of the World* 22 February 1846: 2), on which the article in the *Dispatch* may have been based. All of the other contemporary sources, however, including the 412-page transcript of the in-court proceedings, describe Mr Smith as Mary's father. This leads one to conclude that Mr Smith's (possible) step-parent status was not adverted to at trial. The journalist who reported *Smith* for the *News of the World* either had some insider knowledge or was creating a journalistic canard. The divergence in the newspaper reports nicely highlights the unreliability and inconclusiveness of most historical sources. I am grateful to Arthur Drake for drawing my attention to the 1921 article and the question of Mary Elizabeth's exact relationship with Mr Smith.

mother's side of the family. Her maternal grandfather, a Joseph Erpe, owned the manor house, a handsome three-storey Georgian building, in the neighbouring village of Syerscote and claimed to be descended from the Curzons, the family of Lord Scarsdale.[73] In court, Mary was described as 'a young lady of considerable personal attractions, who had had an excellent education, and most of the accomplishments bestowed upon young ladies in this country...'.[74] While this was the standard claim of counsel in breach-of-promise actions (and therefore to be taken with a grain of salt), we know that she was in the first flush of youth, tall, with dark hair and a good complexion and that she had been to finishing school. A pattern young lady, it would seem, with charms quite sufficient, presumably, to capture the attention even of an earl.

1. Mary Smith's story

According to the story put forward by the Solicitor-General, Sir Fitzroy Kelly, who acted as counsel for Mary Smith, the breach of promise now being tried in February of 1846 had begun six and a half years before, in the autumn of 1839, when the defendant, then styled Viscount Tamworth, came to reside with his private tutor in Mary's home village of Austrey. No sooner had he arrived in Austrey, it was alleged, than he became fervently attached to Mr Smith's 14-year-old daughter. The Smiths, understandably alarmed at the attentions of one 'so immeasurably above their daughter in rank and station',[75] put an end to the budding romance by packing Mary off to school. She did not return to Austrey until after the future earl had left for the Continent.

The second (and decisive[76]) instalment in the story narrated by the Solicitor-General opened in late 1842. Washington Shirley was recalled from abroad to the bedside of the dying earl and, with his grandfather's death, became the 9th Earl Ferrers. According to the Solicitor-General, he lost no time in seeking out his Austrey sweetheart. Within a month of his return, he renewed the acquaintance, insisting at the same time that the romance, which quickly ripened into an engagement, be carried on surreptitiously. His precautions to this end were elaborate. He insisted that he should only come to Mary's house on condition that he could see her alone. His letters were written on scraps of paper, much crossed, and therefore barely legible. Nor did he ever send them through the

---

[73] This, incidentally, would have connected him with Earl Ferrers himself, whose father's cousin had married a Curzon (Cokayne 338).

[74] *Proceedings upon the Trial of the Action Brought by Mary Elizabeth Smith* 3.

[75] Ibid, 4.

[76] As the defendant was a minor in the first period of the alleged acquaintance, any promise of marriage made then would not have been binding upon him. In fact, a defence of infancy (in respect of any promises made before the defendant's coming of age in January of 1843) was pleaded.

post. He had them delivered through confidential servants. Unusual, too, was his mode of present making. All the 'presents'—dresses, jewellery, and books—had been bought by Mary herself (although they were represented by her as having been received from the Earl), on the understanding, so it was said, that the Earl would pay for them (this promise he had signally failed to keep, and Mary's father and grandfather had ended up having to foot the bills).[77] Despite the blatant eccentricity of the Earl's courting habits and despite never having met him, the Smiths were satisfied, 'from his renewing his attentions, that he was sincere in his attachment',[78] and in early 1844 preparations were made for an August wedding.[79] The bright vision of marrying their daughter off to an earl was destroyed, however, when the papers reported the marriage of Earl Ferrers, on 23 July 1844, to Augusta Annabella Chichester, the eldest daughter of the 4th Marquess of Donegall. Mary's hopes, in the words of the Solicitor-General, 'were forever blasted',[80] and her male relatives urged her to sue.

The Earl's immediate response to the suit (and one which he maintained consistently throughout) was that he hardly knew Smith, had never courted her, and that there was not a word of truth in the alleged engagement. Owing to a one and a half year hiatus between the bringing and the hearing of the action,[81] there was ample time for prejudicial gossip to build up. Rumours of Mary Smith's duplicity (and her evident talent for lying and forgery) were set afloat, and Mr Green, the Earl's attorney, went around vowing that he would not rest until he had got her into Warwick jail. When the case finally came on before Mr Justice Wightman and a special jury, the stakes were clearly higher than in most breach-of-promise suits. It was not just a matter of whether Mary Smith would receive adequate compensation for a broken heart. Rather, the point to be established at trial was whether she *had* a heart to match her exterior or

---

[77] This mode of gift giving was one point of attack upon the credibility of the plaintiff's story. Sir Frederick Thesiger, who conducted the case for Earl Ferrers, thought that 'in the history of an attachment of this kind, this is the very first time that any such course of *present making* has ever been adopted, even by the poorest and most destitute person'. See *Proceedings upon the Trial of the Action Brought by Mary Elizabeth Smith* 335 (emphasis in original).

[78] *Proceedings upon the Trial of the Action Brought by Mary Elizabeth Smith* 238.

[79] According to Mary Smith, the wedding was originally planned for May but, at the Earl's request, postponed twice.

[80] *The Times* 16 February 1846: 7.

[81] In November 1844, the case had to be removed from Warwickshire (the original venue) to London. As the defendant had principal residences in Stafford and Leicester (bordering on Warwickshire to the east and west) as well as powerful relatives in Warwickshire itself, it was feared that the plaintiff could not have a fair trial in her home county (*The Times* 23 November 1844: 6). The case stood for trial in London in November 1845, but was again postponed, owing to the pressure of business at Westminster (Mary Smith, *Statement* 27).

whether she was to leave court stripped of her outward guise of true woman-hood and 'stamped for ever with the deepest disgrace and ignominy'.[82]

Mary Smith's evidence in support of the engagement consisted of witnesses—her parents, her 13-year-old sister Ann, and a number of villagers, who claimed to have seen her and Ferrers walking together (though never very close and barely at all in the crucial second period of the claimed attachment)— and 12 incoherent, discursive, and ungrammatical love letters,[83] purportedly written by the Earl (and said by a number of witnesses to be in his handwrit-ing). One, dated February 1844, gives a taste of their characteristic blend of the poetical and the prosaic:

[D]earest; forget not you are the only hope of one to whom a palace would be but a desert, and England no home without you, far dearer to me than each earthly blessing, without which no one or any would be of value. Mary, you are all in all to me, take care of yourself, and mind when you return from walking you change your shoes.[84]

Nearly all of the letters expressed a desire to be united with 'Dearest Mary'[85] and marriage was continually spoken of.

At the conclusion of his speech, the Solicitor-General prepared the minds of the jury for what he knew was to come, namely 'the most extraordinary, and to me the most inconceivable defence that ... I ever met with ... in a court of justice':

Gentlemen, is not the charge upon the very statement of it something approach-ing almost to madness, for a young lady to sit down and forge, that is to imitate the handwriting of a gentleman, of a man, and that not to a signature or to two or three words, but to a long series of letters, of the number and of the length of those I have laid before you.[86]

The Solicitor-General was clearly implying that the outward semblance of the feminine ideal—'a young lady'—could not contain the inner corruption that was alleged; and that Mary Smith, a 21-year-old emblem of domesticity, could not be 'capable of the nearly six years plot that she is accused of'.[87]

---

[82] *Proceedings upon the Trial of the Action Brought by Mary Elizabeth Smith* 38.

[83] The Solicitor-General faulted their 'bad grammar, bad English, a total want of punctuation' and attributed these deficiencies to the Earl's imperfect education, 'below that of a well-educated charity boy at a national school' (*Proceedings upon the Trial of the Action Brought by Mary Elizabeth Smith* 37).

[84] *Proceedings upon the Trial of the Action Brought by Mary Elizabeth Smith* 279–80.

[85] Ibid, 279.

[86] Ibid, 29–30.

[87] Mary Smith, *Statement* 59.

2. Mary Smith's secret

When, on the third day, the Attorney-General, Sir Frederick Thesiger, addressed the jury on behalf of the defendant, 'the most breathless silence prevailed' in a court 'crowded to excess'.[88] The Attorney-General opened by promising his audience the revelation of a great secret:

I promise you, Gentlemen, that if you will but restrain your curiosity, I will explain every thing to your entire and perfect satisfaction. I will clear away every doubt and difficulty...[89]

The audience *had* to restrain their curiosity, for the Attorney-General did not reveal everything at once. Instead, he began by discrediting the evidence supporting the plaintiff's case. Only three creditable witnesses had spoken to the handwriting of the love letters, and these witnesses were not very familiar with the Earl's writing. What is more, the letters themselves were completely nonsensical. They purported to be written from places where the defendant never stayed and discussed family events on the wrong dates. They were peppered with imaginary people, got relations mixed up, and spoke of animals and things the Earl did not own. Whatever correct information they contained was either common knowledge in the county or could have been gleaned from newspaper reports. Counsel for Miss Smith had sought to attribute these inaccuracies to the defendant's 'extraordinary capricious character' and 'strangely wild imagination',[90] but the most straightforward explanation for them was that the letters had not been written by the Earl.[91]

What happened next was climactic. The Attorney-General dramatically produced four anonymous letters, the debris (luckily preserved) of a barrage of anonymous letters his client had apparently received over a number of years. Under his rigorous cross-examination, Mary Smith's mother had proved these letters to be in her daughter's handwriting.[92] These anonymous letters were entirely inconsistent with any idea of an engagement and indeed the whole tale set up in court. In a letter of 5 June 1843, Mary, who signs herself Marie, addresses the Earl as 'the one whom I cannot help but love, though apparently that one a stranger'. A

---

[88] *News of the World* 22 February 1846: 2, 3.

[89] *Proceedings upon the Trial of the Action Brought by Mary Elizabeth Smith* 298.

[90] Ibid, 9.

[91] Another very damning feature of the love letters was that they were variously signed 'W. Ferrers', 'Was. Ferrers', 'Ferrers', and 'Washington Ferrers', rather than merely 'Ferrers'. According to the evidence presented for the Earl, Ferrers always signed with his title of honour only (as is the practice of English noblemen). This evidence is borne out by the fact that private correspondence of the Earl's, dating from the period in question and held at the Warwickshire County Record Office (CR229/158), is invariably signed 'Ferrers'.

[92] The letters were later acknowledged by Mary Smith herself (Mary Smith, *Statement* 21).

little further on she deplores that it is 'in secret I write to you, in secret love you; would we could meet'. In another letter, written at a time when the projected marriage between Smith and Ferrers was supposedly imminent, she tells of her 'secret pleasure in writing to you, knowing you know not me, nor can even dream of the lady's name, or place of abode, that thus addresses you...'.[93]

The thunderclap conclusion had arrived, the secret was out, and the Attorney-General let his claim that the love letters must, like the anonymous letters, have been written by Mary Smith herself, 'artful and ingenious as she has shewn [sic] herself to be',[94] resound through the courtroom. The case was felt to be so conclusive against Mary Smith that her own counsel threw up his brief and Miss Smith upon the world.[95] The public, their curiosity sated, left the court somewhat stunned and subdued, apparently, by the glimpse they had had of what Henry James has called the 'most mysterious of mysteries, the mysteries which are at our own doors',[96] even in the supposed angel in the house. The *News of the World* reports that:

The Court, which had been excessively crowded during the trial, was quickly deserted after the results became known.[97]

* * *

A year on from the trial, Chief Justice Cockburn characterized *Smith v The Earl Ferrers* as 'one of the most remarkable cases ever tried in Westminster Hall since the erection of that venerable edifice' and predicted that it 'would be handed down to posterity as one of the *causes célèbres* of Europe'.[98] If, as has been claimed, a trial 'that threatens the reputation and position of a person of eminence is automatically a *cause célèbre*',[99] then *Smith*, which threatened the reputation, position, and purse of a member of the peerage, was a *cause célèbre* by virtue of its defendant alone. I would suggest, however, that *Smith v The Earl Ferrers* owed its celebrity status to a different and more important reason, and one quite unconnected with the eminence of its defendant. Like every breach-of-promise suit, *Smith v The Earl Ferrers* was a case in which the plaintiff's right

---

[93] *Proceedings upon the Trial of the Action Brought by Mary Elizabeth Smith* 352, 353, 357.

[94] Ibid, 358.

[95] Although, as a consequence of the non-suit, Ferrers did not have to pay any part of the £20,000 damages claimed by Smith, he was left with his costs, which came to the substantial amount of £2,124. This figure is taken from a balance sheet contained in a bundle of letters relating to the Earl's affairs and difficulties in 1847, held at the Warwickshire County Record Office (CR229/158).

[96] Report in Norman Page (ed), *Wilkie Collins: The Critical Heritage*, The Critical Heritage Series (London: Routledge, 1974) 122.

[97] *News of the World* 22 February 1846: 3.

[98] *Smith v Colton*, *The Times* 6 December 1847: 6.

[99] Giles Playfair, *Six Studies in Hypocrisy* (London: Secker & Warbury, 1969) 12.

to *her* position of eminence, the position of an ideal woman, was at stake. *Smith v The Earl Ferrers*, I would contend, owed its *cause célèbre* status first and foremost to the drama of what Lyn Pykett has called 'the improper feminine':[100] to the step-by-step unmasking of a woman 'who looks and (ostensibly) acts like the angel in the house [...and] commits crimes in order to obtain socially sanctioned goals such as a good marriage'.[101] This contention—that the public fascination with *Smith v The Earl Ferrers* was in large measure due to the transgressive femininity of its plaintiff—is borne out by the fact that when the axe came down on Mary Smith's true womanhood on the climactic third day of the trial, interest in the case appeared at once 'to have increased tenfold'.[102]

Lyn Pykett associates the spectacle of the improper feminine with the sensation novels of the 1860s, one of whose 'most sensational aspects... was the transgressive nature of their heroines'.[103] Sensation novels challenged preordained ideological certainties by locating crime at the heart of outwardly respectable womanhood. They habitually focused on the dark secrets of women, secrets, which usually consisted in a 'transgression of the bounds of the proper feminine'.[104] *Smith v The Earl Ferrers*, nineteenth-century court sensation, in fact presents striking similarities with sensation fiction, in terms both of plot (the story being told) and narrativity (the telling of the story).[105] These parallels are perhaps most striking with regard to one sensation novel that, like the *Smith* case, revolves around the titular secret of its (anti-)heroine.[106]

---

[100] Lyn Pykett, *The 'Improper Feminine': The Women's Sensation Novel and the New Woman Writing* (London: Routledge, 1992).

[101] Lyn Pykett, *The Sensation Novel from* The Woman in White *to* The Moonstone, Writers and Their Work (Plymouth: Northcote House, 1994) 50.

[102] *The Sun* 19 February 1846: 4.

[103] Pykett, *'The Improper Feminine'* 9.

[104] Ibid, 84.

[105] Although *Smith* predates the emergence of the sensation novel as a recognized sub-genre in the 1860s, its parallels with sensation fiction are hardly surprising, given the courtroom genesis of sensation fiction itself. Wilkie Collins, credited with being 'the grand inaugurator of the vogue' (Nicholas Rance, *Wilkie Collins and Other Sensation Novelists: Walking the Moral Hospital* (London: Macmillan, 1991) 1), was inspired by a court case (*R v Palmer*) to write *The Woman in White*. His biographer records how Collins was struck by the way each witness in the case rose to contribute a personal fragment to the chain of evidence and how he thought that a series of events in a novel would lend themselves to such an exposition. See Nuel Pharr Davis, *The Life of Wilkie Collins* (Urbana: University of Illinois Press, 1956) 211.

[106] I am not suggesting that Mary Elizabeth Braddon's 1862 novel *Lady Audley's Secret* was inspired by the *Smith* case, although there are some striking points of resemblance. In addition to the features that I discuss, there is the fact that Lady Audley's village is called Audley (Mary Smith's was called Austrey) and that Robert Audley's first brief as a barrister, after vanquishing Lady Audley, involves a breach-of-promise case. These similarities are probably merely accidental, however, as Braddon, according to Jennifer Carnell, was not in the habit of writing *romans à clef*. Jennifer Carnell, *The Literary Lives of M. E. Braddon: A Study of Her Life and Work* (Hastings: Sensation Press, 2000) 158.

Like Mary Elizabeth Braddon's *Lady Audley's Secret*, the Attorney-General's story in *Smith* is about solving the puzzle of a woman's secret identity. It is an instance of the unravelling and exposure of the epitome of conventional Victorian femininity from within, the making visible of the 'thrice guilty principal' inside the body that might have served as 'a model for a medieval saint'.[107] Both stories present an unsettling inversion of Victorian convention: the wicked criminal is female, the besieged victim is male. Thus, the Attorney-General, in a striking reproduction of the rhetoric conventionally put forward on behalf of female breach-of-promise plaintiffs, paints his client as the beleaguered virgin, who 'but for... various accidental circumstances... would have fallen a victim to the snares with which he was encompassed, his honour blasted, his reputation gone...'.[108] The solution to the mystery (pursued so avidly, in both instances, by a barrister) is arrived at through a voyeuristic, almost sexualized spectation of female interiority. Just as Robert Audley, entering through a 'secret passage' into her Ladyship's private chambers, is awakened to Lady Audley's true nature as 'a beautiful fiend'[109] by an inspired pre-Raphaelite portrait of her, so the Attorney-General achieves the 'penetration' of Mary Smith's secret through an 'inspection' of the anonymous letters, 'sibyls' books' these, revelatory of her sexually transgressive, sensuous inner nature.[110] In her letters, Mary Smith orientalizes herself, becomes Salomé-like. She is 'haughty and graceful as a Spaniard, tall and majestic as a Circassian, beautiful as an Italian...'.[111] This vaunting self-description aligns her with the dark-eyed maid or foreign lady of Victorian love songs who, as Tawa has noted, functioned as a counterpoint to idealized womanhood.[112] Mary Smith's letters strip her bare as the 'improper feminine... the domestic ideal's dangerous other'.[113]

The Attorney-General adopts a narrative style well suited to his sensational plot. He self-consciously casts himself as the author of the latest triple-decker, telling his audience that: 'I will not let you into the *third* volume before you have read the *first* and *second*.'[114] According to Wilkie Collins, sensational narrator par excellence, there are two main elements to the attractive telling of all stories: 'the interest of curiosity, and the excitement of surprise'.[115] The

[107] Mary Elizabeth Braddon, *Lady Audley's Secret*, Natalie M Houston (ed), 1862 (Peterborough; Ontario: Broadview Press, 2003) 270, 236–7; vol 2, chs 10, 7.

[108] *Proceedings upon the Trial of the Action Brought by Mary Elizabeth Smith* 351.

[109] Braddon, *Lady Audley's Secret* 104, 107; vol 1, ch 8.

[110] *Proceedings upon the Trial of the Action Brought by Mary Elizabeth Smith* 297, 307, 349.

[111] Ibid, 350.

[112] Tawa 341.

[113] Pykett, '*The Improper Feminine*' 24.

[114] *Proceedings upon the Trial of the Action Brought by Mary Elizabeth Smith* 328. Emphasis in original.

[115] Wilkie Collins, preface, *The Woman in White*, by Collins, 1860 (New York: Modern Library, 2002) xxv.

Attorney-General, by tantalizing his audience with the promised revelation of a great secret ('I will clear away every doubt and difficulty') at the same time as delaying its fulfilment ('restrain your curiosity'[116]), builds up suspense in a manner typical of sensation fiction. Like the sensational narrative, the Attorney-General invites his audience, 'not just to participate in a process of rational inquiry but to enjoy the thrill of being shocked by the unexpected'.[117]

It is to the sensationalism of its subject matter (the improper feminine) and to the sensational rendition of that subject matter, I would contend, that we must look to explain the *cause célèbre* status of *Smith v The Earl Ferrers* and the impact it had on the public perception of breach-of-promise plaintiffs. The overt sensationalism of the case may also account for why the Attorney-General's story was immediately believed by all and sundry. According to Ann Cvetkovich, '[s]ensationalism works by virtue of the link that is constructed between the concreteness of the "sensation-al" event and the tangibility of the "sensational" feelings it produces. Emotionally charged representations produce bodily responses that, because they are physically felt, seem to be natural and thus to confirm the...reality of the event. The tangibility...of feeling...is invested with significance as a sign of the...reality of the representation'.[118] Thus, audience psychology might explain why the Victorians were agreed that Smith had forged the love letters, when a more recent investigation has found the case 'hard to evaluate'.[119]

Smith v The Earl Ferrers both drew strength from and reinforced the growing recognition of the structural inconsistency, a recognition which, as we saw in section I of this chapter, led to the equation of breach-of-promise plaintiffs with fallen, morally corrupted womanhood—the 'improper feminine' in short. Mary Smith perfectly fitted the emergent image of the breach-of-promise plaintiff as dangerously double—scheming, subversive, and false—and her behaviour after the trial had ended only served to accentuate her moral irreconcilability with true womanhood.

For, like Lady Audley, Smith was an unrepentant criminal. Far from hanging her head in shame after the disastrous termination of the proceedings, she rushed into print with a spirited protest of her innocence of all charges (barring the anonymous letters, which she played down as 'the foolish frolic of a foolish girl'[120]). Smith's smartly written pamphlet was her desperate attempt,

---

[116] *Proceedings upon the Trial of the Action Brought by Mary Elizabeth Smith* 298.

[117] Ann Cvetkovich, *Mixed Feelings: Feminism, Mass Culture, and Victorian Sensationalism* (New Brunswick: Rutgers University Press, 1992) 72. The Attorney-General in fact prided himself on the speech he delivered in *Smith*, reminiscing in later life that 'I never did anything better than this while I was at the Bar' (J B Atlay, *The Victorian Chancellors*, vol 2 (London: Smith, 1908) 105). *The Sun* was less complimentary, describing the speech in fairly pejorative terms as 'long and laboured' (*The Sun* 19 February 1846: 4).

[118] Cvetkovich 23.

[119] Frost, *Promises Broken: Courtship, Class and Gender in Victorian England* 118.

[120] Mary Smith, *Statement* 24.

richly laced with rhetoric of victimization and an eagerness to defend herself and her family from calumny,[121] to get her version of events accepted by an English public, if not an English jury. It was received by that public as a defence that betrayed its own hypocrisy, a petition that blindly failed to recognize its own sinfulness even as it confessed it. While endeavouring to defend herself from the charge of falsehood, Smith allowed it to be seen that she had never had any regard for truth. The *Britannia* magazine, for instance, resented that Smith could not even imagine that there was any guilt in having written (and then tried to conceal) the anonymous letters, that she spoke 'of the tissue of deceit . . . as perfectly allowable'.[122] The same article castigated her vengeful desire (incantation-like, Smith's pamphlet had seemed to wish a horrible death on Ferrers—'the guilt . . . will . . . eat into his heart and darken his days—Ay! . . . will make the hour of death terrible indeed!'[123]). The pamphlet, for Smith, was, as the *Britannia* well put it, a leap 'out of the frying-pan into the fire'.[124]

Uncomfortable with the ever-increasing discrepancy between Smith's youth and innocent appearance and what was perceived as her hardened criminality, the public sought ways ideologically to contain and account for her. Like her fictional double, Lady Audley, whose secret ultimately turns out to be not so much bigamy as madness, Smith was 'explained' by being medicalized. To the public, she became a case of 'intellectual malformation':

For some criminals we should feel rather pity than anger, and sentence them to lunatic asylums rather than to severe punishment. This unfortunate girl appears to be afflicted with a propensity to falsehood almost beyond her power to repress.[125]

---

[121] The Attorney-General had accused Smith's mother and sister, both of whom testified on her behalf at the trial, of being implicated in the plot against Earl Ferrers.

[122] 'Miss Smith and Earl Ferrers' *Britannia* 7 November 1846: 729. Smith, whose faults did not include a want of daring, in fact brought a libel action against the publisher of the *Britannia* in respect of this very article, which recovered only contemptuous damages (*Smith v Colton, The Times* 6 December 1847: 6). This suggests that the views expressed in the *Britannia* review were representative of public opinion on the matter. Despite the public's condemnation of her, Smith seems to have had the support of her family throughout. Thus, the pamphlet was composed at her grandfather's, proofread by her father, and presumably published at the family's expense. Her father also testified on her behalf at the libel action, and it is likely that he footed that bill, too.

[123] Mary Smith, *Statement* 39. Ferrers in fact died quite young, at the age of 37, on 13 March 1859 (which, to nip any superstitious surmises in the bud, happens to have been a Sunday, rather than a Friday).

[124] 'Miss Smith and Earl Ferrers' 729.

[125] Ibid, 730. Helen Small has noted that the madwoman, in particular the love-mad woman, provided a 'controllable narrative framework' to contain the threat posed by female transgressiveness. See Helen Small, *Love's Madness: Medicine, the Novel, and Female Insanity 1800–1865* (Oxford: Clarendon Press, 1996) 112. The (predominantly female) condition of moral insanity, 'defined in terms of swerving from the precepts of domestic morality' (Rance 115), constituted a convenient diagnostic peg for women who did not conform to the moral tenets of the nineteenth-century feminine ideal.

The diagnosis given and the treatment suggested for Smith are in fact eerily reminiscent (or prophetic) of the label and regime applied to Braddon's protagonist. Of Lady Audley it is said:

She has the cunning of madness, with the prudence of intelligence. I will tell you what she is, Mr. Audley. She is dangerous!...I believe you could do no better service to society than [...to commit her to a *maison de santé*]; for...the woman...is [...not] to be trusted at large.[126]

Compare the following proposal for dealing with Mary Smith:

This unfortunate girl...is to be pitied; but, as she is dangerous, those who have the charge of her should be careful to keep her under some kind of restraint, and prevent her from exercising her mischievous propensities.[127]

Constructed in court as the subversive anti-heroine of sensation fiction, ideologically contained out of court as mad (and dangerous), there now remained but one 'career' for Mary Smith's future occupation as far as public opinion was concerned. She might assume the mantle of sensation novelist herself, joining the much decried band of (predominantly female) writers associated, like Smith, with 'a betrayal of...essential womanhood',[128] 'widespread corruption',[129] and generally all that was deemed wrong with Victorian society:

She might [...be] quite successful as a writer of vaudevilles. There could be no doubt of her genius for intrigue, or her ingenuity in composition....What an excellent author was spoiled in her through the foolish ambition of setting her mind on a coronet![130]

***

Of course, Mary Elizabeth Smith had never conformed to cultural expectations. And she was not about to start now. Once again disappointing Victorian ideology, she became no real-life Lady Audley, expiating her sin, 'buried alive'[131] in a *maison de santé*, and going to an early grave. Nor did she become a writer of sensation fiction (although she seems to have dabbled in poetry[132]). Instead,

---

[126]   Braddon, *Lady Audley's Secret* 385–6; vol 3, ch 5.

[127]   'Miss Smith and Earl Ferrers' 730. The article went on to hint that greater atrocities than the ones Smith had already committed could not be put past her: 'It is fortunate for her that the nature of her plot did not require more fatal instruments than those she has employed.'

[128]   Pykett, *'The Improper Feminine'* 48.

[129]   Quoted in Rance 10.

[130]   'Miss Smith and Earl Ferrers' 729.

[131]   Braddon, *Lady Audley's Secret* 387; vol 3, ch 6.

[132]   The William Salt Library in Stafford holds an original manuscript letter by Mary Elizabeth Smith to a Mr Thompson (presumably Mr Thompson of Tamworth, a bookseller also mentioned in the trial records) concerning the publication of a poem in several cantos (S.MS.478/19/71). This letter is not dated. It is likely, however, that it postdates the breach-of-promise trial, since it mentions

Mary Elizabeth Smith became just what the Victorian public had most wanted to disqualify her for: an emblem of domesticity, a wife and the mother of four children.

After the trial, Mary Elizabeth Smith seems to have retired to her grand-father's manor house at Syerscote. In an interesting parallel to *Lady Audley's Secret*, she speaks of herself at this time as being '*buried* in the perfect seclusion of this my place of refuge'.[133] This, however, is where any parallel with Braddon's novel breaks down. For, unlike Lady Audley, Mary Smith did not die in her retirement. Instead, she inherited the manor house in 1856[134] and on 3 November 1857 married Kosciusko Hyde Kent Newbolt, two years her senior, and apparently a gentleman of independent means.[135] After their marriage, the Newbolts quit Staffordshire, living in Bath and Weymouth for a time, before settling down in their domestic haven, with the pretty name of Alma Villa, in the Dorsetshire town of Radipole.[136] Mary Newbolt gave birth to four children, Annie, Marion, Rosa, and George (who went on to become a doctor). She died in 1909, a matron of the ripe age of 84, in Liverpool.[137]

In defiance of the future her culture had predicted for her, she had lived out the domestic ideal after all. She had proved herself resistant to ideological construction and containment. In ultimately flouting the 'sticky end' Victorian convention prescribed as the penalty for female transgressiveness, she evokes another of Braddon's sensational heroines. Like Aurora Floyd of Braddon's eponymous novel, Mary Elizabeth Smith lived to exult 'over the cradle of her first-born'.[138]

Ollivier's (the publishing company behind Mary's 1846 *Statement of Facts*) as having declined publication of the poem. Since Mary would probably not have approached Ollivier's for publication of the *Statement* if they had *previously* turned down her poetry, the letter was presumably written after 1846. I am indebted to Lee Wicks for drawing my attention to the manuscript letter.

[133] Mary Smith, *Statement* 65 (emphasis added).

[134] Joseph Erpe, who died on 13 March 1856, left Syerscote Manor to his granddaughters Mary Elizabeth and Ann Smith, subject to legacies and a £20,000 mortgage on the property. Mary (and her husband) and Ann sold the property to Samuel Pole Shaw in March 1858, thus realizing their inheritance (which came to £3,750 each). The deed relating to this sale is held at the Staffordshire Record Office (D984/1/1/13/50).

[135] The 1881 Census Return states no occupation for Kosciusko Newbolt, giving rise to the inference that he must have had some private income. It is possible, of course, that the Newbolts were living off Mary's inheritance. The relevant section of the 1881 Census Return can be seen at the National Archives, film 1341507, RG11, piece 2103, fol 52, p 5.

[136] The Newbolts sold Syerscote Manor in March 1858. My surmise as to their subsequent places of residence is based on the birthplaces of their four children as listed in the 1881 Census Return.

[137] See Register of Deaths in the District of Liverpool, Sub-District of Abercromby, 1909, held at the General Register Office. Mary Newbolt's death is entered under No 499.

[138] Mary Elizabeth Braddon, *Aurora Floyd,* 1863 (London: Virago Press, 1984) 384; ch 39.

III. 'To doubt all maids who of their virtue boast':[139] Feminine Perversion and the Dominance of Satire in High Victorian Breach-of-Promise Fiction

In this section, I should like to continue the investigation, begun in the corresponding section of the preceding chapter, of how the breach-of-promise theme was deployed in contemporary literature. I am especially interested in elucidating the ways in which the legal and contextual changes that we have registered for the high Victorian period were replicated in the high Victorian fictional text. I shall argue that the alterations in the legal and social context had their literary counterpart. They were reflected in a significant change (affecting the prevalent code of representation, the degree of plot-level integration of the breach-of-promise theme, and the dominant mode or tone) that can be observed in the creative rewritings of the breach-of-promise narrative that date from the high Victorian period.

In an exact parallel to the simultaneous increase in the number of actions and the amount of media attention, literary interest in breach of promise went up significantly in the high Victorian period. Little side references to breach-of-promise actions, no doubt frequently lost on the modern reader, are legion in post-1850 texts.[140] In addition to acquiring this subaltern existence in a fair proportion of high Victorian fiction, breach of promise, for the first time since making its entrée into literature in the 1830s, moves centre stage in a few of the high Victorian accounts.

In my analysis of high Victorian breach-of-promise fiction, I shall focus on what I think are the seven major or, at any rate, the seven most illuminating renditions of the theme. Whilst not all of these accounts use breach of promise as their main device of plot construction, each makes what I consider to be

---

[139] William Schwenck Gilbert, *The Palace of Truth, Original Plays* (London, 1876) 324.

[140] These little side references are so numerous that it is impossible to list them all. Among the canonical authors alone, Anthony Trollope refers to breach-of-promise actions in *The Last Chronicle of Barset*, which I include in my analysis, *The MacDermots of Ballycloran*, Robert Tracy (ed),1845 (Oxford: Oxford University Press, 1989), *The Small House at Allington*, and *The Eustace Diamonds*, Stephen Gill (ed), 1873 (London: Penguin, 1986). Dickens has references in *Bleak House*, 1853 (Oxford: Oxford University Press, 1998), which I will discuss, and in *Little Dorrit*. George Augustus Sala touches on breach of promise in his three-volume novel *The Seven Sons of Mammon* (London, 1864), as does George Meredith in *Diana of the Crossways,* 1897 (New York: Charles Scribner's Sons, 1916). References to breach of promise are not absent from the fiction of female novelists, either. Elizabeth Gaskell, for instance, mentions the action in *A Dark Night's Work* (Leipzig, 1863). As we have seen, breach-of-promise actions are also referred to in M E Braddon's *Lady Audley's Secret* (see n 106). This brief run-down is by no means exhaustive of the references to breach-of-promise actions that I came across in the course of my research, and no doubt many more references than the ones I have located could be found.

an important contribution to the high Victorian literary discourse on breach-of-promise actions and on the women bringing them. The earliest account on the list is a short story already familiar from my analysis of early nineteenth-century breach-of-promise fiction (the category to which it technically belongs), but which, as I said before, will not stay confined to the early period: Nathaniel Hawthorne's *Mrs. Bullfrog* (1840). The next depiction of breach of promise that I shall consider (and the first truly high Victorian one) is a three-volume novel with the telltale title *The Breach of Promise*, written by Harriet Maria Smythies (also known as Mrs Gordon) and published in 1845. In 1852, Charles Dickens, past master of the breach-of-promise theme, made comic use of Mr Guppy's (unfounded) fear of a breach-of-promise action in his otherwise sombre novel *Bleak House*.[141] Anthony Trollope bestowed an interesting passing glance on breach of promise in his 1867 novel *The Last Chronicle of Barset*. For the most hilarious romp through the breach-of-promise courtroom, we are indebted to Gilbert and Sullivan's one-act dramatic cantata *Trial by Jury*, which debuted at the Royalty Theatre in London on 25 March 1875.[142] Although not making breach of promise a central feature, T W Robertson's three-act comedy *Home* of 1879, in my opinion, constitutes another major contribution to the literary discourse on breach-of-promise actions in this period.[143] The final item to be included in my list is a collection of comic songs on the breach-of-promise theme, variously authored and dating from between 1863 and 1909. These songs, as we shall see, set up a counter-narrative to the hegemonic literary discourse on breach of promise.

1. The hegemonic literary discourse on breach of promise

Dominant culture, according to Michie, arrives at a self-definition 'by excluding or denying some of its elements'. The elements to be excluded or repressed do not stay the same, but 'vary as the culture changes shape under the pressure of economic, political, and social developments'.[144] In the early nineteenth century, as we have seen, strategies of containment had allowed breach-of-promise plaintiffs to be defined not against, but *within* the respectable or proper feminine and, by implication, *within* the dominant culture. As a consequence, breach-of-promise plaintiffs did not constitute an object of cultural exclusion and attack in the early period. In the high Victorian period, all this changed. An unveiling of the structural inconsistency also unmasked the breach-of-promise

---

[141] See above n 140.
[142] The seeds of *Trial by Jury* were actually sown significantly before 1875. The operetta was conceived from a one-page illustrated sketch by Gilbert published in *Fun* on 11 April 1868.
[143] T W Robertson, *Home* (London, 1879).
[144] Michie 1.

plaintiff as an insidious social transgressor. A definition of the breach-of-prom-ise plaintiff as within the dominant culture being thereby rendered impos-sible, the plaintiff herself became a liminal figure or, in Mary Douglas's more graphic term, a 'polluter'[145] that society positioned itself against and wished to exorcize. In the literature of the high Victorian period, the exorcism of the breach-of-promise plaintiff was sought to be accomplished through laughter: as a figure placed at the periphery (or even outside the pale) of the dominant social community, the laughed-at party in high Victorian breach-of-promise fiction usually turned out to be the breach-of-promise plaintiff herself.[146]

This switch in the butt of derogatory laughter—from the type-woman to the breach-of-promise plaintiff—is implied by a striking change in the dominant code of representation that distinguishes this second generation of breach-of-promise fiction. The early period, as will be remembered, was characterized by an externalization of the conflict, by the creation of a gap between type cast and role, and a concentration on the eccentric. In the second period, by contrast, as the *inherent* inconsistency is revealed, so the conflict is being set up *within* the character of the breach-of-promise plaintiff. Whereas the confrontation in the early period was between two integers, between outward deformity, on the one hand, and sublime role, on the other, there is now a greater effect of chiaroscuro, as light and darkness, the straight and the crooked, angelism and demonism are split between the outside and the inside of a single character. In the high Victorian period, the wall is at last put up within the character of the breach-of-promise plaintiff herself, and innocence becomes irrevoca-bly contaminated. The fictional breach-of-promise plaintiff of this period, a conventional angel figure to all outward appearance, is morally treacherous, a 'daughter of Eve and Evil'.[147] She is the moral, but not the physical opposite of the sublime ideal. In an application of Julia Kristeva's extended metaphor for the abject and perverted, she is 'immoral, sinister, scheming, . . . a terror that dissembles, a hatred that smiles, a passion that uses the body for barter instead of inflaming it, a debtor who sells you up, a friend who stabs you . . .'[148]

We have already seen that the last of the early texts, Nathaniel Hawthorne's *Mrs. Bullfrog*, can be read symbolically as presenting to view a moral, rather than a physical monstrosity, a woman whose angelic appearance is dangerously

[145] Douglas 139.
[146] According to Döring, 'the butt of . . . derogatory laughter invariably turns out to be a social group placed at the periphery of the joke-teller's community and often set up as a slightly strange ver-sion of the socially dominant identity'. See Tobias Döring, 'Freud about Laughter—Laughter about Freud' in Pfister 125.
[147] Smythies 2: 163.
[148] Kristeva 4.

unreflective of her twisted nature.[149] In the high Victorian accounts, this depiction of the breach-of-promise plaintiff as a moral mermaid, an ostensibly lovely woman with fishy extremities, becomes entirely unequivocal. Whereas in the early period, the role of breach-of-promise plaintiff was filled by characters about whom nature seemed to have hesitated before determining whether to make them men or women, in the high Victorian accounts, the whole setting of the palette changes. In the main, outward appearance is now unreliable as a guide to character. Fictional plaintiffs no longer have any giveaway masculine traits, either aesthetically or socially. Rather, these second-generation breach-of-promise plaintiffs display a quintessentially feminine affect and make the most of their womanhood. They constitute a particular manifestation of a new kind of female protagonist 'who appears increasingly at the center of [. . . high] Victorian novels: a woman who manages to think for herself not by breaking with her assigned stereotypic role, but by exaggerating that role in order to exploit it, turning its power back on the male establishment . . . '.[150] Thus, Lucilla Undermine, the plaintiff in Harriet Smythies's *Breach of Promise*, is a 'fine, blooming' young woman with 'a good head, very fine eyes', and 'fine hair.'[151] Realist author Anthony Trollope, never one to present his readers with descriptions of outlandishly beautiful girls, even if they are his avowed heroines, allows his would-be breach-of-promise plaintiff Madalina Demolines the signal distinction of being 'almost sufficiently good-looking to be justified in

[149] On this symbolic reading, Hawthorne's early Victorian text, as I mentioned before, points ahead to the English high Victorian accounts. What I find very interesting in this context is that Hawthorne describes Mrs Bullfrog as having 'personally appeared in court, and . . . borne energetic evidence to her lover's perfidy, and the strength of her blighted affections' (135) in her premarital breach-of-promise suit. This passage should probably not be read as suggesting that the soon-to-be Mrs Bullfrog actually took the witness stand. The United States lagged behind England in the matter of evidence law reform, and it was not until 1848—ie five years after the equivalent enactment in England and a full eight years after Hawthorne penned his short story—that Connecticut became the first American state to permit party testimony in any kind of civil action. See George Fisher, *Evidence*, 2nd edn (New York: Foundation Press, 2008) 351. It is more likely that Hawthorne (who, like his fellow countrymen, was probably quite *au fait* with the conduct of early nineteenth-century breach-of-promise litigation) meant no more than that the future Mrs Bullfrog attended court and sought to convince the jury of her suffering by the 'silent' means of wearing her bridal gown and/or clutching a handkerchief. Even on this reading, however, the passage implies that the strategies of containment (in particular the strategy of detachment) had already been abandoned in America when Hawthorne wrote the story in 1840. This would explain why a code of representation English writers only picked up on after mid-century (and the abandonment of the strategies in this country) was experimented with by an American writer significantly earlier. It also supports my premise that the abandonment of the strategies of containment, the revelation of the structural inconsistency, and the perception of the breach-of-promise plaintiff as internally split or, in a word, false were causally related.

[150] Richard Barickman, Susan MacDonald, and Myra Stark, *Corrupt Relations: Dickens, Thackeray, Trollope, Collins, and the Victorian Sexual System* (New York: Columbia University Press, 1982) 19–20. The authors cite Thackeray's Becky Sharp as an obvious example. Other examples could be found in 1860s sensation fiction.

[151] Smythies 1: 224.

considering herself to be a beauty'.[152] And Gilbert and Sullivan's appropriately named Angelina (*Trial by Jury*) is the very incarnation of outward angelic
loveliness. On her beauty, the judge's instantaneous verdict, wholeheartedly
endorsed by all the jurymen, is that: 'Oh, never, never, never, since I joined
the human race, Saw I so exquisitely fair a face.'[153] If these second-generation
breach-of-promise plaintiffs are betrayed by their physiognomy at all, it is not
because they are unfeminine, but because the marks of their femininity are
exaggerated.[154] Thus, Lucilla Undermine's looks and the adjectives 'blooming', 'buxom', and 'rosy'[155] that Smythies uses in describing her already hint at
her moral nature. Her voluptuousness and strong colouring evoke Victorian
descriptions of the prostitute. Charles Dickens, for instance, presents his prostitutes Nancy and Bet (mediated through the innocent gaze of Oliver Twist) as
two 'quite stout and hearty' girls with 'a great deal of colour in their faces'.[156]
Lucilla Undermine's excessive femininity is her liability, her cloven foot, and
she is well aware of it. Thus, she prepares for the arrival of Sir Felix Archer
(her intended victim), by 'shad[ing] her plump cheeks with a little softening blonde cap' and letting down the curtains of the morning-room so that
'through that... medium, a softening pallor would be given to her very blooming face'.[157] Having become, by those means, 'unusually attractive, *piquante*,
and even delicate',[158] she is virtually indistinguishable from the real thing. In
addition to Smythies's insinuated equation between Lucilla Undermine and the
prostitute,[159] we have, in the preparation scene just considered, the germs of
an equation between Lucilla Undermine and the actress, yet another Victorian
'fallen woman' figure.[160] Lucilla proves herself the consummate actress in the
third volume, when she succeeds in entrapping Sir Felix into giving the appearance (for he never meant to propose) of having offered and then withdrawn his
hand in marriage. Theatrically enacting the appropriate (gendered) responses,

---

[152] Trollope, *The Last Chronicle of Barset* 243; ch 24.

[153] Gilbert and Sullivan 11.

[154] This point is one made by Cvetkovich in respect of Lady Audley. Cvetkovich argues that the
pre-Raphaelite portrait shows Lady Audley as a beautiful fiend because it exaggerates her feminine
traits (49).

[155] Smythies 1: 224, 222, 179.

[156] Charles Dickens, *Oliver Twist,* 1838 (London: Collector's Library, 2003) 101; ch 9.

[157] Smythies 2: 159.

[158] Ibid, 2: 160 (emphasis in original).

[159] This equation is rendered more explicit in the novel's conclusion, which has Lucilla Undermine,
married to the Bill-Sikes-like Rory O'Brien ('a most passionate and violent brute'), 'weep forever the
luckless hour when she first commenced in folly and in sin an action for "BREACH OF PROMISE"'
(3: 310). Breach of promise is here portrayed as having an equally pernicious effect on a woman's life as
a literal fall. Like a fictional prostitute, who, as Lynda Nead has noted, was conventionally portrayed
as haunted by guilt and self-loathing (130), Lucilla Undermine ends in an emotional purgatory, her
self-perceived, irrevocable position as a social outcast her greatest punishment.

[160] See n 40.

she 'with a well-acted hysterical phrenzy' sinks down on the lawn '*as if* in a fainting fit', all the while taking care to time the pretended desertion to coincide with the presence of some elderly maidens, who might prove useful as sympathetic witnesses in court.[161] Trollope's Madalina Demolines is another such veritable actress. Indeed, to John Eames, her intended dupe, she is 'as good as a play'.[162] The fake, but convincing, reproduction of feminine affect by both Lucilla and Madalina reflects the high Victorian suspicion of deceptive representation in the breach-of-promise courtroom. Affect can be learned and acted. Interiority, clearly, is another issue. Unsurprisingly, given that this is the realm of counterfeit, where women are projects of self-fashioning and assimilate acculturated features to further their own ends, many of the male characters in these texts display a veritable obsession with truth, reality, and the natural in women. Thus, Frank Stanley, the hero of *The Breach of Promise*, hopes to marry a woman who combines 'Beauty, Genius, and, *rarer still* [to find]—*truth*... of heart'.[163] Bertie in *Home* makes a point of asking his sweetheart whether she loves him, not only 'devotedly' and 'fondly', but also 'truly'.[164] And Lucilla Temple, herself 'so true, so real', seems to her male contemplator, when compared with her namesake and dark double Lucilla Undermine, like 'moonlight' (the natural) after 'gas' (the unnatural and contrived).[165]

Just as the fictional breach-of-promise plaintiffs of this period are self-constructed rather than organic entities, elaborate simulacra of true womanhood, so the supposed 'engagements' frequently amount to no more than a bit of ingenious pretence. This is certainly the case in *The Breach of Promise*, where Lucilla Undermine accumulates valuable 'evidence' against the unsuspecting Sir Felix by luring him into more and more compromising situations on the pretext of acting as a mere go-between between him and his true love interest, Lucilla Temple. In a similar fashion (but not as successfully), Madalina Demolines seeks to fasten an engagement on Johnny Eames simply by throwing herself into his arms and then claiming that he has proposed to her: 'Twas the word that he said—this moment; before he pressed me to his heart.'[166] This contrasts with the first period, where the engagements, whatever may be said against them, were uniformly above board and irreproachable legally.[167] Even Mrs Bardell made an honest mistake. In *The Pickwick Papers*, as I suggested

---

[161] Smythies 3: 190, 193 (emphasis added).
[162] Trollope, *The Last Chronicle of Barset* 263; ch 25.
[163] Smythies 1: 95 (emphasis added).
[164] Robertson 6.
[165] Smythies 2: 35; 1: 226.
[166] Trollope, *The Last Chronicle of Barset* 855; ch 80.
[167] It will be remembered that Mrs Trapper had secured a watertight written contract, for instance.

earlier, it is the law and the legal profession that are the real villains of the piece, and Martha Bardell is not exempt from their villainy. In the fiction of the high Victorian period, by contrast, we find something akin to an unholy alliance between the plaintiff and the law. Lucilla Undermine, for instance, is an attorney's daughter and 'a sort of Queen among the legal coterie, in which she shone'.[168] Her relationship with the law is quasi-filial: 'I am a child of the law, bred in its bosom, reared in its arms;...Child of the law—the law shall protect and avenge me!'[169] In the second period, the law becomes the plaintiff's nurturer and helpmeet or even, as we shall see when we come to consider *Trial by Jury* later, her dupe.

The fictional breach-of-promise plaintiff of the second period then, brings together all the different aspects of that 'complex of tabooed behaviors and degraded conditions'[170] that the Victorians subsumed under the wide umbrella term of fallenness. She is variously or cumulatively figured as the prostitute, the actress, and the habitual liar, making up engagements that do not exist. What makes the threat of the breach-of-promise plaintiff a particularly insidious one is that inner fallenness and moral perversion coexist with all the outward trappings of true womanhood. The character is internally split, irredeemably heterogeneous. This internal heterogeneity, a co-presence of both the angelic and the fallen, is reflected in the names chosen for many of the fictional plaintiffs of this period. The names, like the plaintiffs' identity, split in two. The Christian name (Lucilla, Madalina, Pamela) usually, and rather obviously, evokes the feminine ideal. Of the name Lucilla, for instance, Sir Felix declares: 'the very name...brings an angel before my eyes',[171] and both Lucilla Undermine and her angelic counterpoint Lucilla Temple bear it. Madalina calls to mind the gushing maiden, and the name Pamela has, at least since Richardson's novel, been synonymous with the ideal in womanhood. In the plaintiff's surname, the 'ominous'[172] Undermine, the foreign Demolines, and the drossy Pinchbeck, however, the squid floats to the surface, and the character's shocking amorphousness is revealed.

The internalization of the inconsistency into the character of the breach-of-promise plaintiff, by splitting that character into external and internal polar opposites, is replicated in a greater plot-level integration of the breach-of-promise theme. In the second period, breach of promise is made vital and brought into the foreground. This is reflected in the fact that a greater proportion of the high Victorian accounts fall into category A ('in-court involvement') of my systematization. In *Trial by Jury*, for instance, the audience is taken into the breach-of-promise courtroom for a first-hand view of the hilarious world

---

[168] Smythies 1: 225.   [169] Ibid, 3: 210.   [170] Anderson 2.
[171] Smythies 2: 182.   [172] Ibid, 3: 66.

of sham, where actions give the lie to surface meaning. And Smythies is only held back from giving the in-court trial more extensive treatment because she fears to 'rush in like a fool where Dickens has deigned to tread'.[173] Even where, as in *Home*, breach of promise does not, at first, seem to be at the centre of the action, the 'trial' (which, in this instance, does not take place in court) in fact, as we shall see, constitutes the major device of plot construction in a narrative of feminine conversion.

These shifts in the dominant code of representation and the degree of plot-level integration are symptomatic of upheavals in perception and reveal the fault-lines of anxiety at work in the high Victorian period. They reflect the growing preoccupation with (and hostility to) the breach-of-promise action and the woman at its centre. That the action and in particular the plaintiff have become objects of cultural obloquy is demonstrated by *Bleak House*. *Bleak House* is to the second period what *Duberly Doubtington* is to the first. Both texts feature a plaintiff figure that is a true woman inside and out. But whereas Ethelinda St Simon Sapsago is a category-B ('out-of-court involvement') plaintiff, who brings and wins her action without being perceived as derogating from true womanhood, Dickens's Esther Summerson constitutes the first-ever category-D ('imputed involvement') plaintiff. She is a plaintiff figure courtesy only of the fact that another character in the novel, old limb of the law William Guppy, entertains the entirely unfounded fear that Esther might sue him for breach of promise of marriage. The split in *Bleak House* is not within Esther herself (she is entirely homogeneous, as indeed is her name, which implies at once Queen Esther, the biblical pillar of womanly virtue, and the summer sun), but between Esther and Guppy's perception of her. The comedy of the 'retraction scene',[174] where Guppy goes to inordinate lengths to ensure that Esther's 'release' of him is legally watertight, relies on the reader's presupposition that a woman like Esther would never so much as consider a breach-of-promise action and that Guppy might have been spared his Herculean exertions. The implication is clear: true womanhood and breach of promise no longer go together, and only a fool like Guppy could think of conjoining the two.

---

[173] Ibid, 3: 301. This is an obvious allusion to Dickens's famous trial scene in *Pickwick*.

[174] Ibid, 567–72; ch 38. Guppy proposes to Esther in chapter 9 of *Bleak House*. His offer is so steeped in law-talk (he 'file[s] a declaration' [138; ch 9] for her hand) that Esther barely understands him. This near-failure to communicate already highlights the inability of the two spheres, the legal and the proper feminine, to share common ground comfortably. Guppy's offer is, of course, refused, although he insists on keeping it open. After Esther's loss of looks, Guppy has a change of heart and is anxious to have it understood that there is no binding promise of marriage. In what I call the retraction scene, Guppy goes to inordinate lengths to ensure that Esther has released him fully and publicly (he even brings in Miss Jellyby as a witness), although a suit for breach of promise is clearly the last thing on Esther's mind.

If the new object of attack and, by implication, the new butt of derogatory laughter is the breach-of-promise plaintiff, the question arises as to the quality of the laughter directed at her. As we have seen, the high Victorian texts thrive on an exploitation of the structural inconsistency. They dramatize the lack of coherence between surface and depth, outside and inside, superficial attractiveness and deeper corruption. Any such discrepancy between profession and practice, between what a person claims and what her actions reveal her to be is the wellspring of satiric humour: the satirist is the 'scourge of appearances' and everything that is 'duplicitous or divided or at odds with one's protests [. . . is] deeply vulnerable to satire'.[175]

Gilbert and Sullivan's *Trial by Jury* contains the period's most luxuriant exploitation of the discontinuity between word and deed, and it is to this text that I should like to turn for an analysis of its satiric humour. The essence of Gilbertian humour has been described as 'satire on a very large scale'[176] and *Trial* as perhaps its finest manifestation.[177] Unfortunately, satire is not a well-defined category, and modern criticism offers surprisingly little to delineate a general design for it. Most critical approaches to satire are intuitive, 'a more sophisticated way of saying, "I know it when I see (or feel) it"'.[178] There is no agreement even on whether the term describes a genre (a specific literary form) or a mode (a tone or quality of art, which one may find in any form).[179] Most attempts at a definition do not seem to go beyond saying that satire is a species of humorous writing. For my analysis of the satiric quality of *Trial by Jury*, I shall be drawing on the theory of satire put forward by Alvin B Kernan in his pair of critical studies *The Cankered Muse* and *The Plot of Satire*.

According to Kernan, the immediate effect that strikes us when we pick up a satiric work is one of disorderly profusion: 'The scene of satire is . . . packed to the very point of bursting. The deformed faces of depravity, stupidity, greed, venality,

---

[175] Gerald L Bruns, 'Allegory and Satire: A Rhetorical Meditation' in *New Literary History* (1979) 127. Although satire is a horribly amorphous and protean term, there is widespread agreement that 'the satirist delights to make much of the discrepancy between profession and practice. Affectation and hypocrisy are ready topics for him at any time.' See Arthur Pollard, *Satire*, The Critical Idiom 7 (London: Methuen, 1970) 12.

[176] Andrew Goodman, *Gilbert and Sullivan at Law* (Rutherford: Fairleigh Dickinson University Press; London: Associated University Presses, 1983) 169.

[177] David Eden, in his chapter on Gilbert's satire, describes *Trial by Jury* as 'a masterpiece, arguably the finest work of Gilbert and Sullivan'. See David Eden, *Gilbert and Sullivan: The Creative Conflict* (Cranbury: Associated University Presses, 1986) 143.

[178] See Peter M Briggs, 'Notes Toward a Teachable Definition of Satire' (1979) 5(3) *Eighteenth-Century Life* 28.

[179] See Northrop Frye, *Anatomy of Criticism* (Princeton: Princeton University Press, 1957) 223.

ignorance, and maliciousness group closely together for a moment . . .'[180] *Trial by Jury* opens on just such a scene of thronging confusion:

> Hark, the hour of ten is sounding:
> Hearts with anxious fears are bounding,
> Hall of Justice crowds surrounding,
> > Breathing hope and fear—[181]

A heterogeneous jumble greets the eye: the stern agents of the law, a judge, barristers, attorneys, and jurymen, a Stentorian-voiced usher vainly clamouring for '*Silence in Court!*',[182] bridesmaids strewing roses, and a bride with orange blossoms in her hair are all indiscriminately commingled together. The publicity of the scene is intense and oppressive, only stressing the very out-of-place-ness of some of the elements at work. There is an overwhelming sense of a violation of the boundaries between private sanctity and public exposure. The bride in her white dress, with her retinue of bridesmaids, so obviously pertains to the realm of the sacred and the church, yet we see her hawking herself up and down in front of a lecherous judge and jury, whose 'compassion' is only a hair's breadth away from patronage and, with that, an assumed right of access:

JUDGE (*to* JURY). How say you? Is she not designed for capture?

FOREMAN (*after consulting with the* JURY). We've but one word,

   my lord, and that is—Rapture.

PLAINTIFF (*curtseying*). Your kindness, gentlemen, quite overpowers!

JURY. We love you fondly and would make you ours![183]

The courtroom is turned into a stage, where the plaintiff, Angelina, in what amounts to a blatant mockery of the domestic ideal her name implies, exhibits herself in attitudes most likely to attract. Just as her wedding clothes function both as erotic traces of femininity and as the costumes of an actress, she differs not in kind, but only in degree from the more obviously sexually available performers of brothel and stage. Both kinds of performance serve as a showcase for female charms that might subsequently be available for a price. Angelina's alluring, siren-like exterior already puts us on the alert as to the values that lie beneath, values that Angelina is actively trying to conceal. For, in a manifestation of another of the tendencies that Kernan has identified as typical of satire,

---

[180] Alvin B Kernan, *The Cankered Muse: Satire of the English Renaissance* (rpt edn) Yale Studies in English 142 (Hamden: Archon Books, 1976) 7. Kernan calls this the mob tendency of satire. See Alvin B Kernan, *The Plot of Satire* (New Haven: Yale University Press, 1965) 65–80.

[181] Gilbert and Sullivan 3.

[182] Ibid.

[183] Ibid, 11.

Angelina tries to magnify herself through the assumption of a mask:[184] rhetoric ('a girl confiding'[185]), feminine gesturing (curtseying, sobbing, reeling as if about to faint), and evocative clothing (bridal attire) are all objective things seeking to substitute for subjective truth. They drive a wedge between appearance and reality and open up a spark-gap for the intervention of irony, Kernan's 'master trope'[186] of satire. The scenic irony in *Trial by Jury* is constructed out of what Angelina does not say, but what the stage business Gilbert has her enact says in spite of her. The stage instructions open up a textual space that may be read against the seemingly hegemonic surface. By offering Angelina's professions and the stage instructions for side-by-side inspection, Gilbert manages to convey a simultaneous double image and in so doing catches the pretence that reveals itself as sham. All of Angelina's professed feminine virtues are shown to be hollow and vicious: passivity is really wiliness, domesticity the most glaring publicity, passionlessness mercenariness, and emotionality cloying hyperbole. Thus, Angelina's affections are anything but fixed and unchangeable. She shifts them between nearly all the males present in the course of a one-act cantata, traversing, with the greatest ease, the romantic trajectory of Edwin-judge-counsel-juror-judge-Edwin-judge by variously reclining on or clinging to these characters. When she sings of Edwin:

> I love him—I love him—with fervour unceasing
> I worship and madly adore;
>
> My blind adoration is always increasing,
> My loss I shall ever deplore . . . [187]

although we, the audience, know that she has a love note from the judge tucked away in her bosom all the while, the untruth of the utterance is brought naked before our eyes, and Angelina stands condemned by the very standards she professes. She is simply lying. It is all about money (after all, her declaration of 'love' for Edwin is part of her address to the jury on damages), and her heart has nothing to do with the matter. Gilbert leads us to judgement by inference from the juxtaposition of stage business and self-profession, forcing us 'to enter into the satire in a much more intimate way than if we had simply been *told* something . . . and hence in a sense [forcing us to become] satirists ourselves'.[188]

---

[184] Kernan calls this the magnifying tendency, the tendency of vice and dullness to create grand and inflated images of themselves. See Kernan, *The Plot of Satire* 36–50.

[185] Gilbert and Sullivan 12.

[186] Kernan, *The Plot of Satire* 90.

[187] Gilbert and Sullivan 16.

[188] James W Nichols, *Insinuation: The Tactics of English Satire* (The Hague: Mouton, 1971) 14 (emphasis in original).

Drawn into the satiric coterie through Gilbert's art of insinuation, we fully appreciate the artificiality of his hard-headed little gold-digger and experience at first-hand what Kernan has called the 'diminishing tendency' of satire, the carrying of 'all that was meaningful and valuable to the lowest levels of being'.[189] We are, quite literally, made eyewitnesses to the substitution of drossy gold for love and of acting for honesty and virtue.

According to Kernan, a typical satiric plot displays not a change or development, but stasis, a 'mere intensification of the unpleasant situation with which the satire opens'.[190] In other words, 'satire resists or even excludes closure'.[191] The conclusion of Gilbert's operetta consists in a parodic re-enactment of the *deus ex machina* that conventionally winds up melodrama. The judge, finally despairing of finding a legal solution to his perplexing case, declares:

> All the legal furies seize you!
>
> No proposal seems to please you,
>
> I can't stop up here all day,
>
> I must shortly go away.
>
> Barristers, and you, attorneys,
>
> Set out on your homeward journeys;
>
> Gentle, simple-minded Usher,
>
> Get you, if you like, to Russ*her*;
>
> Put your briefs upon the shelf,
>
> I will marry her myself![192]

With the union between Angelina and the judge the operetta closes emphatically, but it is precisely in so closing that, paradoxically, it remains open. This is because the parodic closure also creates a typical lack of satiric closure. Gilbert's ending elides the wholesale purgation or catharsis whereby at the climactic end of melodrama the villain is thrown out in a circle of dying stage fire. At the end of *Trial by Jury*, there is no 'hiss the villain(ess)', but Angelina triumphant: in her marriage to the judge, the fallen angel is afforded the ultimate protection and reward, underscoring the inability of the law to guarantee the sanctity of the domestic hearth against the insidious intrusion. The operetta thus closes,

189   Kernan, *The Plot of Satire* 53.

190   Kernan, *The Cankered Muse* 31.

191   Dustin Griffin, 'Satiric Closure' (1985) 18 *Genre* 175.

192   Gilbert and Sullivan 17 (emphasis in original). One of the breach-of-promise songs, *His Lordship Winked at the Counsel, or, the Breach of Promise Case*, words by George Dance, music by Peter Conroy (London, 1887), also marries the plaintiff off to the judge. The song is rather reminiscent of *Trial by Jury*, with the one difference that in the song the judge turns out to be the one who has broken the promise.

its moral vision clear, but the audience's confidence in the triumph of good over evil manifestly shaken.

And such, precisely, is Gilbert's intent. Gilbert, like all satirists, wants 'not to resolve a problem, . . . but to pose a problem, to open an issue, to vex . . . '.[193] The satiric laughter he seeks to evoke in *Trial by Jury* is actuated, I would contend, by immediate reformist impulses.[194] Although he wants his audience to laugh, he wants their laughter to express some serious concern. The laughter he seeks to elicit is no longer the jovial and diffuse laughter associated with the grotesque. Rather, it is a laughter of heightened anxiety, a laughing with a purpose, a resolution. The satiric laughter of the high Victorian period does not just hope to debunk and represent. It wants to be performatively efficacious. It wants to persuade its audience to accept and act on the Victorian ideology that a woman's place is in the home (and not the courtroom) and that her highest duty is to truly embody (and not merely to pay lip-service to) the domestic virtues.

If *Bleak House* and *Trial by Jury* formulate the performative (in the form of encomium and satire respectively[195]), the performative is carried out in *Home*, where Pamela Pinchbeck acts as Dickens and Gilbert (and Victorian society) would have her and every woman act: she says no to breach of promise and gets her reward. Robertson's three-act comedy recounts a narrative of feminine conversion. Pamela Pinchbeck starts out as the opposite of the domestic ideal. A double-barrelled widow, she is well on her way to ensnaring the elderly Mr Dorrison into what, on her side, would clearly amount to a mercenary marriage when the play begins. The comedy's plot revolves around a ruse Dorrison's adult son Alfred devises to open his father's eyes to Mrs Pinchbeck's true mettle. Fighting her 'with her own weapons, fraud, finesse, artifice, deception, and dissimulation',[196] he passes himself off as a German count to dazzle Mrs Pinchbeck with the prospect of an even more

---

[193] Griffin 188. Gilbert's biographers Sidney Dark and Rowland Grey have noted that Gilbert 'was obsessed by the importance of being earnest. He wanted to preach.' Quoted in Leonard R N Ashley, 'Gilbert and Melodrama' in *Gilbert and Sullivan: Papers Presented at the International Conference Held at the University of Kansas in May 1970*, James Helyar (ed) (Lawrence, KS: University of Kansas Libraries, 1971) 4.

[194] The purpose of satire (moral correction) is one of its distinguishing marks. According to Northrop Frye, the 'chief distinction between irony and satire is that satire is militant irony'. See Frye 223. See also Gilbert Highet, *The Anatomy of Satire* (Princeton: Princeton University Press, 1962) 156.

[195] According to Hodgart, the opposite of satire is the encomium, the formal work in praise of women: 'it sets out to praise the ideal woman, but in fact prescribes how women, in men's opinion, ought to behave'. See Matthew Hodgart, *Satire*, World University Library (New York: McGraw-Hill, 1969) 80. It is very fitting that Dickens's story of Esther, an encomium on female docility and excellence duly rewarded in the end, falls into this second period, otherwise distinguished for its satiric treatment of breach-of-promise plaintiffs.

[196] Robertson 21.

brilliant alliance. The ruse succeeds, but in the process Mrs Pinchbeck also recovers 'her native nobility of character' through love.[197] In the words of Lyn Pykett, Mrs Pinchbeck is 'recuperated for True Womanhood through the birth of proper feminine feeling',[198] the outward manifestation of which is her rejection of breach of promise. In the play's functional equivalent of a breach-of-promise trial, the out-of-court settlement of the proposed action, Pamela Pinchbeck recovers her lost virtue, wins everyone's respect, and earns herself the epithet of 'real woman'[199] by tearing up the tendered cheque and dramatically turning her back on breach of promise. Her rejection of breach of promise functions as an epiphany that reveals her true woman's heart: 'I did not...know you,' Alfred declares, 'I [now] recognise in you not only a good woman, but a noble heart.'[200] Issues of morality and breach of promise here mirror each other, functioning as one another's metaphors. In *Home*, to bring or not to bring an action for breach of promise has become the touchstone of true womanhood.

2. A counter-discourse: breach-of-promise songs and the defence of the vulgar

The texts I have been considering thus far constitute the master narrative on breach of promise in the high Victorian period. This hegemonic and, as we have seen, unmitigatedly critical discourse was one 'fed', as it were, by the middling ranks: it was a fictional narrative, written by middle-class authors, addressed to a predominantly middle-class audience, and inscribed with what was, ultimately, very much a middle-class ideal.[201] As an essentially middle-class discourse, it had no notion of the needs and problems of the working-class women, who, as we saw in section I, actually made up the bulk of real-life plaintiffs in the high Victorian period. This dominant discourse has accordingly been labelled a 'skewed version of breach of promise... that most middle-class readers probably never went beyond'.[202] While it is true that the hegemonic middle-class discourse painted a one-sided picture, it does not follow that it stood entirely unopposed. Just as Lynda Nead has noted the emergence of two

---

[197] Ibid, 39.
[198] Pykett, '*The Improper Feminine*' 163.
[199] Robertson 39.
[200] Ibid.
[201] Anna Clark has stressed that 'the image of the delicate wife sheltering at home ... was always an ideal rather than a reality for working people...'. See Anna Clark, *The Struggle for the Breeches: Gender and the Making of the British Working Class*, Studies on the History of Society and Culture 23 (Berkeley: University of California Press, 1995) 231.
[202] Frost, *Promises Broken: Courtship, Class, and Gender in Victorian England* 8. Frost does not mention breach-of-promise songs.

contrasting images of the prostitute (the prostitute as a figure of contagion to be feared and controlled versus the prostitute as a suffering figure, a passive victim of social circumstances[203]), so I observe a fissuring in the representation of the breach-of-promise plaintiff. High Victorian literature was not, in fact, unanimous in its vilification of the suit and of the women making use of it. During the declining decades of the nineteenth century, comic songs on the breach-of-promise theme, addressed to a more working-class audience, which would have been less invested in the middle-class ideal, began to set up a counter-narrative on breach of promise that went some way towards redressing the representational (im)balance.

These songs, productions of widely differing poetical merit, frequently written in dialect and set to simple melodies that make but modest demands on the singer and accompanist, by and large sound a plea for breach of promise.[204] Unlike the hegemonic middle-class discourse, which viewed breach of promise from the high standpoint of feminine delicacy and disinterestedness, the songs do not lose sight of the fact that the law is not only for the refined upper ten thousand but also for the (less particular) masses.[205] In what amounts to an explicitly class-based argument, they stress that it is not the entire female population that can lay claim to (or afford) the niceness of true womanly feeling displayed by an Esther Summerson and scorn a legal remedy against a faithless lover. The songs expose the complexities of the breach-of-promise question, which are entirely absent from the hegemonic narrative. While implicitly acknowledging that breach-of-promise plaintiffs are not the most genteel members of their sex, the songs draw attention to the fact that the consequences of a broken

---

[203] Nead 106. Nead goes on to examine the ways in which these two images were circulated in chapters 4 and 5 of her book.

[204] The breach-of-promise songs do not tell a completely uniform story either. *I Went Like This to the Lady*, words and music by E W Rogers (London, 1895), for instance, chimes in with the dominant satiric representation of the false breach-of-promise plaintiff. This lady has a face that 'made my heart madly, and my head seem'd to be in a whirl'. Yet it turns out:

That a set of false grinders she sported,
And the gold of her tresses was dye.
I wrote saying, 'Girl, you are full of deceit—
From this day all's over, no more we will meet…'

Like Angelina, 'this sweet-tempered miss' gets around the jury and recovers £1,000, which happens to be all the pitiable suitor has in the bank. By and large, however, the songs are overwhelmingly supportive of breach-of-promise plaintiffs. Of the 23 songs I examined, only three expressed any plaintiff-directed criticism.

[205] A similar argument was advanced in journalistic discourse. *The Times*, for instance, published an article exhorting the middle classes and their betters not to impose their 'high poetic standards' on those who 'have not the leisure to cultivate such tastes' ('Mr Herschell's Bill', *The Times* 14 February 1879: 10). The debates pro and contra the breach-of-promise action in legal and social (rather than literary) discourse are documented in Frost, *Promises Broken: Courtship, Class, and Gender in Victorian England* 141–71. See also Steinbach, 'Promises' 241–89.

engagement can in fact be serious and that they tend to be unevenly distributed between the woman and the man. Unlike men, these songs argue, women have a great deal to lose when a romantic relationship fails.

The plaintiffs featured in these songs are economically and sexually vulnerable, but also plucky working girls preyed on by (at best) fickle or (worse) downright opportunistic men. In many of the songs, the girl has given the best years of her life to a man who ultimately deserts her. *They Walked for Miles and Miles*,[206] for instance, stresses the length of a typical working-class courtship:

> They walked for miles and miles and miles,
>
> And talked for hours and hours;
>
> They billed and cooed for days and days,
>
> For lovers have peculiar ways!
>
> They met for weeks and weeks and weeks;
>
> For months and months he'd call;
>
> He courted her for years and years,
>
> Then jilted her after all!

Similarly, in *You'll Hear from My Solicitors*[207] the length of the engagement that is broken off is treated as a serious matter and a legitimate cause for grievance: 'Sal's eyes began to fill with tears; She said, "What! after seven years?"' Songs like these make the point that a Victorian woman's chances on the marriage market declined with age (and a previous attachment), whereas a man's, if anything, increased.[208] Since working-class courtships tended to be longer than middle-class ones,[209] working women were disproportionately vulnerable to breaches and liable to suffer from them far more than their middle- and upper-class sisters.

In addition to underscoring the length of working-class engagements, the songs stress the very real losses, financial or otherwise, which might be incurred by women in the twilight state between starting to go out and getting married. In

---

[206] *They Walked for Miles and Miles*, words by John P Harrington, music by George Le Brunn (London: Francis, Day, and Hunter, 1904).

[207] *You'll Hear from My Solicitors*, words and music by Frank Leo (London: Francis, Day, and Hunter, 1909).

[208] This is pointed out by virtually all historians of the nineteenth century. Frost, for instance, claims that 'men had a wider choice of a spouse and were considered marriageable until an older age'. See Frost, *Promises Broken: Courtship, Class, and Gender in Victorian England* 67.

[209] The working classes aspired to the middle-class ideal without having the financial resources to make the process easy. Although working couples became engaged early, they would frequently have to put off marriage until they could afford to support a family. The resultant lengthy engagements made working-class women particularly vulnerable to breaches. See Frost, *Promises Broken: Courtship, Class, and Gender in Victorian England* 79.

John James Murphy,[210] for instance, the titular Murphy looks upon his relationship with Molly McCue as nothing more than a free-of-charge boarding arrangement:

> Now this Murphy's a flat-footed p'liceman,
>> And this girl used to be on his bate –
> Sure yez all know what divels the coppers
>> Are for rabbit pie, beer, and cowld mate –
> I suppose she gave him many a supper,
>> And she'd think that he'd make a fine hub,
> And while she thought of coortin' and kissin' and love,
>> He was thinking of nothing but grub.

The charge that men might abuse their professed sweethearts as providers, so forcibly made in *John James Murphy*, is reiterated in many of the breach-of-promise songs. In one, sung in a particularly thick Cockney accent, the cheated woman recounts how 'Arry' borrowed five pounds and then used the money to marry another girl.[211] More frequent still are indictments of men who obtain not merely culinary or monetary, but sexual favours. In the first stanza of *A Simple Maiden*,[212] for instance, a city slicker, about to visit a supposedly simple country cousin, relishes the prospect of enjoying a kiss and a squeeze, all at absolutely no cost to himself. We rejoice when the damsel turns out to be one too many for him by bringing a breach-of-promise action. Virtually all of the songs touch on the physical aspects of love. Some—like *The Cuckoo Went 'Cuckoo!'*—do so in fairly decorous language:

> Oh! the moments there were blissful, for the young man he got 'kiss-ful',
>> And the maiden never tried to make him halt;
> Well, you chaps know how men do it, for I guess you've all been thro' it,
>> If you haven't,—well, I'll bet, it's not *your* fault![213]

Most songs, however, exhibit greater vulgarity and coarseness in describing love's physicality. Dialect terms for courting and kissing, such as 'spooning' and 'mashing', abound.[214] Most damning of all, a number of songs, such as

---

[210] *John James Murphy*, words and music by Felix McGlennon (London, 1898).
[211] *Ere's Yer Fine Water-Creases!*, words by John P Harrington, music by Orlando Powell (London: Francis, Day, and Hunter, 1907).
[212] *A Simple Maiden*, words and music by Walter A de Frece (London, 1892).
[213] *The Cuckoo Went 'Cuckoo!'*, words by John P Harrington, music by Orlando Powell (London: Francis, Day, and Hunter, 1908) (emphasis in original).
[214] Examples include: *The Giddy Old Owl*, words by Fred Bowyer, music by Dave Braham (London, 1887) and *The Girl Who Sloshed the Lather*, words by John P Harrington, music by Orlando Powell (London, 1894).

She Went Right Past Her Junction,[215] contain thinly veiled allusions to a fall under promise of marriage: 'Talked about Romano's, and sultanas, and bananas/Can you wonder that the poor girl fell—in love.' In fact, pre-marital intercourse (to test fertility) was common among some sections of the working classes throughout the nineteenth century, but it was usually taken for granted that marriage would ensue if the woman got pregnant.[216] Where working-class women were 'let down' by the men they had expected to marry, they found themselves in an economically precarious state, especially after the New Poor Law of 1834, which until 1844 made mothers solely responsible for the maintenance of illegitimate children.[217]

In the songs, tangible losses on the woman's side are usually compounded by caddish behaviour on the man's. In *The Girl Who Sloshed the Lather*, for instance, a female barber becomes 'perfect spoons' with a gay lothario, not knowing that he already has a wife sitting at home. Songs like this one point to the usefulness of breach of promise as a deterrent against male irresponsibility. Men, the songs suggest, enter into engagements lightly[218] or, which is worse, without any intention of honouring their promises at all. The prospect of having to pay damages for breach might make men think before they speak and help to stamp out dissolute courting behaviour of the kind described in *The Cuckoo went 'Cuckoo!'*:

> Though the blow they try to soften, you will find that, very often,
>> Men grow fickle to the girl they've sworn to love;
> In the summer-time, they court them, but they jilt'em in the autumn;
>> That's what happened with the pair I'm singing of.

Taken together, breach-of-promise songs expose a reverse side to the dominant discourse on breach of promise. They are more alive to the practicalities of working-class courtship: to the reality of long engagements, heavy female investment in relationships, and the widespread (and deplorable) lack of male romantic integrity. Without the action, the songs imply, cheated girls would lack a much-needed remedy against worthless men, who obtain culinary, monetary, or even sexual benefits over the course of long relationships without ever undertaking the offsetting commitment of marriage. The songs make the argument that the hegemonic discourse on breach of promise mistakenly transfers

---

[215] *She Went Right Past Her Junction*, words by C G Cotes, music by Bennett Scott (London, 1898).

[216] Joan Perkin, *Victorian Women* (London: John Murray, 1993) 178.

[217] Perkin 179. See also Kathryn Gleadle, *British Women in the Nineteenth Century*, Social History in Perspective (Basingstoke: Palgrave, 2001) 40.

[218] *As Good and a Great Deal Better*, words by Fred K Burnot, music by George Bicknell (London, 1863), for instance, features an ill-thought-out, drunken proposal.

middle-class standards of feminine excellence to a class wholly different from (and little understood by) the Victorian bourgeoisie. The kind of true womanhood achieved by an Esther Summerson, the songs suggest, requires a too-good-to-be-true Mr Jarndyce in the background and is simply not realizable by poorer women.

Although breach-of-promise songs constituted only a minority discourse, the arguments they put forward could not be gainsaid. That the counter-discourse was not completely drowned out by the hegemonic narrative is reflected in the fact that the breach-of-promise action withstood the sustained and vigorous attack mounted on it, on so many fronts, legal, social, and literary, in the high Victorian period. Breach of promise came in for a sound battering, but it ultimately weathered the high Victorian storm.[219] This shows that the exposure of the plaintiff's structural inconsistency with the feminine ideal, although serving to vulgarize breach-of-promise suits and to bring them into disrepute, could not, by itself, undo them. The age of breach of promise, as the next and final chapter in the historical trilogy will reveal, would only come to an end with the passing of the nineteenth-century feminine ideal. This temporal connection in the decline of both ideal and action once again supports my premise, as did their near simultaneous birth, that the nineteenth-century feminine ideal and the feminized breach-of-promise suit were uneasily and fatally, but nonetheless inextricably entwined.

---

[219] My belief that the breach-of-promise action survived the late nineteenth century largely because it provided much-needed protection for poorer women is shared by Steinbach. Thus, Steinbach notes that although there was widespread hostility to the action, people also 'recognized that it was an aid to working women (as well as a warning to working men). This was the primary reason that breach of promise was not abolished during the late nineteenth century' (298).

5

Breach of Promise in the Post-Victorian Period (1900–40): A Changing Ideal, the Action's Decline, and the Symbolism of Breach of Promise

With the early decades of the twentieth century, fewer and fewer actions for breach of promise were brought and reported on in the newspapers. Section I ties the decline in the incidence and cultural 'visibility' of breach-of-promise actions to the simultaneous change in the prevalent conception of woman, her ideal role in society, sexual relations, and the family. The two World Wars and their aftermath constituted a milestone for women and their public image in England: women became more and more established in the dominant masculine culture and started to assume the personality traits of independence, sexual vigour, and assertiveness. With the advent of women's social and sexual autonomy, the action for breach of promise became as musty and out-of-date as the feminine ideal it enshrined. The modern ideal woman, with intellectual faculties on a par with man's, responsible for her own actions, sexually liberated, and economically self-sufficient, no longer needed what was perceived as a patriarchal and patronizing cause of action. The action for breach of promise accordingly disintegrated in proportion as the nineteenth-century ideology of femininity, which had given it its shape, became fragmented and subject to challenge. In the final decades of its legal existence, the action, cut off from the feminine infusion, which had been its driving force, displayed a marked tendency to revert to its contractual roots or, as illustrated by *Shaw v Shaw*,[1] was put to uses entirely different from those it had previously been concerned with. When the cause of action was finally abolished in 1970, it was on the express ground that it 'seemed to rest upon social assumptions which are no longer valid'.[2]

In the literary and cinematic portrayals that date from this final period, breach of promise, as section II reveals, assumes symbolic meaning, signifying a conception of the nature and status of women, which is, quite simply, passé.

---

[1] [1954] 2 QB 429.   [2] Law Commission 1.

Accounts fall almost exclusively into categories C ('contemplated involvement') and D ('imputed involvement') of my systematization, with female characters being revealed as either old-fashioned 'gimme' girls (C) or 'new women' (D), depending on their attitude to breach of promise. The laughable, in this final period, is constituted by the nineteenth-century feminine ideal, and readers and movie audiences are invited to express their intellectual and moral distance from the outmoded ethos by a Hobbesian laughter of superiority.

I. 'If women were in business, or had a profession, nothing more could, with decency, be heard of breaches of promise':[3] Female Emancipation and the Demise of the Breach-of-Promise Action

After half a century at the forefront of legal and cultural attention in the high Victorian period, the breach-of-promise action went into a decline in the twentieth century. The most obvious symptom of the malaise was a marked drop in the level of breach-of-promise litigation and newspaper reporting. Out of 574 King's Bench actions set down for hearing at the 1905 Easter sittings, for instance, only five were for breach of promise,[4] and by 1920, the numbers had dwindled still further, with only one breach-of-promise case entered in the lists.[5] Just as people were less willing to institute breach-of-promise actions after the turn of the century, so newspapers were less likely to report them for their readers. The *Times* reporting average, for instance, sank to approximately one action per month for the period between 1900 and 1940. In fact, in the second half of this period, *Times* readers could expect to be regaled with a breach-of-promise case every two months at the most. These figures contrast with a reporting peak of 5.5 actions per month in 1870. The downward trend is replicated in the other newspapers I selected for sampling: reporting activity for breach of promise in the *News of the World*, for instance, slumped to about half its former level after 1910.[6] The decline in the incidence of breach-of-promise litigation and in its 'visibility' in the news media indicates that the cause of action had started a descent into relative legal and cultural obscurity by the early 1900s. What had happened to trigger this fall?

---

[3] *The Woman Question: Papers Reprinted from 'The Examiner'* (London, 1872) 61, quoted in Steinbach, 'Promises' 282.

[4] 'King's Bench Actions' *The Times* 26 April 1905: 12.

[5] 'Prospects of a Heavy Divorce List' *The Times* 9 April 1920: 7.

[6] My figures accord quite well with Steinbach's conclusion that the action 'was used less and less frequently after 1920' ('Promises' 304).

The key to the legal and cultural obsolescence of the breach-of-promise action lies in the twentieth-century change in the prevalent conception of woman, her ideal role in society, sexual relations, and the family. The ideal of true womanhood, like all ideology, was not frozen in time, fixed and immutable, but in a constant state of exposure to the pressures of society. The second half of the nineteenth century, as we saw in Chapter 4, had already witnessed a slight straining against the limits of Victorianism. Under the influence of the first women's rights movement, a wider sphere had begun to open up for women, but the numbers that had availed themselves of it had been tiny.[7] Also, the desires of the first women's rights movement, as Ann Oakley has noted, were directed at securing identifiable rights, like women's suffrage and access to higher education, rather than at undercutting 'the influence of less visible ideas and opinions',[8] such as the nineteenth-century ideology of femininity. In fact, most of the early activists accepted the angelic ideal wholesale and believed in 'the natural superiority of man, as . . . in the existence of a God'.[9] As a consequence, the Victorian code had not cracked from within in the nineteenth century. Rather, the ideal of true womanhood had remained in place. So too, as we have seen, had the law of breach of promise.

By the turn of the twentieth century, the first generation of women to have profited from the 'widening sphere' were using their education to change the face of women's employment: 'between 1881 and 1911 there were significant increases in the numbers of women employed in the white-collar sector'.[10] New employment opportunities were rapidly evolving with the advent of the typewriter and the telegraph, the expansion of department stores, and the professionalization of nursing and teaching. With middle-class single women increasingly out to work and 'at least some psychologists, sociologists, and anthropologists . . . coming to understand that many sex

[7] Thus, women had been able to gain a university education since the 1860s. Girton and Newnham Colleges at Cambridge, for instance, were founded in 1869 and 1874 respectively. See Abrams 281. For a detailed account of the movement for the higher education of women, see Josephine Kamm, *Hope Deferred: Girls' Education in English History* (London: Methuen, 1965) 250–70.

[8] Oakley 13.

[9] Norton 172. Caroline Norton, one of the first generation of women's rights activists, presumed that she spoke for 'millions more' in expressing this belief. First-wave feminism was for the most part relational (rather than radical) feminism. Like the dominant ideology of separate spheres, it was based on a belief in the complementariness of women and men. Indeed, first-wave feminists put forward women's supposed moral superiority over men (rather than their equality with them) as the prime argument for granting women access to the public sphere (Abrams 266).

[10] Abrams 284. Of course, women had worked outside the home throughout the nineteenth century. Female involvement in the world of work, however, had previously been regarded as less than ideal, and the work in question had tended to be low-paid factory labour or domestic service.

differences were the result of socialization, not biology',[11] the sharp separation between the sexes was beginning to break down. The pace of change was significantly accelerated by the two great crises of the first half of the twentieth century: the First and the Second World Wars. 'Many accounts of twentieth-century British history assume that the two World Wars inaugurated significant changes for women. The wars are seen as turning points or watersheds bounding well-recognized historical periods and redirecting the course of women's lives.'[12] World War I created a serious labour shortage, which women were called upon to meet. British women responded handsomely, participating in the war effort as well as taking over civilian jobs vacated by men. During the First World War, women were employed in their thousands as tram-conductors, welders, and munitionettes. Employment in the wartime industries allowed women to demonstrate their aptitude for certain 'unfeminine' jobs and to prove that they could do men's work as soon as men stopped blocking their way. While a minority of privileged women had been able to obtain a measure of autonomy in the late nineteenth century, the war instilled a more general sense that tremendous opportunities, a new role and status for women, were there for the taking. Their wartime experiences upped the confidence and sense of independence of women of all classes.[13] 'It seems impossible,' Rosaline Masson opined when the war had ended, 'that they should ever return to the old life of dependence and restriction and aimless days.'[14]

The immediate post-war period displayed some encouraging signs. Women were granted the vote in 1918 and with the passage of the Sex Disqualification (Removal) Act of 1919[15] gained access to professional and public life on the same terms as men. At long last, a culture that was not made up of separate spheres became a distinct possibility. The sexual double standard, which had been so painstakingly constructed over the course of the nineteenth century,

---

[11] Linda K Kerber, 'Separate Spheres, Female Worlds, Woman's Place: The Rhetoric of Women's History' (1988) 75(1) *Journal of American History* 26.

[12] Penny Summerfield, 'Women and the War in the Twentieth Century' in *Women's History: Britain, 1850–1945: An Introduction*, June Purvis (ed) (London: UCL Press, 1995) 307. This view is espoused by Branca 65 and Deirdre Beddoe, *Discovering Women's History: A Practical Guide to Researching the Lives of Women Since 1800*, 3rd edn (London: Longman, 1998) 39. Alice Kessler-Harris, by contrast, disputes that the wars were either a turning point or a milestone for Western women. Alice Kessler-Harris, *Out to Work: A History of Wage-Earning Women in the United States*, 20th anniversary edn (Oxford: Oxford University Press, 2003) 295.

[13] Arthur Marwick, *The Deluge: British Society and the First World War*, 2nd edn (London: Macmillan, 1991) 134.

[14] Rosaline Masson, 'Dark Stars (Unpaid) II.—Unmarried,' *Time and Tide* 11 March 1921, rpt in Dale Spender, *Time and Tide Wait for No Man* (London: Pandora Press, 1984) 199.

[15] 9 & 10 Geo V, c 71.

was another casualty of the post-war period.[16] In the 1920s and 1930s, a new set of sexual conventions emerged, replacing the old ideal of sexual purity with an equally powerful expectation of female sexual availability. As Freud's writings were becoming more widely known, sexual desire in women came to be regarded as normal and even desirable.[17] 'The girl who makes use of the new opportunities for sex freedom,' two prominent sociologists declared, 'is likely to find her experiences have been wholesome...she may be better prepared for marriage by her playful activities than if she had clung to a passive role of waiting for marriage before giving any expression to her sex impulses.'[18] With virtue now resting in the expression rather than the repression of sexuality, passionlessness in women deteriorated from ideal to condition: the passionless Victorian lady re-emerged as the pathological 'frigid woman' of the 1920s.[19]

Women's newfound freedom might not have been long-lived. With the First World War safely over, women were in danger of finding themselves forced out to pasture again. 'The speed with which women had appeared in industry during the war was surpassed by the speed with which they vanished from it. When the war ended, the women were dismissed and their jobs were restored to men.'[20] These atavistic days were not to last, however. In 1939, World War II broke out and history repeated itself. The government and the media embarked on an all-out effort to encourage women to enter the labour force. Hollywood churned out adventuress and career girl movies that cast 'the female as the healthy protagonist, the male as the needy one'.[21] In once more joining the war effort and succeeding in male fields, women undermined the physiological, intellectual, and moral assumptions on which the nineteenth-century concept of femininity was based. Able to earn their own keep, they would never again be dependent on men for their bread and butter. The Second World War and its aftermath brought about the collapse of Victorian gender roles. For one thing, the economic situation after World War II was very different from that after World War I. With the new government launching an export drive, there was a lot of work to be done and hence a continuing and buoyant demand for female labour.[22] Moreover, women had begun to take pleasure in the business world,

---

[16] The new 'single' standard found its legal expression in the introduction of gender-neutral grounds for divorce in 1923 (Thomas 202).

[17] Beddoe 37.

[18] Phyllis Blanchard and Carolyn Manasses, *New Girls for Old* (New York: Macauley Company, 1930) 61, quoted in Rothman 178.

[19] Sheila Jeffreys, 'Women and Sexuality', Purvis 202.

[20] Beddoe 34.

[21] Marjorie Rosen, *Popcorn Venus: Women, Movies and the American Dream* (London: Peter Owen, 1975) 194.

[22] Summerfield 324–5.

which Hollywood portrayed for them as 'exotically attractive'[23] and were eager to stay on. The old ideal began to crumble before these changes in the real world, and a new ideal rose up in its stead. The nineteenth-century dream of the true woman was superseded by the twentieth-century vision of woman as an active and fully competent political subject, capable of self-definition in sexual and in social terms.

The old nineteenth-century law of breach of promise was woefully out of accord with this new feminine image. The breach-of-promise action, as we have seen, had infantilized women, by in effect treating them as legal minors who could sue on, but not in their turn be sued on, the contract. The action's paternalist vision of woman as 'a "perpetual infant," or at best a weak, confiding, half-witted creature',[24] was fundamentally at odds with the new definition of woman as an adult political subject, contractually competent, and able to decide for and look after herself. Indeed, the character traits that were read out of the female sex and condemned in no uncertain terms in the twentieth century were the very self-abnegation, pliancy, and clinginess which had been the key elements of the nineteenth-century ideal.

As the prevailing feminine image and the state of the law became progressively more incongruent, it was to be expected that the latter would adjust. Thus, the twentieth-century decline in the incidence of breach-of-promise actions and their disappearance from the forefront of cultural attention are not at all surprising. In fact, in America, the cause of action started to be abolished from the 1930s onwards.[25] Anti-heartbalm legislation in the United States was typically introduced by women legislators eager to shed the last remnants of their Victorian past: 'Indiana's pioneering bill was introduced by Roberta West Nicholson, at the time Indiana's only woman legislator. Republican Blanche E. Hower and Democrat Alma Smith virtually raced to introduce similar legislation in Ohio.'[26] The autonomous modern woman would not brook the kind of male patronizing enshrined in the breach-of-promise action. In addressing the Indiana Congress before the final vote, Roberta West Nicholson stressed that women 'do not demand rights, gentlemen, they earn them, and they ask no such privileges as these which are abolished in this bill'.[27] Although the cause

---

[23] Rosen 264.

[24] *Englishwoman's Review of Social and Industrial Questions* 10.73 (15 May 1879): 219, quoted in Steinbach, 'Promises' 291.

[25] Beginning in 1935, 25 American states enacted legislation, commonly known as (anti-) heartbalm statutes, abolishing the breach-of-promise action (Homer H Clark 21). The suit, in some shape or form, continues to survive in about half of American jurisdictions. Neil G Williams, 'What to Do When There's No "I Do": A Model for Awarding Damages under Promissory Estoppel' (1995) 70 *Washington Law Review* 1021.

[26] Sinclair 66.

[27] *Indianapolis News* 2 February 1935: 3, quoted in Sinclair 90.

of action was not abolished in England until much later in the century, the in-court processing of breach-of-promise suits changed as English courts adapted the common law to the new mores concerning the status of women.

After being tight-shut against male plaintiffs throughout the nineteenth century, the breach-of-promise action showed signs of opening up. In 1910, a 25-year-old draper's assistant, who had been courted and abandoned by an overeager widow more than twice his age, recovered £100,[28] thus becoming the first male breach-of-promise plaintiff in my sample to be awarded substantial damages since the early 1800s.[29] Mr Justice Grantham, in summing up for Jack Denny Bower, said that he did so on the ground that the 'female sex now claimed to be equal to or better than the male, and he did not see why they should not be treated in the same way'.[30] This increased gender-blindness and marks a rapprochement of the breach-of-promise action to the contractual fold. A similar tendency to revert to strict contract law can be observed in other aspects of the in-court handling of suits after 1900. In a move away from the nineteenth-century position under which unilateral promises to marry were, in substance, valid and enforceable, a 1929 textbook formulated that '[t]he promise to marry must be mutual in order to be effective as a contract.'[31] Similarly, in *Moore v Burrell* (1901), it was stressed that the plaintiff had 'made a definite offer to marry him [the defendant], and he finally refused'.[32] This insistence on the fact that the plaintiff had tendered performance suggests a realignment of the rules on establishing a breach with the contractual mainstream.[33] Finally, in the 1937 case of *Fender v St. John-Mildmay*, Lord Wright used clearly contractual language in 'deciding not to invalidate *a contract* like this'.[34] The courts did not show any signs of suffering from precedent paralysis as regards the defences available to breach-of-promise actions either. In the 1920 case of *Gamble v Sales*,[35] for instance, Mr Justice Darling awarded Caroline Gamble

---

[28] *Bower v Ebsworth*, *The Times* 23 April 1910: 5; 25 April 1910: 3; 28 April 1910: 3.

[29] I found only one other nineteenth-century case (which did not form part of my sample) where a male breach-of-promise plaintiff recovered substantial damages. In *Foster v Mellish*, the male plaintiff was awarded £200. However, *Foster v Mellish* was heard very early in the nineteenth century (1802), and I regard it as a case that pre-dates the emergence of the 'feminized' breach-of-promise action. To me, it seems to belong to the early, pre-1800 period, when the common law action was still in its more strictly contractual phase.

[30] *The Times* 25 April 1910: 3.

[31] George Frederick Emery, *The Law Relating to Husband and Wife, Engagements to Marry, Divorce and Separation, Etc* (London: Effingham Wilson, 1929) 2.

[32] *News of the World* 7 April 1901: 3.

[33] In the nineteenth century, as we saw in Chapter 1, tender of performance by the plaintiff was not required to establish a breach by the defendant. The defendant would be taken to have broken his promise whenever he evinced an unwillingness—towards the plaintiff, her family, or her friends—to do all the running in the relationship.

[34] (1938) AC 1 (37) (emphasis added).

[35] *The Times* 19 March 1920: 4, 5, 17.

contemptuous damages of one farthing and deprived her of her costs, thus effectively allowing the defendant's war wounds to frustrate his pre-war promise. In so doing, Darling came within an inch of overturning the longstanding rule that a breach-of-promise defendant could not rely on the plaintiff's (and much less his own) ill health as an excuse for non-performance.[36] *Gamble v Sales* seemed to be taking the law of breach of promise back to the eighteenth century and Lord Kenyon's formulation that 'if the condition of the parties were changed after the time of making the contract, it was a good cause for either party to break off the connexion'.[37] The 1920s also yield up the first case in my sample where a man's defence of release was successful. In 1921, Hilda Smith lost her case because she had told Harold Wood that she did not want to continue the engagement if he had ceased to care for her.[38] The new stringency of the law was most evident in the area of damages. Deserving cases were no longer identified by the quality of the girl injured, but by the size of the injury, and the size of the injury progressively became a function of the economic loss sustained. Purely emotional suffering, formerly the most significant, was now a suspect head of damage. In *Goodier v Daniels*,[39] for instance, Miss Goodier was only compensated for her 'real' out-of-pocket loss of £25, and not for any emotional injury, although the defendant had taunted her with a Christmas card reading: 'One farthing damages. May no breach occur to the promise of a happy Christmas for you.' Where emotional damages were sought, as in *Kay v Whittaker*,[40] medical evidence was usually given that the plaintiff had suffered severely from nervous shock. This demonstrates that emotional injuries were no longer classed as general damages, arising naturally from a broken engagement and requiring no evidence to support them. With the twentieth-century advent of occupational opportunities and a busy social life for women had gone the idea that female feelings would be irreparably damaged by a courtship gone awry. Outside pursuits were now on hand as the best panacea for a romantic grievance.[41] Similarly, with emotional virginity gone out of fashion and at least some pre-marital sexual experience no longer frowned upon for women, loss

---

[36] Mr Justice Darling in fact thought himself bound by precedent to hold that the defendant's injuries did not constitute a legal defence, but he awarded one farthing and deprived Miss Gamble of her costs on the ground that enforcement of the contract would be contrary to public policy. He thus ensured that, legal defence or no, Caroline Gamble derived no benefit from her breach-of-promise suit.

[37] (1797) Peake's Addl C 103 (124), quoted in Chitty, *Practical Treatise*, 3rd edn, 540.

[38] *Smith v Wood, News of the World* 6 March 1921: 4.

[39] *News of the World* 18 March 1906: 5.

[40] *News of the World* 28 April 1901: 3. This was a particularly heartrending case, where there had once been a strong mutual attachment. The relationship had only ended after several years when the defendant allowed someone else to occupy 'the thoughts that rightfully belonged to you'.

[41] The connection between having something to do and getting over a past attachment is made by Jane Austen's Anne Elliot in accounting for men's superior ability to cope with ill-directed fancies: 'You are forced on exertion. You have always a profession, pursuits, business of some sort or other, to take

of marriage value consequent on the rejection (whether with or without seduction) ceased to be a compensable head of damage.

The courts now gave out stern courtship advice to women, counselling them to look after themselves. Mr Justice McCardie, known as the 'bachelor judge', told women to set a time limit on engagements. Withdrawing oneself from the marriage market for eight years, as Miss Munday had done in the case before him, was not sensible and not the sort of behaviour the law would encourage.[42] As women's new social role continued to evolve, judges and juries became increasingly unresponsive to the musty stories recounted in court. Just how culturally obsolete the action had become, is reflected by *Parsons v Harbourne*.[43] Agnes Parsons got engaged to Sergeant Charles Harbourne when she was 20 years old. He was in the army, quartered first at Cairo and then in India, so they spent most of their 19-year courtship apart. After having kept Agnes waiting for nearly two decades, Sergeant Harbourne decided that, at almost 50, he was too old to marry. In the early nineteenth century or even in the high Victorian period, the story of a woman patiently waiting for nearly 20 years for the final consummation of her one and only true love would have presented a compelling case. If she had brought her action 50 or even 30 years before, Agnes Parsons would have been sure of handsome damages. Coming to court, as she did, in the post-Victorian period, the jury only wondered at this old-fashioned courtship, where the parties had been content to stay apart for almost 20 years and at the woman who had spent her whole youth and middle age writing and receiving the occasional letter instead of intermingling with the world and leading an active existence. Agnes Parsons's Victorian love tragedy had gone stale and no longer made cultural sense in the twentieth century. She recovered a mere £25.

With the demise of the old nineteenth-century ideal, the breach-of-promise action lost its ideological backbone and with that its shape and coherence. In the twentieth century, the action floundered on, bereft of all sense of direction. The best-known breach-of-promise case of the twentieth century is not in fact a 'real' breach-of-promise case at all. In the 1954 action of *Shaw v Shaw*,[44] breach of promise was invoked in an altogether atypical scenario. The plaintiff, Violet Shaw, had married Percy John Shaw at the registry office in Cannock in 1938. She had subsequently lived with him as his wife for 14 years. It was only when Shaw died intestate in 1952 that Mrs Shaw discovered

---

you back into the world immediately, and continual occupation and change soon weaken impressions' (*Persuasion* 233–4).

[42] *Munday v Barber*, *News of the World* 15 March 1931: 4.
[43] *News of the World* 25 March 1906: 1.
[44] [1954] 2 QB 429; *Daily Mail* 26 June 1954: 3, 5.

that the marriage was not legally valid. When he had married her, Shaw had not been a widower as he claimed; his first wife Cecilia did not die until 1950. Mrs Shaw sued her supposed husband's administrators, a son and daughter by his 'legal' wife, basing her claim on breach of a continuing implied warranty by the deceased that he was in a position to marry her and, in the alternative, on breach of promise. A unanimous Court of Appeal upheld her claim on both counts. It found that Shaw had, throughout the Shaws' life together, impliedly warranted that their marriage was valid. This warranty had been finally broken at his death when Mrs Shaw discovered that she was not in fact his widow. In addition to breaking his implied warranty, Shaw had broken his binding 'bigamous' promise of marriage by failing to go through a second marriage ceremony with Mrs Shaw when it became legally possible for him to do so after his first wife's death in 1950.[45] The 'second Mrs Shaw' was awarded £1,000, the sum she would have been entitled to if she had in fact been what she believed she was, Shaw's widow.

In *Shaw v Shaw*, the breach-of-promise action was clearly put to uses entirely different from those it had previously been concerned with. The case did not revolve around Mrs Shaw and her claims to ideal womanhood. Rather, the court was actuated by the perceived need to reach a just result in a hard case. As Lord Justice Singleton observed:

If ever there was a case in which the plaintiff ought to be entitled to succeed, it is the present case, for Shaw persuaded her to marry him, pretended that he was a widower when he was not, and having gone through a form of marriage with her, acquired all her savings from her for use in his affairs, and he did not, in fact, marry her.[46]

Breach of promise, one of the few arguable bases of recovery, was accordingly pressed into service to meet the demands of a difficult case.[47] Its true services, however, crucial throughout the nineteenth century, were no longer called upon.

---

[45] Although Mr Shaw was a married man at the time of making the promise, Mrs Shaw's claim was not excluded on the grounds of public policy, because she did not know that Shaw was married. On 'bigamous promises' to marry (Craig 92), see above Ch 1, n 87.

[46] [1954] 2 QB 429 (438).

[47] That *Shaw v Shaw* was not typical of breach-of-promise actions was recognized by the Law Commission when it considered the action's future in 1969. The Law Commission recommended that a legal remedy should be available in cases like Mrs Shaw's. However, such cases should not be looked at in the context of breach-of-promise actions (where they did not really belong), but in the context of succession rights and family provision legislation. A woman in Violet Shaw's position should be treated like a wife who has contracted a void marriage in good faith and be given a remedy under the Inheritance (Family Provision) Act 1938 (Law Commission 16). The *Shaw* constellation is also given special treatment in American law, where a bigamous marriage exception has been found to the anti-heartbalm statutes (*Snyder v Snyder*, 14 NYS 2d 815).

In the 1960s, parliamentary questions were asked about the breach-of-promise action, which was, by then, long past its cultural sell-by date. However, it was felt that legislation on the subject 'would not be justified in the present state of Parliamentary business'.[48] Abolition of the breach-of-promise action remained on the political backburner until an active and effective awareness of civil rights, a wish to guarantee equality, and a socially engaged Labour administration under Harold Wilson provided the necessary environment for tackling legislative change. In 1969, the Lord Chancellor laid before Parliament Law Commission Report No 26. In the Report, the Law Commission singled out for statutory abolition, under the heading 'miscellaneous matters involving anomalies, obsolescent principles or archaic procedures', the action for breach of promise of marriage upon the ground that it 'seemed to rest upon social assumptions which are no longer valid'.[49] The Law Commission recommended that the action be abolished and replaced by a procedure for settling property disputes analogous to that applied between a divorcing husband and wife. Under the Commission's proposals, most of which became part of the Law Reform (Miscellaneous Provisions) Act 1970,[50] a substantial contribution in money or money's worth to the acquisition or improvement of property was to found a proprietary interest; conditional gifts (most notably engagement rings) were to be recoverable irrespective of fault; and financial losses, such as the purchase of a trousseau or the hiring of a church or hotel for the ceremony, were to go uncompensated. These proposals were in fact a little skewed in favour of men, as under the strict no-fault standard, men would have been able to get back their engagement rings even where they had broken off the engagement, while wedding expenses, which are traditionally incurred by the bride and her family, would have been non-compensable. In the interests of gender equality, Parliament chose to depart from the Commission's recommendations and to impose a different solution in s 3 of the Act: the gift of an engagement ring is now presumed to be an absolute gift, rebuttable by proof of an express or implied condition that the ring be returned in case of the marriage not taking place. Moreover, legal redress for breach of an engagement has been made dependent upon there being 'a definite agreement to marry'.[51] As of 1 January 1971, the day the Act came into force, the English legal system no longer concerns itself with informal promises of marriage.[52]

---

[48] Law Commission 6.
[49] Ibid, 1.
[50] c 33.
[51] Law Commission 15.
[52] The Act does not extend to Scotland or Northern Ireland (s 7(4)). Breach-of-promise actions were abolished in Scotland by the Law Reform (Husband and Wife) (Scotland) Act 1984, c 15, and

II. 'Women are not angels'[53]: 'Gimme' Girls, New Women, and the Symbolism of Breach of Promise

Breach of promise continued to feature in the literature of the post-Victorian period and, with the advent of motion pictures, it was picked up by the nascent film industry. However, just as the real-life breach-of-promise action was increasingly absent from twentieth-century courtrooms and newspapers, so the artistic use made of it became less visible after 1900. Treatment of breach of promise in twentieth-century literature and film tends to be interstitial, rather than central as in the 50 years before. Nearly all of the depictions of the cause of action that date from the final period require careful, breach-of-promise-conscious reading (or viewing) to be identified as portrayals of the cause of action at all. For my analysis of the literary and cinematic representation of breach of promise in the post-Victorian period, I shall concentrate on four twentieth-century accounts. While these four accounts are not exhaustive of the creative use made of breach of promise after 1900, they illustrate the basic representational strategies. Taken together, they cover the main outlines of the breach-of-promise story as re-told in twentieth-century literature and film.

In 1915, the enormously popular and prolific English humorist P G Wodehouse worked breach of promise into the backcloth of one of his earliest pieces—an engaging little novelette called *Something New*.[54] A decade later, Hollywood's own Anita Loos gave the action between-the-lines treatment in what turned out to be 'the surprise best-seller of 1925':[55] the story of a gold-digger's progress in the bathtub-gin days of the 1920s, whose title, *Gentlemen Prefer Blondes*, has become a cultural referent.[56] In 1933, breach of promise put in another blink-and-you'll-miss-it appearance in Busby Berkeley's *Footlight Parade*, a depression-era musical extravaganza starring James Cagney and Joan Blondell.[57] In the same year, the cause of action featured somewhat more prominently in the Mae West vehicle *I'm No Angel*.[58]

Before considering the depiction of breach of promise in these twentieth-century accounts, I should like to return briefly to Nathaniel Hawthorne's *Mrs.*

---

in Northern Ireland by the Family Law (Miscellaneous Provisions) (Northern Ireland) Order 1984, No 1984 (NI 14).

[53] Hawthorne, 'Mrs. Bullfrog' 136.

[54] P G Wodehouse, *Something New*, 1915 (Mineola, NY: Dover Publications, 2000).

[55] Gary Carey, *Anita Loos: A Biography* (London: Bloomsbury Publishing, 1988) 98.

[56] Anita Loos, *Gentlemen Prefer Blondes: The Illuminating Diary of a Professional Lady*, 1925 (New York: Liveright, 1973).

[57] *Footlight Parade*, Lloyd Bacon (dir), James Cagney and Joan Blondell (perf), Warner, 1933.

[58] *I'm No Angel*, Wesley Ruggles (dir), Mae West and Cary Grant (perf), Paramount, 1933.

Bullfrog. When I first discussed this short story in the context of Chapter 3, I claimed that Hawthorne's text cut across an orderly temporal separation into three distinct historical periods and had to be seen in multiple time frames; that it was multi-layered and spoke not only to the early nineteenth century and to the high Victorian period, but to the post-Victorian period as well. On the two readings of the story that I have considered thus far, *Mrs. Bullfrog* had seemed complicit with (rather than critical of) the Victorian value system. Both readings see the story as building on the Victorian dream of an angel in the house and the concomitant fear that the supposed seraph might turn out to be a creature of another stamp, a physical or a psychic monster. To leave it at these two interpretations, however, would be to miss the richness, not to mention the point, of Hawthorne's text. For *Mrs. Bullfrog* does not, ultimately, so much represent as expose and condemn Victorian sexual values.

In Hawthorne's text, Mr Bullfrog starts out with the preconceived Victorian notion that his wife is a goddess worthy of his adoration, only to be awakened to the base and disillusioning facts. In the course of the narrative, he discovers that his etherealized angel has physical needs, a will of her own, and a past that includes a breach-of-promise suit:

I, the most exquisitely fastidious of men, and whose wife was to have been the most delicate and refined of women, with all the fresh dew-drops glittering on her virgin rosebud of a heart! I thought of the glossy ringlets and pearly teeth—I thought of the Kalydor—I thought of the coachman's bruised ear and bloody nose—I thought of the tender love secrets, which she had whispered to the judge and jury, and a thousand tittering auditors—and gave another groan![59]

In this passage, Mr Bullfrog is clearly testing his wife against the idealized image and finds her wanting. However, it is crucial to point out that Mrs Bullfrog is found wanting as an angel, and not as a human being. Hawthorne, it would seem, is not so much making fun of Mrs Bullfrog as of how Mr Bullfrog thinks about her and, by implication, of how the Victorians thought about women generally. To have bodily functions and needs, such as a need for food, for instance, is merely human, but Mr Bullfrog's mental categories, made rigid by cultural ideology, will not allow his wife to be human. Having swallowed nineteenth-century mythology wholesale, he confidently expects his Laura to exist on some 'airy diet…for a week together'[60] and never stops to reflect that this would require a physiological miracle. As a result of his exposure to the feminine mystique, Mr Bullfrog's mental vision of women has narrowed to the point where he can no longer accommodate the real thing. When he is presented with reality in

[59] Hawthorne, 'Mrs. Bullfrog' 136.
[60] Ibid, 132.

the course of Hawthorne's text, he confuses different realms of knowledge. He confuses facts (the Kalydor and the breach-of-promise suit) with values (his wife's worth); he confuses aesthetics with morals; he confuses the ideal with the real; and, finally, like all Victorian men happily living according to a double standard, he confuses subject and object: he has the same functions and needs and obeys the same motives[61] as Mrs Bullfrog does, but he does not quite find this a reason for being disgusted with himself. In *Mrs. Bullfrog*, the nineteenth-century feminine ideal itself—its practical attainability and its social desirability—are put into question. 'Women,' Hawthorne tells his readers, 'are not angels.'[62] And men, who claim the privilege of being less than perfect themselves, are hardly in a position to require them to be. Although Hawthorne's story dates from my first period, ie the early nineteenth century, its most plausible reading is one critical of the feminine ideal. Such ideal-directed criticism is otherwise absent from breach-of-promise fiction until my third period, ie until the early twentieth century. In its muted critique of the nineteenth-century ideal and the sexual double standard it enshrined, *Mrs. Bullfrog* is thus nearly 100 years ahead of its time. While the story is certainly neither the only nor the earliest nineteenth-century text to mock Victorian gender ideals,[63] it is the only piece within the (limited) canon of nineteenth-century breach-of-promise fiction to do so. This puts Hawthorne (usually thought of as a conservative as regards gender issues) significantly ahead of those of his contemporaries who also chose to incorporate a breach-of-promise element into their writings. His short story foreshadows the literary and cinematic portrayals of the final, post-Victorian period, all of which deploy breach of promise obliquely in what is really an attack upon the outdated feminine mystique.

In the post-Victorian period, the object of attack is no longer merely, or even mainly, constituted by the breach-of-promise plaintiff as such. The twentieth-century shift in the prevailing feminine image had placed the nineteenth-century ideal woman at the fringes of the dominant community. The

---

[61] The money motive may serve as an example. When Bullfrog finds out about his wife's breach-of-promise suit, he initially deplores that she did not live up to his ideal by 'treat[ing] the villain with the silent contempt he merited'. However, when Mrs Bullfrog tells him that the suit brought her $5,000, which will now be available for her dear Bullfrog's benefit, he calls it a 'blessed law-suit' and declares all her 'little defects and frailties...forgiven' (137). This incident proves that while Bullfrog might expect his wife to be free from the taint of mercenariness, he himself is clearly no stranger to the emotion.

[62] Hawthorne, 'Mrs. Bullfrog' 136.

[63] American author Sara Willis Parton (better known under her pseudonym of Fanny Fern), for instance, wrote enormously popular books and stories in this period mocking conventional gender ideals, and Louisa May Alcott's splendid four-part novella *Behind a Mask* has an ostensibly beautiful heroine, who—like Mrs Bullfrog—operates with powder and false hair to perform ideal femininity successfully as a script with which to secure the prize of marriage. See Louisa May Alcott, *Behind a Mask, or, A Woman's Power,* 1866 (London: Hesperus, 2004).

paradigm shift had made the former ideal a cultural misfit, a social 'pollution' the dominant identity defined itself against, condemned, and wished to exorcize. At long last, after the type-woman and the breach-of-promise plaintiff, the nineteenth-century ideal found itself at the dangerous 'periphery of the joke-teller's community'[64] and, by implication, at the centre of comic attack. In the breach-of-promise comedy of the final period, readers and movie audiences were invariably invited to express their intellectual and moral distance from the outmoded nineteenth-century ethos by scoffing and scorning the old Victorian mystique.

One of the most striking features of this third generation of breach-of-promise plaintiffs is their affinity with the nineteenth-century ideal. The fictional and cinematic plaintiffs of this period display many of the characteristics the Victorians valorized in women. They are domestic, passive, male-dependent, and childlike. However, these very qualities have become wrenched from their customary positive connotations and now bear the opposite value. In the twentieth-century accounts, the Victorian lady's distinguishing graces, her vine-like dependence on male support and her 'majestic childishness',[65] are filtered through the alienating prism of a changed ideology and transformed into the social diseases of female parasitism and she-philistinism respectively. The nineteenth-century ideal woman reappears in an altogether negative incarnation: as a mindless gold-digger and 'gimme' girl.

Anita Loos's characterization of her protagonist Lorelei Lee typifies the period's simultaneous evocation and repudiation of the sublime ideal. Loos leaves her readers in no doubt as to Lorelei's Victorian ancestry, but she also leaves them in no doubt as to her condemnation of it. Her gold-digging blonde enacts a critique on the system of commodification and objectification that nineteenth-century gender ideology upholds. Savvy to the economics of pleasure and romance and unfailingly accurate about how old-fashioned values for women are materialist at heart, Lorelei acts the part of socially constructed femaleness to her own rhetorical and financial advantage. Lorelei has more than a few overtones of the old feminine ideal. The very story she inhabits, recounting, as it does, Lorelei's entrée into the world (not even omitting the obligatory début scene), is redolent of popular nineteenth-century novels, like Maria Edgeworth's *Belinda*, that dramatized a sheltered girl's first encounters with the social world. The association is strengthened by Lorelei's self-introduction as 'a professional lady'[66] and 'an old fashioned girl'.[67] Through her choice

---

[64] Döring 125.
[65] Ruskin 14.
[66] The subtitle of Loos's novel is 'The Illuminating Diary of a Professional Lady'.
[67] Loos, *Gentlemen Prefer Blondes* 139.

of sobriquets, Lorelei reveals her conscious kinship with the Victorian ideal woman, whose career, like Lorelei's own, exhausted itself in the practice of 'professional ladyhood'—in functioning as a male adornment, a status symbol showing forth and conspicuously consuming male wealth. Lorelei's Victorianism is not limited to self-description, but absorbed into all her actions and attitudes. Having retired from the screen when a male patron 'made me give it all up',[68] she is now thoroughly domestic, with shopping (always regarded as a proper feminine preserve) her most public activity. Lacking any gainful occupation, Lorelei is traditionally passive and dependent on men for her material support. She even displays the infantile airs expected of the Victorian idol: to her, a male patron is simply 'Daddy'.[69] However, Loos telescopes and makes strange the familiar image, painting a startling tableau of what adherence to the ideal will reduce women—and relations between the sexes—to. True to her vision of Lorelei as 'a symbol of the lowest possible mentality of [. . . the] nation',[70] Loos shows her up as a female imbecile, ignorant of the rules of grammar and spelling and drained of all human thought outside insatiable consumerism.[71] Lorelei's less brilliantly rendered double, Vivian Rich in *Footlight Parade*, is another perfect little she-philistine, ridiculed for her French malapropisms and abortive attempts at quoting Ruskin.[72] Just as childishness in women receives a decidedly negative coloration in these post-Victorian accounts, feminine dependence on men is seen with alienated eyes. Lorelei's dependence on male support not only objectifies Lorelei herself, transforming her into a bit of arm-candy sported by a succession of well-heeled males, it transforms her entire world into a world of objects: Lorelei's designation 'shopper'[73] for gentlemen distinguished by their capacity to go shopping with a girl at any hour deprives men of their individuality, of their humanity even. In Loos's novel, a stubborn embrace of the nineteenth-century ideal dehumanizes both women and men,

---

[68] Ibid, 17.

[69] Ibid, 15.

[70] Anita Loos, Introduction: the biography of a book, Loos xii.

[71] Despite her lack of formal education, Lorelei is, however, keenly aware of the power dynamics that shape the relations between men and women, and she uses her astute recognition of the frailties and foibles of (male) human nature to alter this dynamic, have fun, and get the better of the men who woo her.

[72] For yet another twentieth-century account with a similar take on breach of promise, see *Adventure in Blackmail*, Harold Huth and Roland Pertwee (dir), Clive Brook and Judy Campbell (perf), 1943, videocassette, Nostalgia Family Video, 1996. In this British production, the character bringing the breach-of-promise action only pretends to be a worthless gold-digger. Her real purpose is the honourable one of avenging her brother. However, as in *Gentlemen Prefer Blondes* and *Footlight Parade*, the breach-of-promise action is clearly used to invoke the gold-digger paradigm. Its purpose is to endow the female character in question with the (in this case pretended) attributes of mercenariness and parasitism.

[73] Loos, *Gentlemen Prefer Blondes* 26.

reducing them to status symbols and meal tickets respectively, to parasites and hosts united by the cash nexus.

Gentlemen Prefer Blondes and *Footlight Parade* directly target the old ideal, hoisting it on its own petard and ideologically subverting it. Unsurprisingly, given that the real object of attack is the former feminine mystique, the breach-of-promise element has receded into the background. Both *Gentlemen Prefer Blondes* and *Footlight Parade* fall into category C ('contemplated involvement') of my systematization. Lorelei's and Vivian's involvement with breach of promise is contemplative rather than actual. Lorelei merely flirts with the idea of goading her fiancé ('a gentleman who gets on a girls [sic] nerves quite a lot'[74]) into breaking his engagement, so she can sue him for breach of promise, 'take what I can get out of it and be satisfied'.[75] And Vivian Rich issues a single threat to sue and attach everything but her fiancé's garters. Neither woman goes on to bring an action. While breach of promise no longer fulfils a vital or, indeed, any kind of plot-serving function, it is powerful as a method of characterization. Ideologically loaded with nineteenth-century femininity, breach of promise is invoked for its symbolic rather than its literal meaning—as a prime signifier for the outdated feminine mystique. Lorelei's readiness to contemplate an action for breach of promise, like her description of herself as 'an old fashioned girl',[76] reveals her deep affinity with the ideal the cause of action codified and enshrined. It 'places' her as a woman in the traditional Victorian mould, content to be dependent, childlike, and devoid of a role outside one parasitical on men.

By the same token, the symbolic qualities of breach of promise could be invoked to mark a break with, rather than a continuation of, the old ideal. Joan Valentine, heroine of *Something New*, is a 'textual New Woman',[77] typical of Wodehouse's 'festive young female squirts' and 'androgynous mischief-makers',[78] who, as Richard Usborne has noted, could well be masculine in terms of their name (Joan/John), lifestyle, and easy companionship with men.[79] Unlike Lorelei and Vivian, Joan is not prepared to exchange the possibility of a fully individuated humanity for the chivalry doled out to women patterning themselves after the old ideal. Wodehouse repeatedly invokes the old conception of women as inferior, weak, and in need of special protection for the sole purpose of allowing Joan to define herself against it. One guise the

---

[74] Ibid, 170.
[75] Ibid, 197.
[76] Ibid, 139.
[77] Sally Ledger, *The New Woman: Fiction and Feminism at the Fin de Siècle* (Manchester: Manchester University Press, 1997) 13.
[78] Richard Usborne, *Wodehouse at Work: A Study of the Books and Characters of P. G. Wodehouse across Nearly Sixty Years* (London: Herbert Jenkins, 1961) 130.
[79] Ibid, 129–31.

old ideal assumes in Wodehouse's text is that of an action for breach of promise. Joan roundly rejects breach of promise, even though she would, technically, have a case (having been the unwilling recipient of the Honourable Frederick Threepwood's amorous epistles) and is in desperate need of money. But, significantly, unlike Pamela Pinchbeck in the preceding period, Joan turns down breach of promise not in order to regain her lost true womanhood, but to renounce it. In rejecting breach of promise, Joan is also, symbolically, rejecting a vision of herself as a traditional nineteenth-century lady, 'a weak creature to be shielded and petted'.[80] Her abdication of breach of promise amounts to a simultaneous abdication of the angelic pedestal—a pedestal that would 'cripple' her, make her 'forfeit [. . . her] independence of action',[81] and ultimately leave her with no scope to develop her individuality. In *Something New*, the symbolic breach-of-promise action is used to accentuate a break with the past and to reveal Joan Valentine in her full glory as a 'formidable modern woman'—'another man',[82] in short.

The three accounts I have discussed thus far are typical of the post-Victorian period. They attack the nineteenth-century mystique and assign breach of promise a supporting and symbolizing function. The final account to be considered constitutes the only exception to that rule. In *I'm No Angel*, breach of promise is given considerably more substantial treatment, with an in-court trial the climax of the action. As a category-A ('in-court involvement') account in a period otherwise distinguished for its interstitial treatment of breach of promise, *I'm No Angel* occupies a position reminiscent of the *The Pickwick Papers*, another standout in a period when a 'sidelining' of the breach-of-promise element was the norm. Released in 1933, nearly 100 years after the publication of *Pickwick*, *I'm No Angel* marks a fitting conclusion to my consideration of the literary and cinematic representation of breach of promise throughout the nineteenth and early twentieth centuries: in *I'm No Angel*, the curtain rises on a scene nearly identical to that found in *Pickwick*, but the movie brings things full circle and ends on the opposite note.

The trial scene in *I'm No Angel*, like the trial scene in *Pickwick*, brings the nineteenth-century ideal and its opposite into an illuminating conjunction. Both scenes dramatize the direct confrontation between the sublime role invoked by the breach-of-promise paradigm and the incongruous actress cast in it. As a 'brashly sexual and persistently autonomous woman',[83] Mae West's Tira is

---

[80] Wodehouse 125.
[81] Ibid, 126.
[82] Ibid, 125.
[83] Ramona Curry, *Too Much of a Good Thing: Mae West as Cultural Icon* (Minneapolis: University of Minnesota Press, 1996) 28.

the complete antithesis of the old ideal and a worthy successor of the virago-cum-lusty-widow line of early-period breach-of-promise plaintiffs, exemplified by Martha Bardell. In fact, Tira far surpasses Mrs Bardell in the degree to which she embodies both the mannish woman and the woman of unbridled sensuality. Mrs Bardell's social masculinity was limited to her occupation as a landlady. Mae West's Tira, by contrast, is a lion-tamer, who, at the beginning of the movie, performs the Amazonian stunt of placing her head in a lion's mouth. And whereas Mrs Bardell's sexual experience was the result of a single prior marriage, West's Tira is a serial monogamist, a self-declared 'one-man-at-a-time woman', who, in the words of film critic Marjorie Rosen, transforms 'the idea of passive feminine sexuality into an aggressive statement of fact'.[84] While *I'm No Angel* presents the same, only accentuated, comedic gap between type cast and role as *Pickwick*, the treatment it gives to it could not be more different. Where *Pickwick* championed, *I'm No Angel* turns on and systematically contradicts the action's inbuilt nineteenth-century ideals. Unlike Mrs Bardell, who vainly strove to fulfil her assigned role of 'sensitive and confiding female',[85] only grotesquely to fail in and be ridiculed for the attempt, West's Tira deliberately flouts the Victorian script. Instead of remaining demurely silent, she bypasses her lawyer and conducts the case herself, cross-examining the witnesses and proving that she has the nous to show them up. Her central narrative position, as Ramona Curry has noted, makes her the scene's identificatory centre.[86] It allows her to transcend Mrs Bardell's position as the butt of comic laughter and to become instead the joke-teller, who delivers the punch line.[87] In *I'm No Angel*, the quintessential oversexed 'great (wo)man'[88] of Hollywood reverses the Pickwickean power relation: where *Pickwick* ridiculed the oversexed man-woman, *I'm No Angel* ridicules the nineteenth-century ideal. West's performance re-appropriates breach of promise, transforming it into a showcase for her quick wit, red-blooded eroticism, and panache that makes the old ideal look positively feeble by comparison. Tira's brilliant cross-examinations, outshining even Sergeant Buzfuz's own, invert traditional gender relations and demolish the nineteenth-century vision of modest, chaste, and emotional womanhood: having been 'the love-interest in more than one guy's life' and, presumably, the sexual partner of more than one also, Tira refuses to let her past determine her

[84] Rosen 155.
[85] Dickens, *Pickwick* 426; ch 34.
[86] Curry 92.
[87] According to her biographers George Eells and Stanley Musgrove, West consistently refused to make her characters the butt of humour. George Eells and Stanley Musgrove, *Mae West: A Biography* (New York: William Morrow, 1982) 160–1.
[88] Curry has called Mae West the ' "Great (Wo)Man" in Hollywood History' (25). West's ambiguous gender positioning is frequently remarked upon. See, for instance, Pamela Robertson, *Guilty Pleasures: Feminist Camp from Mae West to Madonna* (Durham: Duke University Press, 1996) 29–34.

present; and far from nursing her injured emotions, she snaps: 'Don't ruin my character!' when her maid reveals that she had actually cared for her ex-fiancé Jack Clayton (Cary Grant). Unlike *Pickwick*, which situated Mrs Bardell as the comedic butt and concluded in her narrative containment and defeat, *I'm No Angel* allows West's Tira the central heroic position in the film's narrative. The breach-of-promise trial demonstrates Tira's mettle, endears her to the judge and jury, and wins back Clayton himself, who settles for the amount asked and ends the film crooning: 'You are everything to me.' While the curtain rose on a situation nearly identical to that found in *Pickwick*, it goes down on its mirror image. At the end of *I'm No Angel*, the modern, highly sexualized (wo)man is affirmed and the old effete ideal utterly vanquished. Solid and sensual, joyously autonomous, the complete antithesis of the nineteenth-century ideal had, after years as taboo, finally become totem. The age of the Victorian lady and the age of the ladies' action were both, irrevocably, over.

Epilogue: The Power of the Image

The action for breach of promise of marriage has rarely been the subject of legal scholarship and is conventionally regarded as one of the ephemera of a bygone era. But, for all its hoary quaintness, it holds an important place in legal history as a salutary reminder of the law's responsiveness to cultural mythology. An analysis of breach-of-promise actions through the centuries supports the argument advanced by a number of scholars in recent years that the structure and the method of the law are gendered. Hidden and powerful assumptions and expectations, deriving from generalizations on the grounds of a person's sex, are all-pervasive in legal life, manifesting themselves in legal doctrine and in the thinking of legal actors. In the area of criminal law, for example, stereotypes of conventional femininity have found expression in the female gendering of particular defences, such as mental incapacity defences like diminished responsibility (as opposed to 'masculine' defences like provocation and self-defence)[1], and in the apparent 'leniency' towards women, as regards both prosecution levels and the treatment of women coming to the notice of the criminal justice system, which, as Nicola Lacey has shown, can be observed at every level of the criminal process from the mid-eighteenth century onwards.[2] The same conception of womanhood, as Albie Sachs and Joan Hoff Wilson have demonstrated, influenced Victorian judges to use whatever powers the legal system granted them to rule in favour of male privilege and against female advancement.[3]

The history of the breach-of-promise action, too, shows it to have been adaptive to the prevalent myth of the ideal woman. In the nineteenth century, women were regarded as by nature domestic, frail, and virtuous, and the breach-of-promise action changed to accommodate the dominant ideal. In the twentieth century, the 'true' nature of woman came to be regarded as not materially different from man's, and the cause of action was abolished. During the century and a half or so of its legal existence, the 'feminized' breach-of-promise suit, marred by a fatal structural inconsistency, sat astraddle two conflicting images of woman. It embodied an irreconcilable double perspective on femininity, which cut across the dualities of private and public, passivity and

---

[1] Susan S M Edwards, *Women on Trial: A Study of the Female Suspect, Defendant, and Offender in the Criminal Law and Criminal Justice System* (Manchester: Manchester University Press, 1984).

[2] Lacey 89–90.

[3] Sachs and Wilson 125.

agency, submission and resistance. As a Janus-faced cause of action, enshrining the pious true woman of the Victorian period at the same time as anticipating the egalitarian new woman of the twentieth century, it was at once anachronistic and prophetic.

While this study has been an examination of the reproduction of a particular feminine mythology in a specific legal context in the past, it is framed by the recognition that we are still part of this history of discourses and representations. It is not an empty slogan, but a fundamental statement of truth to say that no one can completely break free from the prison of their own culture. But examining the work of particular orders of representation in the past is the first step towards understanding the politics and effects of representation today and in the future. The rise and fall of the breach-of-promise action serves as a metaphor for fundamental changes in women's identity, agency, and social role between the late eighteenth and the early twentieth century, highlighting the fact that definitions of femininity vary according to who does the defining and when. The historical changeability of the dominant conception of woman should make us wary of arguments from the eternal verities of nature as the justificatory bedrock of our current socio-cultural ideal. 'Men do not have with myth a relationship based on truth but on use: they depoliticize according to their needs.'[4] A heightened historical awareness of both the power and the malleability of the feminine image can help us break through the wall of myth and mystification to question and probe the public image of woman, which, however little it may have to do with women themselves, has so frequently had 'the power to shape too much of their lives'.[5]

---

[4] Roland Barthes, *Mythologies*, Annette Lavers (trans) (London: Cape, 1972) 144.
[5] Betty Friedan, *The Feminine Mystique* (New York: Norton, 2001) 75.

References

Primary Sources

Archival Sources

General Register Office. Register of Deaths in the District of Liverpool, Sub-District of Abercromby, 1909.

The National Archives. Film 1341507, RG11, piece 2103, fol 52, p 5, 1881 Census Return for Alma Villa in Radipole, Dorset.

Staffordshire Record Office. D984/1/1/13/50, deed conveying the equity of redemption of the manor of Syerscote from the devisees and mortgagees of the late Mr Joseph Erpe to Samuel Pole Shaw, 25 March 1858.

Warwickshire County Record Office. CR229/158, personal records of the Shirley family, 1837–1849.

William Salt Library, Stafford. S.MS.478/19/71, undated letter from Mary Elizabeth Smith to Mr Thompson, publisher, about correcting the proofs of her poem.

Printed Sources

'The Action for Breach of Promise of Marriage' *The Times* 12 February 1878: 9.

Alcott, Louisa May, *Behind a Mask, or, A Woman's Power,* 1866 (London: Hesperus, 2004).

Arnold, F O, *The Law of Damages and Compensation*, 2nd edn (London: Butterworths, 1919).

As Good and a Great Deal Better, words by Fred K Burnot, music by George Bicknell (London, 1863).

Austen, Jane, *Mansfield Park,* 1814. Kathryn Sutherland (ed) (London: Penguin, 2003).

—— *Persuasion,* 1818 (London: Penguin, 1994).

—— *Pride and Prejudice,* 1813 (New York: Bantam Books, 1981).

—— *Sense and Sensibility,* 1811 (London: Penguin, 1994).

The Bench and the Bar (London, 1837).

Blackstone, William, *Commentaries on the Laws of England* (Philadelphia, 1879).

Bodichon, Barbara Leigh Smith, *A Brief Summary, in Plain Language, of the Most Important Laws Concerning Women* (London, 1854).

Braddon, Mary Elizabeth, *Aurora Floyd,* 1863 (London: Virago Press, 1984).

—— *Lady Audley's Secret,* 1862. Natalie M Houston (ed) (Peterborough, Ontario: Broadview Press, 2003).

'Breach of Promise' *The Times* 7 May 1879: 9.

'Breaches of Promise' *News of the World* 9 April 1871: 2.

Brown, Robert C, 'Breach of Promise Suits' (1929) 77 *University of Pennsylvania Law Review* 474–96.

Buckstone, John Baldwin, *The Breach of Promise: Or, Second Thoughts Are Best,* 1832 (New York: O A Roorbach, n d).

Byron, Lord, *Don Juan*, T G Steffan, E Steffan, and W W Pratt (eds) (Harmondsworth: Penguin, 1973).

Cairns, Alexander, *Eversley's Law of the Domestic Relations: Husband and Wife, Parent and Child, Guardian and Ward, Infants, Master and Servant*, 4th edn (London: Sweet & Maxwell, 1926).

Chitty, Joseph, *A Practical Treatise on the Law of Contracts*, 3rd edn (London, 1841); 4th edn (London, 1850); 9th edn (London, 1871).

—— *Precedents in Pleading: With Copious Notes on Pleading, Practice and Evidence* (London, 1847).

Collins, Wilkie, Preface, *The Woman in White*, by Collins, 1860 (New York: Modern Library, 2002) xxiii–xxv.

The Cuckoo Went 'Cuckoo!', words by John P Harrington, music by Orlando Powell (London: Francis, Day, and Hunter, 1908).

Dickens, Charles, *Bleak House,* 1853. Stephen Gill (ed) (Oxford: Oxford University Press, 1998).

—— 'The Boarding House', 1834, in *Sketches* (Leipzig, 1843) 283–322.

—— *The Letters of Charles Dickens*, Madeline House and Graham Storey (eds), Vol 1 (1820–39) (Oxford: Clarendon Press, 1965).

—— *Little Dorrit,* 1857 (London: Everyman's Library, 1992).

—— *Oliver Twist,* 1838 (London: Collector's Library, 2003).

—— *The Pickwick Papers,* 1837. James Kinsley (ed) (Oxford: Oxford University Press, 1998).

Ellis, Henry Havelock, *The Erotic Rights of Women, and the Objects of Marriage* (London: British Society for the Study of Sex Psychology, 1918).

Ellis, Sarah Stickney, *The Daughters of England* (London, 1845).

—— *The Women of England: Their Social Duties and Domestic Habits* (New York, 1843).

Emery, George Frederick, *The Law Relating to Husband and Wife, Engagements to Marry, Divorce and Separation, Etc* (London: Effingham Wilson, 1929).

'Ere's Yer Fine Water-Creases, words by John P Harrington, music by Orlando Powell (London: Francis, Day, and Hunter, 1907).

A Familiar Compendium of the Law of Husband and Wife; in Two Parts; to Which Is Added a Third Part; Comprising the Laws Relating to Breach of Promise of Marriage, Seduction and Abduction of Women (London, 1831).

Feinsinger, Nathan P, 'Legislative Attack on "Heart Balm"' (1935) 33(7) *Michigan Law Review* 979–1009.

Gahan, Frank, *The Law of Damages* (London: Sweet & Maxwell, 1936).

Gaskell, Elizabeth, *A Dark Night's Work* (Leipzig, 1863).

—— *The Letters of Mrs Gaskell*, J A V Chapple and Arthur Pollard (eds) (Manchester: Manchester University Press, 1966).

—— *Wives and Daughters,* 1866. Frank Glover Smith (ed) (London: Penguin, 1986).

The Giddy Old Owl, words by Fred Bowyer, music by Dave Braham (London, 1887).

Gilbert, William Schwenck, *The Palace of Truth. Original Plays* (London, 1876) 251–324.

Gilbert, William Schwenck and Arthur Sullivan, *Trial by Jury*, 1875, *The Savoy Operas: Being the Complete Text of the Gilbert and Sullivan Operas As Originally Produced in the Years 1875–1896* (London: Macmillan, 1926) 1–19.

The Girl Who Sloshed the Lather, words by John P Harrington, music by Orlando Powell (London, 1894).

Graves, A J, *Girlhood and Womanhood; or, Sketches of My Schoolmates* (Boston, 1844).

Great Britain. Law Commission. *Breach of Promise of Marriage*. Law Com No 26 (London: HMSO, 1969).

Greg, William Rathbone, 'Prostitution' (1850) 53 *Westminster Review* 448–506.

—— *Literary and Social Judgments* (Boston, 1873).

Gregory, John, *A Father's Legacy to His Daughters* (London, 1822).

Hansard Parliamentary Debates, (series 3), vols 195, 198 (London, 1869).

Hawthorne, Nathaniel, 'Mrs. Bullfrog', 1840, *The Centenary Edition of the Works of Nathaniel Hawthorne*, William Charvat, Roy Harvey Pearce, and Claude M. Simpson (eds) Vol 10 (N p: Ohio State University Press, 1974) 129–37.

—— 'Young Goodman Brown', 1835, *Young Goodman Brown and Other Tales*, Brian Harding (ed) (Oxford: Oxford University Press, 1998) 111–24.

Hershell, John, 'Review of *The Mechanism of the Heavens*' (1832) *Literary Gazette and Journal of the Belles Lettres* 806–7.

His Lordship Winked at the Counsel, or, the Breach of Promise Case, words by George Dance, music by Peter Conroy (London, 1887).

Horace, *Satires, Epistles and Ars Poetica*, (trans) H Rushton Fairclough, Loeb Classical Library 194 (London: William Heinemann; New York: G P Putnam's Sons, 1926).

Hunt, Leigh, *Wit and Humour, Selected from the English Poets; with an Illustrative Essay and Critical Comments* (London, 1846).

I Went Like This to the Lady, words and music by E W Rogers (London, 1895).

John James Murphy, words and music by Felix McGlennon (London, 1898).

Kelly, Hugh, *Memoirs of a Magdalen, or, the History of Louisa Mildmay*, 1767, The Flowering of the Novel (New York: Garland Publishing, 1974).

'King's Bench Actions' *The Times* 26 April 1905: 12.

Lawyer, George, 'Are Actions for Breach of the Marriage Contract Immoral?' (1894) 38 *Central Law Journal* 272–5.

Loos, Anita, *Gentlemen Prefer Blondes: The Illuminating Diary of a Professional Lady*, 1925 (New York: Liveright, 1973).

—— Introduction: The Biography of a Book, Loos vii–xvi.

MacColla, Charles J, *Breach of Promise: Its History and Social Considerations; to Which Are Added a Few Pages on the Law of Breach of Promise and a Glance at Many Amusing Cases since the Reign of Queen Elizabeth*, 1879 (Littleton: Fred B Rothman, 1993).

McCormick, Charles T, *Handbook on the Law of Damages*, Hornbook Series (St Paul: West Publishing, 1935).

Meredith, George, *Diana of the Crossways*, 1897 (New York: Charles Scribner's Sons, 1916).

'Miss Smith and Earl Ferrers' *Britannia* 7 November 1846: 729–30.

'Mr Herschell's Bill' *The Times* 14 February 1879: 10.

Neal, Joseph Clay, 'Duberly Doubtington: The Man Who Couldn't Make Up His Mind' in *Charcoal Sketches; or, Scenes in a Metropolis* (Philadelphia, 1838) 82–92.

Norton, Caroline, *English Laws for Women in the Nineteenth Century*, 1854 (rpt edn) (Westport: Hyperion Press, 1981).

Oliphant, Margaret, *The Literary History of England in the End of the Eighteenth Century and the Beginning of the Nineteenth Century*, 3 vols, 1882 (New York: AMS Press, 1970).

Patmore, Coventry, The Angel in the House *together with* The Victories of Love, introduction by Alice Meynell (London: Routledge, 1905).

'Prospects of a Heavy Divorce List' *The Times* 9 April 1920: 7.

Reade, Charles, *The Jilt and Other Stories* (London, 1884).

Robertson, T W, *Home* (London, 1879).

Ruskin, John, *Of Queens' Gardens*, Norbert Thomé (ed), Schöninghs Englische Lesebogen (Paderborn: Ferdinand Schöningh, 1947).

Sala, George Augustus, *The Seven Sons of Mammon* (London, 1864).

Salmond, John W, *The Law of Torts: A Treatise on the English Law of Liability for Civil Injuries* (London: Stevens & Haynes, 1907).

Shakespeare, William, *Hamlet*, Harold Jenkins (ed), The Arden Edition of the Works of William Shakespeare (London: Methuen, 1982).

She Went Right Past Her Junction, words by C G Coates, music by Bennett Scott (London, 1898).

A Simple Maiden, words and music by Walter A de Frece (London, 1892).

Smith, Mary Elizabeth, *A Statement of Facts Respecting the Cause of* Smith v. The Earl Ferrers, *Tried before Mr Justice Wightman, in Westminster Hall, on the 14th, 16th, 17th, and 18th Days of February, 1846; with an Examination of the Speech for the Defendant, of the Late Attorney-General Sir Frederic Thesiger* (London, 1846).

Smythies, Harriet Maria, *The Breach of Promise*, 3 vols (London, 1845).

'Some Early Breach of Promise Cases' (1891) 3 *Green Bag* 3–6.

Sterne, Lawrence, *Tristram Shandy*, 1760. Howard Anderson (ed) (New York: W. W. Norton, 1980).

Street, Harry, *Principles of the Law of Damages* (London: Sweet & Maxwell, 1962).

Swinburne, Henry, *A Treatise of Spousals, or Matrimonial Contracts: Wherein All the Questions Relating to That Subject Are Ingeniously Debated and Resolved* (London, 1686).

They Walked for Miles and Miles, words by John P Harrington, music by George Le Brunn (London: Francis, Day, and Hunter, 1904).

Trollope, Anthony, *Can You Forgive Her?* 1864–65 (London: Oxford University Press, 1972).

—— *The Eustace Diamonds*, 1873. Stephen Gill (ed) (London: Penguin, 1986).

—— *The Last Chronicle of Barset*, 1867. Stephen Gill (ed) (Oxford: Oxford University Press, 2001).

—— *The Macdermots of Ballycloran*, 1845. Robert Tracy (ed) (Oxford: Oxford University Press, 1989).

—— *The Small House at Allington*, 1862–64 (London: Oxford University Press, 1963).

Trollope, Frances, *The Widow Barnaby* (London, 1840).

Wharton, J J S, *An Exposition of the Laws Relating to the Women of England* (London, 1853).

White, J Dundas, 'Breach of Promise of Marriage' (1894) 38 *Law Quarterly Review* 13–42.

Wodehouse, P G, *Something New*, 1915 (Mineola, NY: Dover Publications, 2000).

Wollstonecraft, Mary, *Maria, Or, The Wrongs of Woman*, 1798 (Mineola, NY: Dover Publications, 2005).

Woolf, Virginia, *A Room of One's Own* (London: Hogarth Press, 1974).

You'll Hear from My Solicitors, words and music by Frank Leo (London: Francis, Day, and Hunter, 1909).

Non-Print Sources

Adventure in Blackmail, (dir) Harold Huth and Roland Pertwee, (perf) Clive Brook and Judy Campbell, 1943 (Videocassette. Nostalgia Family Video, 1996).

Footlight Parade, (dir) Lloyd Bacon, (perf) James Cagney and Joan Blondell (Warner, 1933).

I'm No Angel, (dir) Wesley Ruggles, (perf) Mae West and Cary Grant (Paramount, 1933).

Secondary Sources

Printed Sources

Abrams, Lynn, *The Making of Modern Woman: Europe 1789–1918*, Longman History of European Women 5 (London: Longman-Pearson Education, 2002).

Ames, James Barr, *Lectures on Legal History and Miscellaneous Legal Essays* (Cambridge, MA: Harvard University Press; London: Humphrey Milford, 1913).

Anderson, Amanda, *Tainted Souls and Painted Faces: The Rhetoric of Fallenness in Victorian Culture*, Reading Women Writing (Ithaca: Cornell University Press, 1993).

Ashley, Leonard R N, 'Gilbert and Melodrama' in *Gilbert and Sullivan: Papers Presented at the International Conference Held at the University of Kansas in May 1970*, James Helyar (ed) (Lawrence, KS: University of Kansas Libraries, 1971) 1–6.

Atiyah, Patrick S, *An Introduction to the Law of Contract*, 5th edn, Clarendon Law Series (Oxford: Clarendon Press, 1995).

—— *The Rise and Fall of Freedom of Contract* (Oxford: Clarendon Press, 1979).

Atlay, J B, *The Victorian Chancellors*, Vol 2 (London: Smith, 1908).

Austin, John L, *How to Do Things with Words* (Cambridge, MA: Harvard University Press, 1962).

Baker, J H, *An Introduction to English Legal History*, 4th edn (London: Butterworths, 2002).

—— (ed), *The Oxford History of the Laws of England*, Vol 6 (Oxford: Oxford University Press, 2003).

Bakhtin, Mikhail, *Rabelais and His World*, (trans) Helene Iswolsky (Bloomington: Indiana University Press, 1984).

Barickman, Richard, Susan MacDonald, and Myra Stark, *Corrupt Relations: Dickens, Thackeray, Trollope, Collins, and the Victorian Sexual System* (New York: Columbia University Press, 1982).

Barker, Hannah, and Elaine Chalus (eds), *Gender in Eighteenth-Century England: Roles, Representations, and Responsibilities* (London: Longman, 1997).

Barker-Benfield, G J, *The Culture of Sensibility: Sex and Society in Eighteenth-Century Britain* (Chicago: University of Chicago Press, 1992).

Barret-Ducrocq, Françoise, *Love in the Time of Victoria: Sexuality, Class and Gender in Nineteenth-Century London* (London: Verso, 1991).

Barthes, Roland, *Mythologies*, (trans) Annette Lavers (London: Cape, 1972).

Basch, Norma, *Framing American Divorce: From the Revolutionary Generation to the Victorians* (Berkeley: University of California Press, 1999).

Beale, H G, W D Bishop, and M P Furmston, *Contract: Cases and Materials*, 5th edn (Oxford: Oxford University Press, 2008).

Beddoe, Deirdre, *Discovering Women's History: A Practical Guide to Researching the Lives of Women since 1800*, 3rd edn (London: Longman, 1998).

Benjamin, Marina (ed), *Science and Sensibility: Gender and Scientific Enquiry, 1780–1945* (Oxford: Basil Blackwell, 1991).

Bennett, W Lance, and Martha S Feldman, *Reconstructing Reality in the Courtroom* (London: Tavistock Publications, 1981).

Branca, Patricia, *Women in Europe since 1750* (London: Croom Helm, 1978).

Briggs, Peter M, 'Notes Toward a Teachable Definition of Satire' (1979) 5(3) *Eighteenth-Century Life* 28–39.

Bruns, Gerald L, 'Allegory and Satire: A Rhetorical Meditation' (1979) 11 *New Literary History* 121–31.

Burke, Edmund, 'Modernity's Histories: Rethinking the Long Nineteenth Century, 1750–1950' in *University of California World History Workshop. Essays and Positions from the World History Workshop*, Paper 1, 25 May 2000 <http://repositories.cdlib.org/ucwhw/ep/1>.

Carey, Gary, *Anita Loos: A Biography* (London: Bloomsbury Publishing, 1988).

Carnell, Jennifer, *The Literary Lives of M. E. Braddon: A Study of Her Life and Work* (Hastings: Sensation Press, 2000).

Cecil, David, *The Fine Art of Reading and Other Literary Studies* (London: Constable, 1957).

Clark, Anna, *The Struggle for the Breeches: Gender and the Making of the British Working Class*, Studies on the History of Society and Culture 23 (Berkeley: University of California Press, 1995).

Clark, Homer H, Jr, *The Law of Domestic Relations in the United States*, 2nd edn, Vol 1, Hornbook Series (St Paul: West Publishing, 1987).

Clayborough, Arthur, *The Grotesque in English Literature* (Oxford: Clarendon Press, 1965).

Cokayne, G E, *The Complete Peerage of England, Scotland, Ireland, Great Britain, and the United Kingdom, Extant, Extinct, or Dormant*, Vicary Gibbs and H A Doubleday (eds), Vol 5 (London: St Catherine Press, 1926).

Coombe, Rosemary J, ' "The Most Disgusting, Disgraceful and Inequitous Proceeding in Our Law": The Action for Breach of Promise of Marriage in Nineteenth-Century Ontario' (1988) 38 *University of Toronto Law Journal* 64–108.

Coombs, Mary, 'Agency and Partnership: A Study of Breach of Promise Plaintiffs' (1989) 2(1) *Yale Journal of Law and Feminism* 1–23.

Cott, Nancy F, 'Passionlessness: An Interpretation of Victorian Sexual Ideology, 1790–1850' (1978) 4(2) *Signs* 219–36.

Craig, Randall, *Promising Language: Betrothal in Victorian Law and Fiction* (Albany: State University of New York Press, 2000).

Curry, Ramona, *Too Much of a Good Thing: Mae West as Cultural Icon* (Minneapolis: University of Minnesota Press, 1996).

Cvetkovich, Ann, *Mixed Feelings: Feminism, Mass Culture, and Victorian Sensationalism* (New Brunswick: Rutgers University Press, 1992).

Dabney, Ross H, *Love and Property in the Novels of Dickens* (London: Chatto & Windus, 1967).

Davidoff, Leonore, Megan Doolittle, Janet Fink, and Catherine Holden, *The Family Story: Blood, Contract and Intimacy, 1830–1960*, Women and Men in History (London: Longman, 1999).

Davidoff, Leonore, and Catherine Hall, *Family Fortunes: Men and Women of the English Middle Class, 1780–1850*, Women in Culture and Society (Chicago: University of Chicago Press, 1987).

Davis, Nuel Pharr, *The Life of Wilkie Collins* (Urbana: University of Illinois Press, 1956).

Donahue, Charles, Jr, *Law, Marriage, and Society in the Later Middle Ages: Arguments About Marriage in Five Courts* (New York: Cambridge University Press, 2007).

Döring, Tobias, 'Freud about Laughter—Laughter about Freud' in Pfister 121–35.

Douglas, Mary, *Purity and Danger: An Analysis of Concepts of Pollution and Taboo* (London: Routledge, 1966).

Duffin, Lorna, 'The Conspicuous Consumptive: Woman as Invalid' in *The Nineteenth Century Woman: Her Cultural and Physical World*, S Delamont and Lorna Duffin (eds) (London: Croom Helm; New York: Barnes & Noble, 1978) 26–56.

Dunbar, Janet, *The Early Victorian Woman: Some Aspects of Her Life (1837–57)* (Westport: Hyperion Press, 1979).

Eden, David, *Gilbert and Sullivan: The Creative Conflict* (Cranbury: Associated University Presses, 1986).

Edwards, Susan S M, *Female Sexuality and the Law: A Study of Constructs of Female Sexuality as They Inform Statute and Legal Procedure*, Law in Society Series (Oxford: Martin Robertson, 1981).

—— *Women on Trial: A Study of the Female Suspect, Defendant, and Offender in the Criminal Law and Criminal Justice System* (Manchester: Manchester University Press, 1984).

Eells, George and Stanley Musgrove, *Mae West: A Biography* (New York: William Morrow, 1982).

Fisher, George, *Evidence*, 2nd edn (New York: Foundation Press, 2008).

Friedan, Betty, *The Feminine Mystique* (New York: Norton, 2001).

Friedman, Lawrence M, *Contract Law in America: A Social and Economic Case Study* (Madison: University of Wisconsin Press, 1965).

Frost, Ginger S, 'Promises Broken: Breach of Promise of Marriage in England and Wales 1753–1970', diss Rice University, 1991.

—— *Promises Broken: Courtship, Class, and Gender in Victorian England*, Victorian Literature and Culture Series (Charlottesville: University Press of Virginia, 1995).

—— ' "I Shall Not Sit Down and Crie": Women, Class and Breach of Promise of Marriage Plaintiffs in England, 1850–1900' (1994) 6(2) *Gender and History* 224–45.

Frye, Northrop, *Anatomy of Criticism* (Princeton: Princeton University Press, 1957).

Gabel, Peter, and Jay Feinman, 'Contract Law as Ideology' in *The Politics of Law: A Progressive Critique*, David Kairys (ed), 3rd edn (New York: Basic Books, 1998) 497–510.

Garfinkle, Ann M, Carol Lefcourt, and Diane B Schulder, 'Women's Servitude under Law' in *Law against the People: Essays to Demystify Law, Order and the Courts*, Robert Lefcourt (ed) (New York: Random House, 1971) 105–22.

Gash, Norman, *Aristocracy and People: Britain 1815–1865*, The New History of England 8 (London: Edward Arnold, 1979).

Gérin, Winifred, *Elizabeth Gaskell: A Biography* (Oxford: Clarendon Press, 1976).

Gleadle, Kathryn, *British Women in the Nineteenth Century*, Social History in Perspective (Basingstoke: Palgrave, 2001).

Goodman, Andrew, *Gilbert and Sullivan at Law* (Rutherford: Fairleigh Dickinson University Press; London: Associated University Presses, 1983).

Gorham, Deborah, *The Victorian Girl and the Feminine Ideal* (Bloomington: Indiana University Press, 1982).

Green, Anna, and Kathleen Troup, 'Gender and History' in *The Houses of History: A Critical Reader in Twentieth-Century History and Theory*, Anna Green and Kathleen Troup (eds) (Manchester: Manchester University Press, 1999) 253–62.

Greenberg, Janelle, 'The Legal Status of the English Woman in Early Eighteenth-Century Common Law and Equity' in *Studies in Eighteenth-Century Culture*, Harold E Pagliaro (ed), Vol 4 (Madison: University of Wisconsin Press, 1975) 171–81.

Griffin, Dustin, 'Satiric Closure' (1985) 18 *Genre* 173–89.

Grossberg, Michael, *Governing the Hearth: Law and the Family in Nineteenth-Century America*, Studies in Legal History (Chapel Hill: University of North Carolina Press, 1985).

Hall, Catherine, *White, Male and Middle Class: Explorations in Feminism and History* (Cambridge: Polity Press, 1992).

Hanft Korobkin, Laura, *Criminal Conversations: Sentimentality and Nineteenth-Century Legal Stories of Adultery*, The Social Foundations of Aesthetic Forms (New York: Columbia University Press, 1998).

Harding, Alan, *A Social History of English Law* (rpt edn) (Gloucester, MA: Peter Smith, 1973).

Hardy, Barbara, *The Moral Art of Dickens* (London: Athlone Press, 1970).

Harrison, Michael, *Painful Details: Twelve Victorian Scandals* (London: Max Parish, 1962).

Hellerstein, Erna Olafson, Leslie Parker Hume, and Karen M Offen, *Victorian Women: A Documentary Account of Women's Lives in Nineteenth-Century England, France, and the United States* (Brighton: Harvester Press, 1981).

Highet, Gilbert, *The Anatomy of Satire* (Princeton: Princeton University Press, 1962).

Hill, Nancy K, *A Reformer's Art: Dickens' Picturesque and Grotesque Imagery* (London: Ohio University Press, 1981).

Hodgart, Matthew, *Satire*, World University Library (New York: McGraw-Hill, 1969).

Holcombe, Lee, *Wives and Property: Reform of the Married Women's Property Law in Nineteenth-Century England* (Toronto: University of Toronto Press, 1983).

Holdsworth, William Searle, *A History of English Law* (London: Methuen, 1923).

Holmes, Oliver Wendell, Jr, 'The Path of the Law' (1897) 10(8) *Harvard Law Review* 457–78.

Horwitz, Morton J, 'The Historical Foundations of Modern Contract Law' (1974) 87 *Harvard Law Review* 917–56.

Houghton, Walter E, *The Victorian Frame of Mind, 1830–1870* (New Haven: Yale University Press; London: Oxford University Press, 1957).

Howe, Daniel Walker, 'Victorian Culture in America' in *Victorian America*, Daniel Walker Howe (ed) (N p: University of Pennsylvania Press, 1976) 3–28.

Ibbetson, David, *A Historical Introduction to the Law of Obligations* (Oxford: Oxford University Press, 2001).

Irigaray, Luce, *This Sex Which Is Not One*, (trans) Catherine Porter and Carolyn Burke (Ithaca: Cornell University Press, 1985).

Jackson, Bernard S, 'Narrative Models in Legal Proof' in *Narrative and the Legal Discourse: A Reader in Storytelling and the Law*, David Ray Papke (ed), Legal Semiotics Monographs (Liverpool: Deborah Charles, 1991) 158–78.

Jacobs, Kathryn, *Marriage Contracts from Chaucer to the Renaissance Stage* (Gainesville: University Press of Florida, 2001).

Jeffreys, Sheila, 'Women and Sexuality' in Purvis 193–216.

Jenks, Edward, *A Short History of English Law: From the Earliest Times to the End of the Year 1927*, 4th edn (London: Methuen, 1928).

Johnson, Edgar, *Charles Dickens: His Tragedy and Triumph*, 2 vols (New York: Simon and Schuster, 1952).

Kamm, Josephine, *Hope Deferred: Girls' Education in English History* (London: Methuen, 1965).

Kayser, Wolfgang, *The Grotesque in Art and Literature*, (trans) Ulrich Weisstein (New York: Columbia University Press, 1981).

Kellogg, Karin L, ' "Blighted Prospects and Wounded Feelings": Breach of Promise in Victorian Law and Literature', Master's thesis, University of Alberta, 1995.

Kerber, Linda K, 'Separate Spheres, Female Worlds, Woman's Place: The Rhetoric of Women's History' (1988) 75(1) *Journal of American History* 9–39.

Kernan, Alvin B, *The Cankered Muse: Satire of the English Renaissance* (rpt edn), Yale Studies in English 142 (Hamden: Archon Books, 1976).

—— *The Plot of Satire* (New Haven: Yale University Press, 1965).

Kessler-Harris, Alice, *Out to Work: A History of Wage-Earning Women in the United States*, 20th anniversary edn (Oxford: Oxford University Press, 2003).

Kleinberg, S Jay (ed), *Retrieving Women's History: Changing Perceptions of the Role of Women in Politics and Society*, Berg/Unesco Comparative Studies (Oxford: Berg; Paris: Unesco, 1988).

Kristeva, Julia, *Powers of Horror: An Essay on Abjection*, (trans) Leon S Roudiez, European Perspectives (New York: Columbia University Press, 1982).

Kronman, Anthony T, 'Paternalism and the Law of Contracts' (1983) 92(5) *Yale Law Journal* 763–97.

Lacey, Nicola, *Women, Crime, and Character: From Moll Flanders to Tess of the D'Urbervilles* (Oxford: Oxford University Press, 2008).

Latta, Robert L, *The Basic Humor Process: A Cognitive-Shift Theory and the Case against Incongruity*, Humor Research 5 (Berlin: Mouton de Gruyter, 1999).

Ledger, Sally, *The New Woman: Fiction and Feminism at the Fin de Siècle* (Manchester: Manchester University Press, 1997).

Leeper, Thomas K, 'Alienation of Affections: Flourishing Anachronism' (1977) 13 *Wake Forest Law Review* 585–601.

Logan, Deborah Anna, *Fallenness in Victorian Women's Writing: Marry, Stitch, Die, or Do Worse* (Columbia: University of Missouri Press, 1998).

Marwick, Arthur, *The Deluge: British Society and the First World War*, 2nd edn (London: Macmillan, 1991).

McBride, Theresa M, 'The Long Road Home: Women's Work and Industrialization' in *Becoming Visible: Women in European History*, Renate Bridenthal and Claudia Koonz (eds) (Boston: Houghton Mifflin, 1977) 280–95.

McGregor, Harvey, *McGregor on Damages*, 17th edn (London: Sweet & Maxwell, 2003).

McKendrick, Ewan, *Contract Law*, Palgrave Macmillan Law Masters (Basingstoke: Palgrave Macmillan, 2007).

McLaren, John P S, 'Nuisance Law and the Industrial Revolution—Some Lessons from Social History' (1983) 3 *Oxford Journal of Legal Studies* 155–221.

Metcalf, Greg, 'The Soul in the Meatsuit: Ivan Albright, Hannibal Lecter and the Body Grotesque' in *Literature and the Grotesque*, Michael J Meyer (ed), Rodopi Perspectives on Modern Literature 15 (Amsterdam: Rodopi, 1995) 153–70.

Meyer, Michael, 'The Pleasures of Men and the Subjection of Women' in *In the Footsteps of Queen Victoria: Wege zum Viktorianischen Zeitalter*, Christa Jansohn (ed), Studien zur englischen Literatur 15 (Münster: LIT Verlag, 2003) 177–99.

Michie, Elsie B, *Outside the Pale: Cultural Exclusion, Gender Difference, and the Victorian Woman Writer*, Reading Women Writing (Ithaca: Cornell University Press, 1993).

Millett, Kate, 'The Debate over Women: Ruskin vs. Mill' in Vicinus 121–39.

Mintz, Steven, *A Prison of Expectations: The Family in Victorian Culture* (New York: New York University Press, 1983).

Morgan, Kenneth O (ed), *The Oxford Illustrated History of Britain* (Oxford: Oxford University Press, 1997).

Morreall, John (ed), *The Philosophy of Laughter and Humor*, Suny Series in Philosophy (Albany: State University of New York Press, 1987).

Mullan, John, *Sentiment and Sociability: The Language of Feeling in the Eighteenth Century* (Oxford: Clarendon Press, 1988).

Nead, Lynda, *Myths of Sexuality: Representations of Women in Victorian Britain* (Oxford: Basil Blackwell, 1988).

Nichols, James W, *Insinuation: The Tactics of English Satire* (The Hague: Mouton, 1971).

Oakley, Ann, *Sex, Gender and Society* (rev edn), Towards a New Society (Aldershot: Gower Publishing, 1985).

Page, Norman (ed), *Wilkie Collins: The Critical Heritage*, The Critical Heritage Series (London: Routledge, 1974).

Paulos, John Allen, *Mathematics and Humor* (Chicago: University of Chicago Press, 1980).

Pearl, Cyril, *The Girl with the Swansdown Seat* (London: Frederick Muller, 1955).

Perkin, Joan, *Victorian Women* (London: John Murray, 1993).

Pfister, Manfred (ed), *A History of English Laughter: Laughter from Beowulf to Beckett and Beyond*, Internationale Forschungen zur Allgemeinen und Vergleichenden Literaturwissenschaft 57 (Amsterdam: Rodopi, 2002).

Playfair, Giles, *Six Studies in Hypocrisy* (London: Secker & Warbury, 1969).

Plessner, Helmut, 'Lachen und Weinen' in *Ausdruck und Menschliche Natur*, Gesammelte Schriften 7, Günther Dux, Otto Marquard, and Elisabeth Stroeker (eds) (Frankfurt: n p, 1982) 210–389.

Pollard, Arthur, *Satire*, The Critical Idiom 7 (London: Methuen, 1970).

Poovey, Mary, *The Proper Lady and the Woman Writer: Ideology as Style in the Works of Mary Wollstonecraft, Mary Shelley, and Jane Austen*, Women in Culture and Society (Chicago: University of Chicago Press, 1984).

Purvis, June (ed), *Women's History: Britain, 1850–1945* (London: UCL Press, 1995).

Pykett, Lyn, *The 'Improper Feminine': The Women's Sensation Novel and the New Woman Writing* (London: Routledge, 1992).

—— *The Sensation Novel from* The Woman in White *to* The Moonstone, Writers and Their Work (Plymouth: Northcote House, 1994).

Rance, Nicholas, *Wilkie Collins and Other Sensation Novelists: Walking the Moral Hospital* (London: Macmillan, 1991).

Robertson, Pamela, *Guilty Pleasures: Feminist Camp from Mae West to Madonna* (Durham: Duke University Press, 1996).

Rosen, Marjorie, *Popcorn Venus: Women, Movies, and the American Dream* (London: Peter Owen, 1975).

Rubinstein, David, *Before the Suffragettes: Women's Emancipation in the 1890s* (Brighton: Harvester Press, 1986).

Sachs, Albie and Joan Hoff Wilson, *Sexism and the Law: A Study of Male Beliefs and Legal Bias in Britain and the United States*, Law in Society Series (Oxford: Martin Robertson, 1978).

Sanders, Valerie, *The Private Lives of Victorian Women: Autobiography in Nineteenth-Century England* (New York: St. Martin's Press, 1989).

Sayers, Janet, *Biological Politics: Feminist and Anti-Feminist Perspectives* (London: Tavistock Publications, 1982).

'Scarlett, James, first Baron Abinger (1769–1844)', rev Elisabeth A Cawthon, *Oxford Dictionary of National Biography*, Oxford University Press, 2004, online edn, Jan 2009 <http://www.oxforddnb.com/view/article/24783>, accessed 12 October 2009.

Schor, Hilary M, *Scheherezade in the Marketplace: Elizabeth Gaskell and the Victorian Novel* (New York: Oxford University Press, 1992).

Scott, Joan Wallach, 'The Problem of Invisibility' in Kleinberg 5–29.

Shanley, Mary Lyndon, *Feminism, Marriage, and the Law in Victorian England, 1850–1895* (London: I B Tauris, 1989).

Shoemaker, Robert, *Gender in English Society 1660–1850: The Emergence of Separate Spheres?* (London: Longman, 1998).

Simpson, A W B, *A History of the Common Law of Contract: The Rise of the Action of Assumpsit* (rpt edn) (Oxford: Clarendon Press, 1987).

—— *Leading Cases in the Common Law* (New York: Oxford University Press, 1995).

—— 'The Horwitz Thesis and the History of Contracts' (1979) 46(3) *University of Chicago Law Review* 533–601.

Sinclair, M B W, 'Seduction and the Myth of the Ideal Woman' (1987) 5(33) *Law and Inequality* 33–102.

Slater, Michael, *Dickens and Women* (London: J M Dent, 1983).

Small, Helen, *Love's Madness: Medicine, the Novel, and Female Insanity 1800–1865* (Oxford: Clarendon Press, 1996).

Smith, Grahame, *Dickens, Money, and Society* (Berkeley: University of California Press, 1968).

Spender, Dale, *Time and Tide Wait for No Man* (London: Pandora Press, 1984).

Staves, Susan, 'British Seduced Maidens' (1980) 14(2) *Eighteenth-Century Studies* 109–34.

Steinbach, Susie L, 'Promises, Promises: Not Marrying in England 1780–1920', diss Yale University, 1996 (Ann Arbor: UMI, 1996) 9632509.

—— *Women in England 1760–1914: A Social History* (London: Weidenfeld & Nicolson, 2004).

Stone, Lawrence, *Broken Lives: Separation and Divorce in England, 1660–1857* (Oxford: Oxford University Press, 1993).

—— *Road to Divorce: England 1530–1987* (Oxford: Oxford University Press, 1990).

—— *Uncertain Unions: Marriage in England, 1660–1753* (New York: Oxford University Press, 1992).

Summerfield, Penny, 'Women and the War in the Twentieth Century' in Purvis 307–32.

Thomas, Keith, 'The Double Standard' (1959) 20 *Journal of the History of Ideas* 195–216.

Thomson, Philip, *The Grotesque*, The Critical Idiom 24 (London: Methuen, 1972).

Tiffany, Grace, *Erotic Beasts and Social Monsters: Shakespeare, Jonson, and Comic Androgyny* (London: Associated University Presses, 1995).

Tomalin, Claire, *The Life and Death of Mary Wollstonecraft* (London: Weidenfeld & Nicolson, 1974).

Tönnies, Merle, 'Laughter in the Nineteenth-Century British Theatre: From Genial Blending to Harsh Distinctions' in Pfister 99–119.

Trudgill, Eric, *Madonnas and Magdalens: The Origins and Development of Victorian Sexual Attitudes* (New York: Holmes and Meier, 1976).

Usborne, Richard, *Wodehouse at Work: A Study of the Books and Characters of P. G. Wodehouse across Nearly Sixty Years* (London: Herbert Jenkins, 1961).

Utter, Robert Palfrey and Gwendolyn Bridges Needham, *Pamela's Daughters* (New York: Russell & Russell, 1972).

VanderVelde, Lea, 'The Legal Ways of Seduction' (1996) 48 *Stanford Law Review* 817–901.

Vicinus, Martha (ed), *Suffer and Be Still: Women in the Victorian Age* (Bloomington: Indiana University Press, 1973).

Vickery, Amanda, 'Golden Age to Separate Spheres? A Review of the Categories and Chronology of English Women's History' (1993) 36(2) *Historical Journal* 383–414.

Wadlington, Walter and Monrad G Paulsen, *Cases and Other Materials on Domestic Relations*, 3rd edn, University Casebook Series (Mineola, NY: Foundation Press, 1978).

Watt, Ian, 'The New Woman: Samuel Richardson's Pamela' in *The Family: Its Structure and Functions*, Rose L Coser (ed) (New York: St Martin's Press, 1964) 267–89.

Welter, Barbara, 'The Cult of True Womanhood: 1820–1860' (1966) 18 *American Quarterly* 151–74.

Williams, Neil G, 'What to Do When There Is No "I Do": A Model for Awarding Damages under Promissory Estoppel' (1995) 70 *Washington Law Review* 1019–69.

Zimmermann, Reinhard, *The Law of Obligations: Roman Foundations of the Civilian Tradition* (Oxford: Oxford University Press, 1996).

Personal Communications

Cretney, Stephen, email to the author, 18 January 2004.

Donahue, Charles, Jr, email to the author, 2 March 2009.

Index